SEMAPRO 2016

The Tenth International Conference on Advances in Semantic Processing

October 9 - 13, 2016

Venice, Italy

SEMAPRO 2016 Editors

Özgü Can, Ege University - Izmir, Turkey

Floriano Scioscia, Politecnico di Bari, Italy

Printed from e-media with permission by:

Curran Associates, Inc.
57 Morehouse Lane
Red Hook, NY 12571

Some format issues inherent in the e-media version may also appear in this print version.

Printed by Curran Associates, Inc. (2016)

International Academy, Research, and Industry Association (IARIA)
412 Derby Way
Wilmington, DE 19810

Phone: (408) 893-6407
Fax: (408) 527-6351

petre@iaria.org

Additional copies of this publication are available from:

Curran Associates, Inc.
57 Morehouse Lane
Red Hook, NY 12571 USA
Phone: 845-758-0400
Fax: 845-758-2633
Email: curran@proceedings.com
Web: www.proceedings.com

TABLE OF CONTENTS

SEMAPRO 5 / SOON: SEMANTIC-BASED OPPORTUNISTIC OBJECT NETWORKS

SEMAPRO 2016

Forward

The Tenth International Conference on Advances in Semantic Processing (SEMAPRO 2016), held between October 9 and 13, 2016 in Venice, Italy, continued a series of events related to the complexity of understanding and processing information.

Semantic processing considers contextual dependencies and adds to the individually acquired knowledge emergent properties and understanding. Hardware and software support and platforms were developed for semantically enhanced information retrieval and interpretation. Searching for video, voice and speech [VVS] raises additional problems to specialized engines with respect to text search. Contextual searching and special patterns-based techniques are current solutions.

With the progress on ontology, web services, semantic social media, semantic web, deep web search /deep semantic web/, semantic deep web, semantic networking and semantic reasoning, SEMAPRO 2016 constituted the stage for the state-of-the-art on the most recent advances.

The event was very competitive in its selection process and very well perceived by the international scientific and industrial communities. As such, it has attracted excellent contributions and active participation from all over the world. We were very pleased to receive a large amount of top quality contributions.

The conference had the following tracks:

- Semantic applications/platforms/tools
- Healthcare Information and Management Systems
- Semantic Technologies
- Semantic-based Opportunistic Object Networks

We take here the opportunity to warmly thank all the members of the SEMAPRO 2016 technical program committee, as well as the numerous reviewers. The creation of such a high quality conference program would not have been possible without their involvement. We also kindly thank all the authors that dedicated much of their time and effort to contribute to SEMAPRO 2016. We truly believe that, thanks to all these efforts, the final conference program consisted of top quality contributions.

Also, this event could not have been a reality without the support of many individuals, organizations and sponsors. We also gratefully thank the members of the SEMAPRO 2016 organizing committee for their help in handling the logistics and for their work that made this professional meeting a success.

We hope SEMAPRO 2016 was a successful international forum for the exchange of ideas and results between academia and industry and to promote further progress in the area of semantic processing.

We also hope that Venice, Italy, provided a pleasant environment during the conference and everyone saved some time to enjoy the unique charm of the city.

SEMAPRO Advisory Committee

Wladyslaw Homenda, Warsaw University of Technology, Poland
Bich-Lien Doan, SUPELEC, France
Alexey Cheptsov, High Performance Computing Center Stuttgart (HLRS), Germany
Sule Yildirim Yayilgan, Gjøvik University College, Norway
Jesper Zedlitz, Christian-Albrechts-Universität Kiel, Germany
Soon Ae Chun, City University of New York, USA
Fabio Grandi, University of Bologna, Italy
David A. Ostrowski, Ford Motor Company, USA
Andrea Perego, European Commission - Joint Research Centre, Ispra, Italy

SEMAPRO Industry/Research Liaison Chairs

Riccardo Albertoni, IMATI-CNR-Genova, Italy
Panos Alexopoulos, iSOCO S.A., Spain
Sofia Athenikos, IPsoft, USA
Isabel Azevedo, ISEP-IPP, Portugal
Sam Chapman, The Floow Limited, UK
Daniele Christen, Parsit Company, Italy
Frithjof Dau, SAP Research Dresden, Germany
Thierry Declerck, DFKI GmbH, Germany
Alessio Gugliotta, Innova SpA, Italy
Shun Hattori, Muroran Institute of Technology, Japan
Tracy Holloway King, eBay Inc., USA
Lyndon J. B. Nixon, STI International, Austria
Zoltán Theisz, evopro Innovation LLC, Hungary
Thorsten Liebig, derivo GmbH - Ulm, Germany
Michael Mohler, Language Computer Corporation in Richardson, USA

SEMAPRO Publicity Chairs

Felix Schiele, Reutlingen University, Germany
Bernd Stadlhofer, University of Applied Sciences, Austria
Ruben Costa, UNINOVA, Portugal
Andreas Emrich, German Research Center for Artificial Intelligence (DFKI), Germany

SEMAPRO 2016

Committee

SEMAPRO Advisory Committee

Wladyslaw Homenda, Warsaw University of Technology, Poland
Bich-Lien Doan, SUPELEC, France
Alexey Cheptsov, High Performance Computing Center Stuttgart (HLRS), Germany
Sule Yildirim Yayilgan, Gjøvik University College, Norway
Jesper Zedlitz, Christian-Albrechts-Universität Kiel, Germany
Soon Ae Chun, City University of New York, USA
Fabio Grandi, University of Bologna, Italy
David A. Ostrowski, Ford Motor Company, USA
Andrea Perego, European Commission - Joint Research Centre, Ispra, Italy

SEMAPRO Industry/Research Liaison Chairs

Riccardo Albertoni, IMATI-CNR-Genova, Italy
Panos Alexopoulos, iSOCO S.A., Spain
Sofia Athenikos, IPsoft, USA
Isabel Azevedo, ISEP-IPP, Portugal
Sam Chapman, The Floow Limited, UK
Daniele Christen, Parsit Company, Italy
Frithjof Dau, SAP Research Dresden, Germany
Thierry Declerck, DFKI GmbH, Germany
Alessio Gugliotta, Innova SpA, Italy
Shun Hattori, Muroran Institute of Technology, Japan
Tracy Holloway King, eBay Inc., USA
Lyndon J. B. Nixon, STI International, Austria
Zoltán Theisz, evopro Innovation LLC, Hungary
Thorsten Liebig, derivo GmbH - Ulm, Germany
Michael Mohler, Language Computer Corporation in Richardson, USA

SEMAPRO Publicity Chairs

Felix Schiele, Reutlingen University, Germany
Bernd Stadlhofer, University of Applied Sciences, Austria
Ruben Costa, UNINOVA, Portugal
Andreas Emrich, German Research Center for Artificial Intelligence (DFKI), Germany

SEMAPRO 2016 Technical Program Committee

Nasser Alalwan, King Saud University - Riyadh, Saudi Arabia
Riccardo Albertoni, IMATI-CNR-Genova, Italy
José F. Aldana Montes, University of Málaga, Spain
Panos Alexopoulos, iSOCO S.A., Spain
Mauricio Almeida, Federal University of Minas Gerais, Brazil
Mario Arrigoni Neri, University of Bergamo, Italy
Sofia Athenikos, Flipboard, USA
Agnese Augello, ICAR - CNR, Italy
Isabel Azevedo, ISEP-IPP, Portugal
Bruno Bachimont, Universite de Technologie de Compiegne, France
Ebrahim Bagheri, Ryerson University, Canada
Renata Baracho, Federal University of Minas Gerais, Brazil
Helmi Ben Hmida, Fraunhofer Institute for Computer Graphics Research IGD, Germany
Jorge Bernardino, ISEC - Polytechnic Institute of Coimbra, Portugal
Dilletta Romana Cacciagrano, University of Camerino, Italy
Nicoletta Calzolari, CNR-ILC (Istituto di Linguistica Computazionale del CNR), Italy
Ozgu Can, Ege University, Turkey
Tru Hoang Cao, Vietnam National University - HCM & Ho Chi Minh City University of Technology, Vietnam
Rodrigo Capobianco Guido, São Paulo State University, Brazil
Sana Châabane, ISG - Sousse, Tunisia
Sam Chapman, The Floow Limited, UK
Chao Chen, Capital One, USA
Alexey Cheptsov, High Performance Computing Center Stuttgart (HLRS), Germany
Dickson Chiu, University of Hong Kong, Hong Kong
Smitashree Choudhury, UK Open University - Milton Keynes, UK
Sunil Choenni, Ministry of Security and Justice, Netherlands
Daniele Christen, Parsit Company, Italy
Soon Ae Chun, City University of New York, USA
Paolo Ciancarini, Università di Bologna, Italy
Timothy Clark, Harvard Medical School, USA
Francesco Corcoglioniti, Fondazione Bruno Kessler - Trento, Italy
Ruben Costa, UNINOVA - Instituto de Desenvolvimento de Novas Tecnologias, Portugal
Frithjof Dau, SAP Research Dresden, Germany
Tom De Nies, Ghent University - iMinds, Belgium
Cláudio de Souza Baptista, Computer Science Department, University of Campina Grande, Brazil
Thierry Declerck, DFKI GmbH, Germany
Gianluca Demartini, University of Fribourg, Switzerland
Chiara Di Francescomarino, Fondazione Bruno Kessler - Trento, Italy
Gayo Diallo, University of Bordeaux, France
Alexiei Dingli, The University of Malta, Malta
Christian Dirschl, Wolters Kluwer, Germany
Bich Lien Doan, SUPELEC, France
Milan Dojčinovski, Czech Technical University in Prague, Czech Republic

Elio Masciari, ICAR-CNR, Italy
Miguel Félix Mata Rivera, Laboratorio de Computo Móvil - IPN-UPIITA, Mexico
Dennis McLeod, University of Southern California - Los Angeles, USA
Muntazir Mehdi, National University of Ireland, Galway, Ireland
Michele Melchiori, Università degli Studi di Brescia, Italy
Ana Meštrović, University of Rijeka, Croatia
Elisabeth Métais, Cedric-CNAM, France
Vasileios Mezaris, Informatics and Telematics Institute (ITI) and Centre for Research and Technology Hellas (CERTH) - Thermi-Thessaloniki, Greece
Michael Mohler, Language Computer Corporation in Richardson, U.S.A.
Shahab Mokarizadeh , Royal Institute of Technology (KTH) - Stockholm, Sweden
Anne Monceaux, Airbus Group Innovations, France
Alessandro Moschitti, Qatar Computing Research Institute, Qatar
Mir Abolfazl Mostafavi, Université Laval - Québec, Canada
Fleur Mougin, University of Bordeaux, France
Ekawit Nantajeewarawat, Sirindhorn International Institute of Technology / Thammasat University, Thailand
Vlad Nicolicin Georgescu, SP2 Solutions, France
Lyndon J. B. Nixon, STI International, Austria
Csongor Nyulas, Stanford Center for Biomedical Informatics, USA
David A. Ostrowski, Ford Motor Company, USA
Vito Claudio Ostuni, Polytechnic University of Bari, Italy
Peera Pacharintanakul, TOT, Thailand
Andrea Perego, European Commission - Joint Research Centre, Ispra, Italy
Max Petrenko, NTENT / Ontological Semantics Technology Lab - Texas A&M University-Commerce, USA
Livia Predoiu, University of Oxford, UK
Hemant Purohit, Wright State University, USA
Filip Radulovic, Universidad Politécnica de Madrid, Spain
Jaime Ramírez, Universidad Politécnica de Madrid, Spain
Isidro Ramos, Valencia Polytechnic University, Spain
Werner Retschitzegger, Johannes Kepler University Linz, Austria
Kate Revoredo, Federal University of the State of Rio de Janeiro (UNIRIO), Brazil
German Rigau, IXA NLP Group. EHU, Spain
Juergen Rilling, Concordia University, Canada
Tarmo Robal, Tallinn University of Technology, Estonia
Renato Rocha Souza, Fundação Getulio Vargas & Universidade Federal de Minas Gerais, Brazil
Alejandro Rodríguez González, Centre for Biotechnology and Plant Genomics, UPM-INIA, Spain
Marco Ronchetti, Universita' degli Studi di Trento, Italy
Marco Rospocher, Fondazione Bruno Kessler (FBK), Italy
Gaetano Rossiello, University of Bari Aldo Moro, Italy
Thomas Roth-Berghofer, University of West London, U.K.
Michele Ruta, Technical University of Bari, Italy
Gunter Saake, University of Magdeburg, Germany

Melike Sah Direkoglu, Near East University, North Cyprus
Satya Sahoo, Case Western Reserve University, USA
Domenico Fabio Savo, Department of Computer, Control, and Management Engineering "Antonio Ruberti" - Sapienza University of Rome, Italy
Adriano A. Santos, Universidade Federal de Campina Grande, Brazil
Minoru Sasaki, Ibaraki University, Japan
Frederik Schadd, Maastricht University, Netherlands
Felix Schiele, Hochschule Reutlingen, Germany
Raoul Schönhof, High Performance Computing Center Stuttgart (HLRS), Germany
Kinga Schumacher, German Research Center for Artificial Intelligence (DFKI) - Berlin, Germany
Wieland Schwinger, Johannes Kepler University Linz, Austria
Floriano Scioscia, Politecnico di Bari, Italy
Giovanni Semeraro, University of Bari "Aldo Moro", Italy
Kunal Sengupta, Wright State University - Dayton, USA
Luciano Serafini, Fondazione Bruno Kessler, Italy
Md. Sumon Shahriar, Tasmanian ICT Centre/CSIRO, Australia
Nuno Silva, School of Engineering - Polytechnic of Porto, Portugal
Sofia Stamou, Ionian University, Greece
Vasco N. G. J. Soares, Instituto de Telecomunicações / Polytechnic Institute of Castelo Branco, Portugal
Ahmet Soylu, University of Oslo, Norway
Mari Carmen Suárez-Figueroa, Universidad Politécnica de Madrid (UPM), Spain
Lars G. Svensson, German National Library, Germany
Cui Tao, Mayo Clinic - Rochester, USA
Saïd Tazi, LAAS-CNRS, Université de Toulouse / Université Toulouse1, France
Zoltán Theisz, evopro Innovation LLC, Hungary
Tina Tian, Manhattan College, U.S.A.
Ioan Toma, University of Innsbruck, Austria
Tania Tudorache, Stanford University, USA
Christina Unger, CITEC - Bielefeld University, Germany
Willem Robert van Hage, SynerScope B.V. / Innovation Lab TU Eindhoven, Netherlands
Luc Vouligny, Hydro-Québec Research Institute, Canada
Holger Wache, University of applied Science and Arts Northwestern Switzerland, Switzerland
Shenghui Wang, OCLC Research, Netherlands
Peter Wetz, Vienna University of Technology, Austria
Mari Wigham, Food and Biobased Research, Wageningen UR, Netherlands
Wai Lok Woo, Newcastle University, UK
Honghan Wu, University of Aberdeen, UK
Hongyan Wu, Database Center for Life Science, Research Organization of Information Systems, Japan
Sule Yildirim Yayilgan, Gjøvik University College, Norway
Fouad Zablith, American University of Beirut, Lebanon
Filip Zavoral, Charles University in Prague, Czech Republic
Yuting Zhao, The University of Aberdeen, UK

Hai-Tao Zheng, Tsinghua University, China
Ingo Zinnikus, German Research Center for Artificial Intelligence (DFKI), Germany
Amal Zouaq, Royal Military College of Canada, Canada

Copyright Information

For your reference, this is the text governing the copyright release for material published by IARIA.

The copyright release is a transfer of publication rights, which allows IARIA and its partners to drive the dissemination of the published material. This allows IARIA to give articles increased visibility via distribution, inclusion in libraries, and arrangements for submission to indexes.

I, the undersigned, declare that the article is original, and that I represent the authors of this article in the copyright release matters. If this work has been done as work-for-hire, I have obtained all necessary clearances to execute a copyright release. I hereby irrevocably transfer exclusive copyright for this material to IARIA. I give IARIA permission or reproduce the work in any media format such as, but not limited to, print, digital, or electronic. I give IARIA permission to distribute the materials without restriction to any institutions or individuals. I give IARIA permission to submit the work for inclusion in article repositories as IARIA sees fit.

I, the undersigned, declare that to the best of my knowledge, the article is does not contain libelous or otherwise unlawful contents or invading the right of privacy or infringing on a proprietary right.

Following the copyright release, any circulated version of the article must bear the copyright notice and any header and footer information that IARIA applies to the published article.

IARIA grants royalty-free permission to the authors to disseminate the work, under the above provisions, for any academic, commercial, or industrial use. IARIA grants royalty-free permission to any individuals or institutions to make the article available electronically, online, or in print.

IARIA acknowledges that rights to any algorithm, process, procedure, apparatus, or articles of manufacture remain with the authors and their employers.

I, the undersigned, understand that IARIA will not be liable, in contract, tort (including, without limitation, negligence), pre-contract or other representations (other than fraudulent misrepresentations) or otherwise in connection with the publication of my work.

Exception to the above is made for work-for-hire performed while employed by the government. In that case, copyright to the material remains with the said government. The rightful owners (authors and government entity) grant unlimited and unrestricted permission to IARIA, IARIA's contractors, and IARIA's partners to further distribute the work.

Ontologies-based Optical Character Recognition-error Correction Method for Bar Graphs

Sarunya Kanjanawattana
Graduate School
Shibaura Institute of Technology
Tokyo, Japan
e-mail: nb14503@shibaura-it.ac.jp

Masaomi Kimura
Information Science and Engineering
Shibaura Institute of Technology
Tokyo, Japan
e-mail: masaomi@sic.shibaura-it.ac.jp

***Abstract*— Graphs provide an effective method for briefly presenting significant information appearing in academic literature. Readers can benefit from automatic graph information extraction. The conventional technique uses optical character recognition (OCR). However, OCR results can be imperfect because its performance depends on factors such as image quality. This becomes a critical problem because misrecognition provides incorrect information to readers and causes misleading communication. Numerous publications have appeared in recent years documenting OCR performance improvement and OCR result correction; however, only a few studies have focused on the use of semantics to solve this problem. In this study, we propose a novel method for OCR-error correction using several techniques, including ontologies, natural language processing, and edit distance. The input of this study includes bar graphs and associated information, such as their captions and cited paragraphs. We implemented five conditions to cover all possible situations for acquiring the most similar words as substitutes for incorrect OCR results. Moreover, we used DBpedia and WordNet to find word categories and part-of-speech tags. We evaluated our method by comparing performance rates, i.e., accuracy and precision, with our previous method using only the edit distance technique. As a result, our method provided higher performance rates than the other method. Our method's overall accuracy reached 81%, while that of the other method was 54%. Based on the evidence, we conclude that our solution to the OCR problem is effective.**

Keywords- OCR-error correction; dependency parsing; ontology; edit distance; two-dimensional bar graphs.

I. Introduction

Scientific literature has grown remarkably in recent years, and document recognition plays an important role in extracting information from the literature [1]. Typically, to understand the principal idea of a particular item of literature, readers must gradually read a detailed part of the literature. However, acquiring only descriptive details can result in unclear explanations. Imagine that an author endeavors to explain experimental results and presents some measurement data to readers. In such a case, the most suitable means might be to use a graph to present the data and their tendencies. A graph contains a lot of essential information that people can interpret easily; therefore, developing a system that can extract information from graphs can be expected to be particularly useful for gaining new knowledge more easily than ever; see, e.g., [2] and [3]. Optical character recognition (OCR) is the most basic and effective method for extracting information from graphs. However, this technique cannot guarantee perfect outcomes because OCR performance depends on many factors, such as image quality, specific language requirement, and image noise. As a result, if OCR is sensitive to such factors, error recognition can negatively affect our desired information. To alleviate this difficulty, there have been many studies proposing efficient methods based on several techniques, such as image processing and semantics. In addition, our aim in this study is to mitigate the difficulty of incorrect character recognition as well as develop an automatic system for extracting and correcting OCR errors from graphs based on ontologies.

OCR is an indispensable technique for information extraction from graphs. It has long been well known as an image processing approach that solves such problems as detecting and recognizing text in complex images and video frames [4][5]. Recently, OCR has been used extensively in many applications, such as the medical article citation database MEDLINE [6] and academic applications. For example, Kataria et al. [2] proposed an efficient method for automatically extracting elements (e.g., axis-labels, legends, and data points) from within a two-dimensional graph. Huang et al. [3] also presented a study targeting the association of recognition results of textual and graphical information contained in scientific chart images. They individually recognized text and graphical regions of an input image and combined the results of graph components to achieve a full understanding of an input image. These studies focused on investigating effective methods for extracting important graph components, similarly to our study. In contrast to this previous study, we solved OCR problems practically that might have occurred in our results. We not only extracted graph components using the OCR technique, but also addressed an OCR error problem by correcting errors using our methods.

In general, there are two types of word errors that can be found in our study, non-word and real-word errors [7]. A non-word error occurs when OCR extracts a source text as a string that does not correspond validly to any vocabulary item in the dictionary. If an extracted word matches an item in the dictionary, but is not identical with the source-text

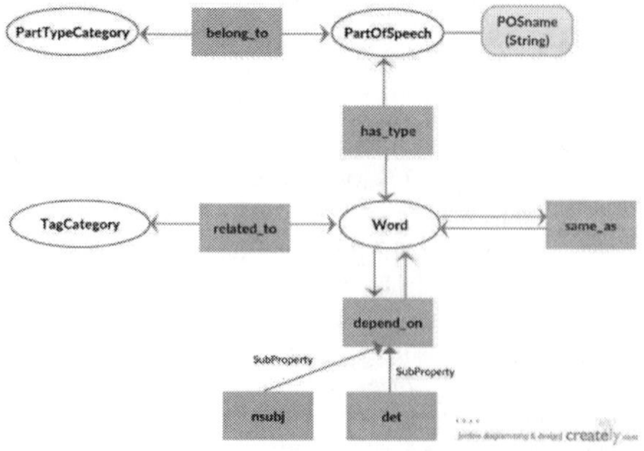

Figure 1. Illustration of our ontology structure to describe classes, properties, and relations.

word, we call it a real-word error. For example, if a source text "A dog is cute" is rendered as "A doq is rule" using OCR, then "doq" is a non-word error, and "rule" is a real-word error.

Over several years, a great deal of effort has developed several techniques for correcting such OCR errors [8]. Nagata [9] proposed an OCR-error correction method for Japanese consisting of a statistical OCR model, an approximate word-matching method using character shape similarity, and a word segmentation algorithm using a statistical language model. However, items such as numbers, acronyms, and transliterated foreign words cannot be extracted properly using his method, which differs from ours, because our method can correct words universally as long as they appear in the source document. Lasko et al. [6] suggested five methods for matching words mistranslated by OCR, viz., an adaptation of the cross-correlation algorithm, the generic edit distance algorithm, the edit distance algorithm with a probabilistic substitution matrix, Bayesian analysis, and Bayesian analysis on an actively thinned reference dictionary, and their accuracy rates were compared. They found that the Bayesian algorithm produced the most accurate results. As our interest, we focus on the results of the generic edit distance algorithm. This suggests a minimum edit distance between two words defined as the smallest number of deletions, insertions, and substitutions required to transform either word into the other word. They obtained an overall accuracy of approximately 77.3% for the generic edit distance. Using only this algorithm was inadequate to correct OCR results, as also occurred in our previous study [10].

Current studies related to OCR-error correction tend to use ontology and semantics to address OCR problems [11] [12]. Jobbins et al. [13] developed a system for automatic semantic-relations identification between words using an existing knowledge source, Roget's Thesaurus. The thesaurus contains explicit links between words, including related vocabulary items for each part of speech (e.g., noun and verb), unlike an ordinary dictionary. However, we consider that this previous study might encounter a problem, if dealing with words in a sentence, because it is possible to obtain a real-word error with a word that is also in the same category or cross-reference. To mitigate this shortcoming, it is necessary to use not only the word categories, but also the dependencies of English grammar to obtain a suitable solution, because each word in the sentence will definitely contain at least one dependency on some other word. Zhuang et al. [14] presented an OCR post-processing method based on multiple forms of knowledge, i.e., language knowledge and candidate distance information provided by the OCR engine, using a huge set of Chinese characters as input data.

The input of our system is a collection of biological bar graphs gathered from PubMed. The input must contain at least an X-category, a Y-title, and optionally, a legend. Moreover, we also use related contents of documents (i.e., image captions and corresponding paragraphs) to create our own ontology.

We propose here a novel method of OCR-error correction using edit distance, natural language processing (NLP), and multiple ontologies applied to two-dimensional bar graphs. The edit distance algorithm was used to measure similarities between OCR results and tokens in documents. Moreover, each word is scored to determine its similarity and then collected in a list of individual images ordered by ascending score. The top five words are selected as candidates to be used to replace incorrect OCR results. We designed a structure for our ontology that supports dependency parsing of English text and word categories queried from DBpedia (e.g., [15]). Our objectives in this study were to develop a new OCR-error correction method utilizing ontologies applied to the bar graphs. Our system clearly contributes some benefit to society, particularly in regard to academics, by suggesting a new means of correcting erroneous recognitions that can be adapted to other applications for enhancing their performance.

The remainder of the paper is organized as follows. In Section 2, we present the details of the methodology used in our study. Section 3 evaluates and describes the results, followed by discussion in Section 4. Section 5 concludes and suggests future work.

II. METHODOLOGY

A. *Dataset*

The dataset used in this study is a collection of two-dimensional bar graphs from journal articles. A bar graph is a chart that represents data grouped in categories by bars with lengths proportional to their corresponding values. Typically, a bar graph in our study has two axes, X and Y. For the Y-axis, the bar graph presents an axis-title as a sentence, a noun phrase, or a single word. In contrast, the X-axis contains several words representing categories, for example, names of medicines or periods of time. In addition, a legend identifies a label for each bar. Extracting characters from the legend is a challenging task, because its position is changeable, depending on the graph space and the author.

B. Ontology Creation

Our ontology is created using captions and corresponding paragraphs from all documents used in this study. We systematically designed an ontology, shown in Fig. 1, that stores word categories gathered from DBpedia, parts of speech (POS), and grammar dependency data extracted using the Stanford dependency parser. It consists of four entity types (i.e., Word, TagCategory, PartOfSpeech, and PartTypeCategory classes), many object properties (e.g., belong_to, has_type, depend_on), and a data property (i.e., full names of POS).

The Word entity represents every individual word tokenized from captions and corresponding paragraphs. The TagCategory entity collects category names of each word in documents, such as mammal, plant, and medicine. Such categories are obtained by querying DBpedia via its SPARQL endpoint; moreover, we also use the Stanford Named Entity Recognizer (Stanford NER) to classify words in sentences into seven classes, i.e., Location, Person, Organization, Money, Percent, Date, and Time. The PartOfSpeech entity provides information about the POS tagging of each word. The total number of individuals is fixed at 36 instances, whose names come from Penn treebank nodes, such as CC, VB, and NNP. The last entity is PartTypeCategory, representing groups of POS taggings. For instance, NNP indicates a singular proper noun belonging to the Noun group.

There are several properties described in our ontology, belong_to, has_type, related_to, same_as, and depend_on, object properties that connect entities to specify their relations. The same_as property represents relations of at least two synonymous words. For example, the word "Japan" appears as JPN, Nihon, and more, which are related by the same_as property. This property is useful for covering words expressing the same concept.

Another crucial property is depend_on, representing dependency relationships between paired words parsed from sentences. We created 67 sub-properties of dependencies used by the Stanford parser, e.g., conj, dep, and nsubj.

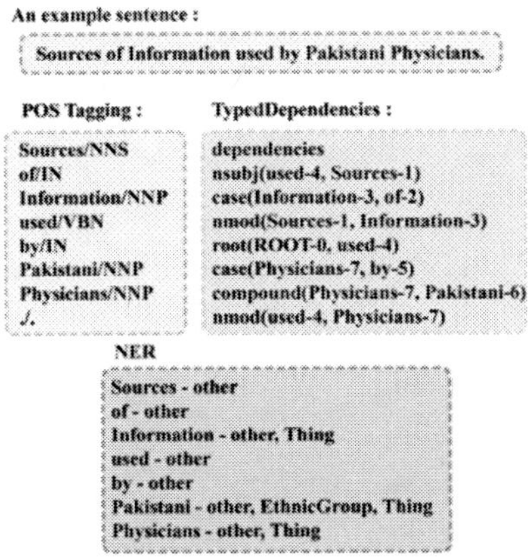

Figure 2. Example of grammar dependency parsing and its results, such as POS tags and typed dependencies, including NER classes queried from DBpedia.

C. Our Proposed Method

In this study, we propose a new method of OCR-error correction combining the edit distance technique and the ontology concept. We divide our system into three major steps: word selection based on edit distance, ontology creation, and OCR-error correction.

1) Word selection based on edit distance: Our input consists of bar graphs that contain an X-category, a Y-title, and optionally, a legend. We use the OCR library to obtain results from the axis descriptions (i.e., X-category and Y-title) and the legend; however, the OCR might produce some recognition errors as a result of unpredictable effects.

The major purpose of this step is to use the edit distance technique to measure the similarity of two words, one of which comes from an OCR result and the other from the caption or paragraphs. The similarity value varies with the distance scale, as shown in (1).

$$\mathrm{Sim}(A, B) = 1-(\mathrm{EditDis}(A, B)/(L(A) + L(B))) \qquad (1)$$

A and B represent two strings. EditDis(A, B) is the edit distance between the strings A and B representing the difference between words. L(A) and L(B) are the lengths of string A and B, respectively. Sim(A, B) is the similarity of strings A and B.

After we make a list of the compared words and their similarities, we sort the records in ascending order of distance. The number of lists is equal to the number of tokens of OCR results. The minimum edit distance score represents the highest similarity between two compared words.

After measuring word similarities, we select only the top five words closest to each OCR result and discard those with smaller similarities. We selected five words as candidates, because this quantity is reasonable in terms of utilization and resource management. For example, in an image, we have a word "well" incorrectly rendered as "woll." Our system can select candidates ordered by ascending scores, for example, welt, will, wall, well, and more. This example obviously illustrates that if the number of candidates is too small (e.g., one or three), we miss a correct word, "well." Moreover, if there are too many candidates, more memory space is consumed unnecessarily. Consequently, we obtain lists of similar words corresponding to OCR results.

2) Ontology creation: We construct our ontology following the design procedure in Section II-B. Before building the ontology, we must properly prepare our inputs for storage in our database, including several essential kinds of information regarding bar graphs, such as images' captions and paragraphs, and axis descriptions extracted using OCR.

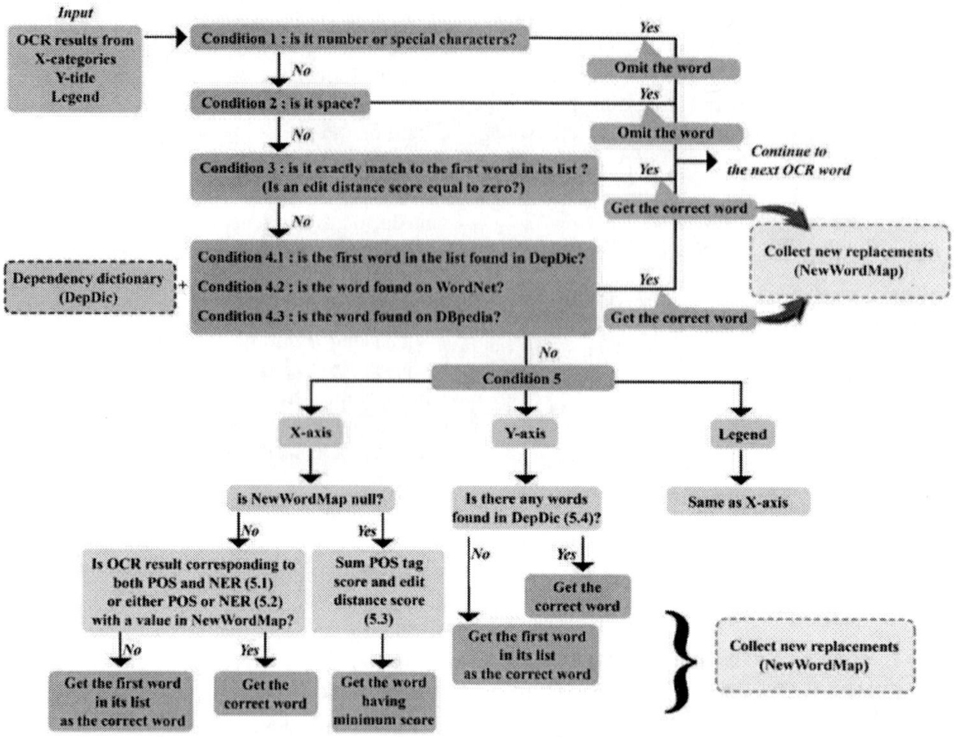

Figure 3. Third step of our method presenting five conditions to correct OCR errors.

We implement a tokenizing program to break the captions and the corresponding paragraphs into tokens. Then, we apply a dependency parser (Stanford parser) to analyze sentences and obtain their NER classes and POS. We separate this step into three minor parts.

First, our system automatically obtains POS tags for each token from the Stanford parser. Second, concurrently, it also obtains the typed-dependency of each pair of words in sentences based on grammar dependency parsing. Fig. 2 shows an example of the dependency parsing process. Third, we endeavor to find the categories that each word belongs to, by querying in DBpedia, all instances of which are represented in the form of triples including the subject, predicate, and object. Here, to acquire the categories, we focus only on the class hierarchies of each token that are queried on the predicate name "rdf:type" or "rdfs:subClassOf." Finally, we obtain our ontology.

3) OCR-error correction: The final step is the core of our system. After we acquire lists of similar words and our ontology from previous steps, we are ready to correct the error recognition.

Initially, we begin to create a mapping dictionary, called DepDic. This records the chain dependencies of the tokens contained in the axis description or the legend. In each image, we can create this mapping if we have at least one OCR result exactly matching the first word in its own list. We use this as the head of the dependency chains. For example, a Y-title contains a word "Information" that also appears in the example sentence. Suppose OCR correctly recognizes it. After following links of dependency relationships, we can obtain a dependency chain of "Information" that includes "Sources," "of," "used," "Physicians," "Pakistani," and "by."

To cover all possible situations for correcting errors, we divide our processes into five core conditions (Fig. 3).

The first condition is whether the OCR result is numeric. In general, the graph component descriptions must be described by alphabet letters, rather than in numerical terms. Numerical representation is inappropriate for our study, because we use the axis descriptions and a legend, which are mostly expressed in letters; on the other hand, numerical terms often appear as measurements. Moreover, we eliminate escape characters in sentences that interfere. It can be troublesome, if a sentence contains escape characters (such as /, -, <, >, and *), because they are reserved characters of SPARQL. If any OCR result contains such characters, our system ignores it.

The next condition is whether the OCR result contains only spaces. We omit it, because we cannot obtain information from it.

The third condition is whether the OCR result finds an exact match in a list. Our system examines the similarity between the OCR result and the first word of its list whose similarity is maximal. If the distance score is equal to zero, the paired words are identical. Hence, we do not need a replacement, because the OCR result is accurate. Further, we collect it into NewWordMap, which is used to store the OCR results and their new replacements.

The basic idea of our study is that in a graph image, a component description must correspondingly appear at its own caption or referred paragraph(s), since the OCR result, which is extracted from the component descriptions, is expected to have found a matched token in the caption or paragraph(s). However, the description might not appear anywhere in the item of literature, even in the caption or paragraph(s). In this situation, we obtain a list containing words with high distance scores that becomes an obstacle for our correcting system. The fourth condition has been proposed as a solution for this case.

Condition 4 is whether OCR provides correct results that match nothing in the caption or paragraph(s). In this condition, we designed three further sub-conditions. First is whether the first word of the list is matched in DepDic (Condition 4.1). If the matched word has been found, our system suggests using it as a new replacement, because it not only has the smallest distance score but is also collected in the same dependency chain. Otherwise, our system moves to the second sub-condition (Condition 4.2), whether the OCR result actually exists, by querying WordNet. If the system receives a return value from the SPARQL endpoint, this vocabulary exists exactly and can be used itself as the new replacement. Then, it is recorded in NewWordMap. For this sub-condition, its list of similar words is not used. The process of the third sub-condition (Condition 4.3) is similar to the second, but it differs in using DBpedia instead of WordNet. In general, we apply these conditions in the order 4.1, 4.2, 4.3. However, the order of conditions is changed in the case in which the distance score exceeds a threshold, following Conditions 4.2, 4.3, 4.1.

In Condition 5, ideas for correcting the OCR results are separated depending on the types of graph components. For the X-axis, we introduce a method for extracting the X-category based on the generality of bar graphs. Each word in the description of the X-axis must be classified into the corresponding category. For example, a graph might present some descriptions in the X-axis as follows: Suc, Fru, Glc, Gol, Raf, and Sta. After querying DBpedia, we acknowledge that these are names of soluble sugars and have the same POS tags, which are nouns. Based on this method, we obtain the correct OCR results from the X-axis. Initially, the system checks whether NewWordMap is available. Condition 5.1 is satisfied if it is not null, hence we select one of the replacements already stored in NewWordMap to find its POS tags and NER class by querying our ontology. Simultaneously, considering the current OCR result, we also query the POS tag and NER class of the first word in its list with our ontology. If the POS tags and NER class for them are consistent, the first word of the list is taken as the new replacement. Condition 5.2 is an extended version of Condition 5.1. If either the POS tag or NER class is matched, we also flexibly accept the first word of the list as the new replacement.

In contrast, Condition 5.3 checks whether NewWordMap is unavailable or null, hence we compute new scores based on both edit distance score and POS tags for all elements in the list. We assign scores to the POS tags to order their priorities for choosing the new replacement based on our experience of the tags' appearance on the X-axis. The tagging scores are assigned as follows: noun (score = 0), adjective (score = 1), verb (score = 2), article (score = 3), adverb (score = 4), preposition (score = 5), conjunction (score = 6), interjection (score = 7), others (score = 8), and number (score = 9). Nouns are assigned as minimum score, because descriptions of X-categories are mostly nouns. The new replacement of the OCR result is to be the word in the list that contains the lowest score. Note that the minimum score is typically assigned to the noun with the least distance.

Regarding the Y-axis, Condition 5.4 is satisfied if the OCR result is found in DepDic. The idea differs from that of the X-axis, because it contains a description as a title, not a group of words. Commonly, a description of a Y-title often appears as a sentence, a noun phrase, or a single word. Each token in a title must be connected in a chain of dependency; thus, using DepDic is an appropriate idea for selecting the most similar word in the list as a new replacement. Correcting OCR results located at the legend resembles the process at the X-axis. Moreover, as described above, Condition 4.1 also uses DepDic, which is similar to Condition 5.4. However, Condition 4.1 uses only the first word of the list to search in DepDic, whereas Condition 5.4 uses words in the list to explore DepDic until a match is retrieved. Whole words in the list are the top five with the closest distance to the OCR result; therefore, it might be necessary to use every word in the list to find candidates to be a new replacement.

In addition to the cases mentioned above, the OCR result can also be replaced by the first word of the list because of its lowest edit distance score.

III. EXPERIMENTAL RESULTS

We conducted an experiment to compare performance differences between the method used in our previous study (Setting 1) [10] and the method proposed in this study (Setting 2). In the previous study, we proposed a method for correcting OCR results only using the edit distance technique.

After running both systems, we obtained a total of 1,112 OCR tokens from 100 bar graphs. We evaluated both settings by verifying the differences between the OCR results and their new replacements through comparison with actual words showing in the graphs. Setting 1 was tested using the edit distance method based on the previous study, while our method was tested and shown in Setting 2.

We compared accuracies from both settings, as presented in Fig. 4. Our method provided a higher accuracy rate, reaching 81%, and also produced an improvement over the previous method's 54%. Moreover, the precision rate of Setting 2 is approximately 81%.

Fig. 5 presents the accuracy rates of each condition implemented in our method. Moreover, the proportion of correct and incorrect replacements for each condition is also presented there. There were conditions in which the number of correct replacements was greater than the number of incorrect ones, i.e., Conditions 1 or 2, Condition 3, Condition

4.1, Condition 4.2 and Condition 4.3, which attained accuracies of 86%, 97%, 85%, 62%, and 55%, respectively. The highest accuracy was attained in Condition 3, with Condition 5.4 attaining the lowest accuracy.

In addition, we examined the significant differences between these two settings. We observed that our outputs were of the nominal type, classified as "Wrong" or "Correct." We collected the results from both settings and tested them using McNemar's test. This is a statistical test used on paired nominal data to examine a change between two different sets of data that are obtained from before and after treatment. We calculated a two-tailed probability value (p), which we used to decide to accept or reject a null hypothesis. It was less than 0.0001. A small p value indicates a significant difference.

IV. DISCUSSION

This paper presents a solution for OCR-error correction based on multiple ontologies, NLP, and edit distance. The focus is to develop a system that can effectively correct OCR's errors and enhance its performance (i.e., accuracy and precision rates) over traditional methods. Moreover, our method is not limited only to biology, but is available also for use with other domains, as long as there is a related ontology to apply it with. In this study, we evaluated our method by comparison with the method in our previous study, in which we used only the edit distance to correct OCR results. We applied these two systems to the same dataset containing 100 images of bar graphs and 1,112 OCR tokens.

Reviewing the accuracy rates of Settings 1 and 2, we see that the second setting provided better performance than the first for two reasons. First, our method potentially classifies irrelevant OCR results, which are not to be recorded in NewWordMap. For example, some tokens are meaningless, because they do not come from descriptions of the graph but from other sources, e.g., a part of a bar. OCR can misleadingly recognize such tokens as characters, such as "l-l" or "III." Our method used Conditions 1 and 2 to detect this case, differently from the method of Setting 1, which cannot distinguish relevant from irrelevant characters. This is a shortcoming of Setting 1, which causes many recognition errors. Second, the method of Setting 1 is limited to using the least distance. It can provide an incorrect replacement, because the lowest score represents only a similar word, except for the case of a distance score equal to zero. On the other hand, our system applied many techniques to overcome the OCR difficulty. In addition to using the edit distance to find a list of similar words for each OCR result, we also used ontologies to discover the most suitable replacements for correcting OCR errors.

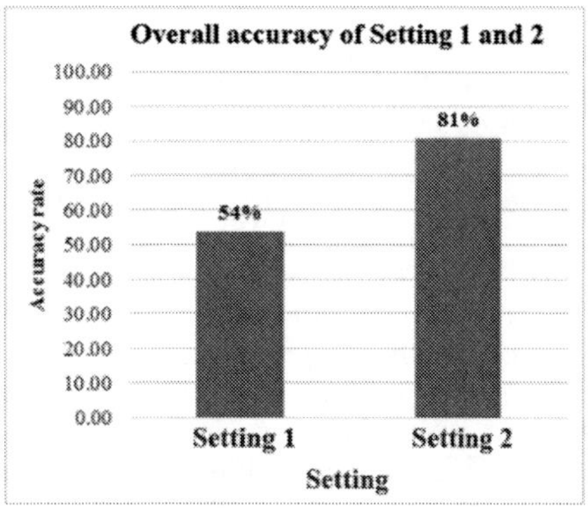

Figure 4. Overall accuracy of Settings 1 and 2.

In other respects, we analyzed some errors that occurred during the experiment and discovered two possible causes. First, some axis descriptions are originally compound nouns. When OCR was used to process the graphs to extract the descriptions, it independently separated them into tokens. On the other hand, to extract words from captions and paragraphs, we used the dependency parser to handle compound nouns. Thus, when our system compared a similarity between OCR results and tokens from captions or paragraphs, we might not be able to find a match. For example, the word "part-of-speech" was a compound noun. OCR divided this word into three independent words, i.e., "part," "of," and "speech." Simultaneously, the dependency parser extracted the caption and obtained this word "part-of-speech" without separation. Hence, we could not find a match between the separated and non-separated words. Second, some OCR results were not mentioned anywhere in a caption or in paragraphs in the text body. We consider that there are two reasons why the words found in a bar graph are not mentioned in its caption or in the paragraphs. First, a token described in axis descriptions is either too general or completely explains itself. For example, if a graph appearing in a biological journal contains some sugar names on the X-axis, an author who is familiar with biology might find these words too general for other researchers who work in related areas; hence, he or she omits explanations in the paper. Second, the extracted token might not be definitely related to the study.

Condition 1 and 2 were very useful due to reduced number of errors by discarding irrelevant OCR results. These

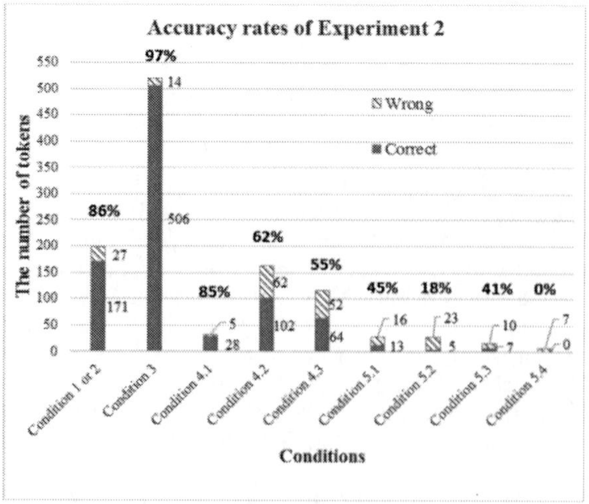

Figure 5. Illustration of accuracy rates in Setting 2 and the proportion of correct and incorrect replacements of each condition.

conditions are also a main reason that makes our method much better than the previous method. They accurately detect irrelevant characters and provide good accuracy rate, 86%.

For Condition 3, we obtained the best accuracy (97%), because OCR was an effective application; moreover, we prepared the input data efficiently. At the beginning, we collected the bar graphs and cleaned them by decreasing noise, omitting irrelevant parts, and increasing sharpness. Based on this evidence, we admit that this condition highly impacts our method's performance. However, we know that other conditions also substantially supported our system, because the accuracy rate was reduced to 45%, if our system used only Condition 3.

For Condition 4, we used ontologies and dependency relationships to correct OCR errors. Obviously, Condition 4.1 provided appropriate accuracy. It applied our chain dependency dictionary to find a match by using the first words of the lists. We proved that the viewpoint of using grammar dependencies was acceptable, because we obtained accurate results, 84%. Moreover, we also used ontologies (i.e., WordNet and DBpedia) to overcome the difficulty of OCR errors. We used them in this study, because we needed to confirm that the words existed. Owing to the advantage of ontology, the recognition errors were moderately reduced; furthermore, the average accuracy rate of this condition was approximately 60%.

However, under these conditions, we encountered errors if the length of a word was too short, especially for two or three characters. The short-length words were often represented as prepositions (such as "in," "on," or "at"), conjunctions (such as "so" or "as") and abbreviations (such as CG and NLP). We realized that every sentence regularly contained at least one preposition or conjunction, since in the DepDic, short-length words (such as prepositions) were ordinarily stored. As a consequence, it was easy for a short-length word to be replaced accidentally by an incorrect selection, because candidates (such as prepositions), even incorrect ones, had usually been found in DepDic. For instance, we assume that we have a word "so," and the first word in its list is "hi," as recorded in DepDic. It is clear that these two example words are totally different, but their distance score is only two. In this case, the system assigns the word "hi" as an incorrect replacement for the OCR result, "so." It was essential to reduce the probability to counter the incorrect matching in DepDic, in particular for short-length words. We decided to rearrange the order of conditions based on the distance score and the word length. If the length of a word was greater than five characters, and the distance score was less than three, then the word was processed through Conditions 4.1, 4.2, and 4.3, respectively. Otherwise, we began the process by querying ontologies (Condition 4.2 and 4.3) to confirm the word's existence and then applying DepDic (Condition 4.1). To evaluate this idea, we conducted a minor test of the order of conditions. As the result, the sequence of conditions definitely impacted the accuracy of the system. After rearranging, the accuracy rate increased dramatically from 39% to 59%.

Observing the results of Condition 5, we see that the overall accuracy rate was approximately 31%. We obtained this low accuracy because we could not find a match in the ontologies (WordNet and DBpedia), since it was impossible to acquire a correct word category. Investigation of why the ontologies had not returned any results revealed that the word might have many equivalents or different spellings.

Moreover, we attempted to compare the results of our study with those of another existing approach. The evaluation presented in [14] aimed to compare results obtained from the proposed method and a basic method that created lists of candidates of each character based on distances. After comparing the differences in the experimental results, which proposed method reduced errors better than the basic method by approximately 29%. Similarly, in our study, our method also attained remarkable results that were much improved over the edit distance method. The error reduction was approximately 27%. Based on this finding, the results from our method and the other method were in agreement, because the key idea of using semantics to reduce OCR errors and the obtained results were in agreement.

Regarding the statistical evidence, we conclude that the difference of both settings (i.e., the edit distance method and ours) is considered to be extremely statistically significant, because the two-tailed p value is very small.

V. Conclusion and Future Work

A graph can represent data visually, rendering them easy for a human to interpret and understand. However, automatic information extraction obtained from OCR is desirable. In order to acquire information correctly, in this paper, we proposed a novel OCR-error correction method utilizing the concepts of ontology, NLP, and edit distance. We constructed our ontology to support sentence dependencies, POS tagging, and word categories (NER). Moreover, we also used DBpedia and WordNet by querying via their endpoints to obtain useful information. Sentence dependencies were very efficient in handling the difficulty of OCR errors. We created a dictionary based on the dependency relationships. The edit distance is a traditional technique that we also used in the previous study. However, in this study, we used it only for ranking similar words based on distance scores and storing them in a list corresponding to each OCR result. Our objective was to find a suitable solution for correcting OCR errors that would provide better accuracy and precision than the previous method.

As noted above, we evaluated our method by conducting an experiment with two different settings and then comparing the outcomes. Explicitly, our method provided better results than the previous one. Based on the experimental results of this study, Condition 3 clearly provided the highest accuracy rates, definitely improving the overall performance of our method. Without other supportive conditions, it would not likely reach such high accuracy (81%); therefore, the idea of using dependency relationships and ontologies in Conditions 4 and 5 was very fruitful.

In our future research, we will continue to develop a semantic system based on this method. We will extract significant information from the graph and apply it to available ontologies. Moreover, other types of graphs will also be of concern and will be used in the future as target data.

REFERENCES

[1] Y. LeCun, L. Bottou, Y. Bengio, and P. Haffner, "Gradient-based learning applied to document recognition," Proceedings of the IEEE, vol. 86, no. 11, Nov 1998, pp. 2278–2324.

[2] S. Kataria, W. Browuer, P. Mitra, and C. L. Giles, "Automatic extraction of data points and text blocks from 2-dimensional plots in digital documents." in AAAI, vol. 8, pp. 1169–1174, 2008.

[3] W. Huang, C. L. Tan, and W. K. Leow, "Associating text and graphics for scientific chart understanding," in Document Analysis and Recognition, Proceedings. Eighth International Conference on. IEEE, pp. 580–584, 2005.

[4] D. Chen, J.-M. Odobez, and H. Bourlard, "Text detection and recognition in images and video frames," Pattern Recognition, vol. 37, no. 3, pp. 595–608, 2004.

[5] C.-J. Lin, C.-C. Liu, and H.-H. Chen, "A simple method for Chinese video ocr and its application to question answering," Computational linguistics and Chinese language processing, vol. 6, no. 2, pp. 11–30, 2001.

[6] T. A. Lasko and S. E. Hauser, "Approximate string matching algorithms for limited-vocabulary ocr output correction," in Photonics West 2001-Electronic Imaging. International Society for Optics and Photonics, pp. 232–240, 2000.

[7] X. Tong and D. A. Evans, "A statistical approach to automatic ocr error correction in context," in Proceedings of the fourth workshop on very large corpora, pp. 88–100, 1996.

[8] D. D. Walker, W. B. Lund, and E. K. Ringger, "Evaluating models of latent document semantics in the presence of ocr errors," in Proceedings of the 2010 Conference on Empirical Methods in Natural Language Processing. Association for Computational Linguistics, pp. 240–250, 2010.

[9] M. Nagata, "Japanese ocr error correction using character shape similarity and statistical language model," in Proceedings of the 17th international conference on Computational linguistics-Volume 2. Association for Computational Linguistics, pp. 922–928, 1998.

[10] S. Kanjanawattana and M. Kimura, "A proposal for a method of graph ontology by automatically extracting relationships between captions and X- and y-axis titles," Proceedings of the International Conference on Knowledge Engineering and Ontology Development (KEOD 2015), vol. 2, pp. 231–238, Nov 2015. [Online]. Available from: http://dx.doi.org/10.5220/0005602102310238

[11] M. Jeong, B. Kim, and G. G. Lee, "Semantic-oriented error correction for spoken query processing," in Automatic Speech Recognition and Understanding, ASRU'03. 2003 IEEE Workshop on. IEEE, pp. 156–161, 2003.

[12] Y. Bassil and M. Alwani, "Ocr post-processing error correction algorithm using google online spelling suggestion," arXiv preprint arXiv:1204.0191, 2012.

[13] A. Jobbins, G. Raza, L. Evett, and N. Sherkat, "Postprocessing for ocr: Correcting errors using semantic relations," in LEDAR. Language Engineering for Document Analysis and Recognition, AISB 1996 Workshop, Sussex, England, 1996.

[14] L. Zhuang and X. Zhu, "An ocr post-processing approach based on multi-knowledge," in Knowledge-Based Intelligent Information and Engineering Systems, Springer, pp. 157–157, 2005.

[15] A. Garcia, M. Szomszor, H. Alani, and O. Corcho, "Preliminary results in tag disambiguation using dbpe-dia," 2009.

[16] E. Loggi, F. K. Bihl, C. Cursaro, C. Granieri, S. Galli, L. Brodosi, G. Furlini, M. Bernardi, C. Brander, and P. Andreone, "Virus-specific immune response in hbeag-negative chronic hepatitis b: relationship with clinical profile and hbsag serum levels," PloS one, vol. 8, no. 6, p. e65327, 2013.

A Classification Method to Select a Mashup Creating Tool Based on Prior Knowledge of the End-User

Sofía Oraá Pérez

Grupo Reconocido de Investigación en Recuperación de Información y Bibliotecas Digitales (GRINBD)
Universidad de Valladolid
Email: sofiaoraa@gmail.com

María Mercedes Martínez-González

Departamento de Informática
Universidad de Valladolid
Edificio T.I.T., Campus 'Miguel Delibes' s/n, 47011 Valladolid
Email: mercedes@infor.uva.es

***Abstract*—Over the years, several tools and frameworks have appeared with the aim to facilitate the creation of mashups for the end user. These tools aim to integrate semantic and nonsemantic information available on the Web. However, not all users have the necessary technological knowledge to use them interchangeably. In this article, we propose a two stage classification for this set of tools that will allow users to select the most suitable tool based on their previous knowledge. In the first stage, we focus on the interface for the construction of the mashup provided by the system, enabling users to choose the technology they feel most comfortable with. In the second stage, a set of criteria for the choice of a particular tool are presented.**

Keywords–Mashups; Classification method; Selection of a tool.

I. Introduction

A mashup is a Web application that provides new functionality by combining, incorporating and transforming the resources and the services available on the net. These applications collect and process structured data from different sources and then display it for the users, while changing the original look-and-feel [1]. Mashups are particularly interesting because they facilitate the integration of information for a wide range of users. Thus, they become a way for users with little technical knowledge to perform this kind of tasks. An example of this technology is *Neighborhood Scout* [2] which allows users to select the best neighborhood to buy a house based on available data on schools, lifestyle or crime levels, among other factors.

As we have stated before, the purpose of this technology is to enable users to control relevant data, instead of software developers. However, the use of mashups involves programmers who must first study the data sources used to extract the necessary information in order to be able to reuse them. This task is quite complex, time consuming and it also undermines the main objective of this technology: to allow as much end users as possible to perform their own integration of information [1]. To overcome this problem, in recent years several tools and frameworks have been developed to facilitate obtaining information from different sources without the need to have developer knowledge [3].

Our objective is to help users without the necessary technological knowledge to choose the most suitable mashup creation tool. To do so, we provide a two-stage method of classification that facilitates the selection of a tool for mashups based on the user's prior knowledge. The existing classifications in the literature for these kinds of tools focus on a set of mashups, without a comprehensive review of them, or provide unclear and hard to apply criteria for the selection of a suitable tool when the user is inexperienced.

The first stage of our proposal classifies tools according to their interface, helping users to choose the tools with the most familiar technology from all available categories. Thus the number of tools available for the user will be limited, preventing them being overwhelmed and facilitating selection within a smaller set. The second stage provides a number of additional criteria that will help the user to select a specific tool from all available tools in that category. For example, a person who has studied statistics will be more familiar with using spreadsheets, so a tool using this technology will be the most appropriate one.

The rest of the paper is organized as follows: Section 2 contains a brief description of how this classification has been done in previous studies; in Section 3, we present the proposed method of classification; in Section 4 some of the existing tools are analyzed using the proposed method of classification; Section 5 contains an overall analysis of the tools studied; finally, Section 6 contains ideas for future work and the conclusions of our study.

II. State of the Art

1) Classification based on 4 criteria: Yu et al. [4] talks about the five most popular tools for building mashups in 2008. Two of them are no longer available. Whilst explaining their functionality, they enumerate their characteristics. This article divides the tools using four factors: the component model (type, interface or scalability), the composition (outputs, orchestration, data passing or ability to handle exceptions), the development (tool for inexperienced users or developers) and the runtime environment (browser plug-in or application standalone).

This article does not make a proper classification of the available tools. It simply makes a list of the characteristics of the five tools analyzed. Some of the criteria provided may be useful to some users; however, no further explanation is offered so as to understand or to extract concepts, meaning technical knowledge is required to use this classification.

2) Classification based on prior technical knowledge of the user: In 2009, Fischer et al. [5] divided the tools into six major types: programming paradigm, script language, spreadsheet, wiring, programming by demonstration and automatic creation. Their goal was to do a study of the tools to state if an inexperienced user could use them or if prior knowledge on programming would be needed to do so.

Categories established in this classification do not serve as a prefilter based on user's profile to choose the right tool for two reasons: in each category they mix easy to use tools with more complex ones without proper clarification. In addition, the selected classification is not intuitive; that is, a user with no previous technological knowledge would not be able to use it for the selection of a concrete tool.

3) Classification based on the use of semantic knowledge: In his book *"A developer's guide to the semantic Web"* (2014) [1], Yu divided the tools into semantic and nonsemantic. The first ones to appear were the nonsemantic. An example of this technology are the *"map mashups"* [6] that allowed inexperienced users to exploit the usefulness of maps without having prior knowledge of programming or graphic mapping. These mashups had many limitations mainly due to the heterogeneity of the data; a change in the structure of this data forced them to reprogram their entire operation. That is why semantic mashups appeared, using Resource Description Framework (RDF) (as a data model) and SPARQL Protocol and RDF Query Language (SPARQL) (for task execution) allowing for effective organization, finding and representation of data regardless of the syntax. Therefore, they are better suited for change. An example of this technology is *Revyu* [7]. *Revyu* is a Web page to create reviews using RDF without having any knowledge of semantics.

Sorting mashups into semantic and nonsemantic does not provide enough information for people unfamiliar with this terminology; that is, for users without any knowledge of necessary technology, who will be the ones that will need more support to perform the selection of a suitable tool.

4) Classification based on 3 criteria: In her thesis (2014), Aghaee [8] developed a tool for creating mashups using natural language. She uses three criteria to classify existing tools: the usability of the systems based on the end-user's programming skills; how these users interact with the system and their various features; and the amount of aid provided by the system for the user to create their own mashup.

The classification focuses solely on mashups based on natural language, so it is insufficient to provide an overview of existing tools.

As has been observed during the evaluating of the existing classifications, none of them fits our objective and it is necessary to create a new classification method. The existing categorizations provide difficult to apply or unclear criteria, or else they are solely focused on a set of tools without an overall review. However, some of the supplied criteria can be useful and will be reused after being refined to achieve our goal: for a user to be able to select the right tool to develop mashups guided by our method of classification. To do this, we use a classification in two stages: first, using the interface provided by the tool for the user, which will determine the necessary knowledge about the technology that the user should have, and will allow users make a first filter selecting those tools that best fit their knowledge; the second, which will provide additional criteria allowing further refining of the selection by focusing on those features that make the tool unique.

III. Method of Classification. A proposal

A. *First phase of classification*

In the first stage of our classification, tools are divided based on the interface provided, allowing the user to select a set of them according to their previous knowledge. A summary of these categories can be found in Table I. What follows is a brief explanation of the selected criteria:

- Mashups tools **based on programming by demonstration** allow the users to generate their own mashup through a series of examples. It is the most appropriate technology for a person without previous knowledge of programming when they want to make the integration of information on pages whose structure hardly varies, for example, a news page. Their use is very simple. The user only needs to copy and paste pieces of the website indicating which content they want. After that, the tool will automatically be able to get the rest of the information on a particular topic following the structure indicated. Their functionality is limited.
- Mashups tools **based on databases** are very similar to those based on programming by demonstration, with the difference that they are able to adapt to changes in the structure of the Web pages consulted. This set of tools processes each of the existing Web pages as if it were a table in a database. It is therefore the appropriate technology for people without previous knowledge if the structure of the pages varies. These tools are able to integrate information following the HTML structure of the Web pages. As in the previous case, its functionality is limited, although it can adapt to the variation of the structure of the web making suggestions of possible integration. They require human intervention if the change in the structure is large.
- Mashups tools **based on widgets** contain graphic components used to create the mashup as an alternative to writing code. This type of technology is suitable for inexperienced users with little knowledge about technology who wish to do integration with more complex functionality than in the two previous cases. For example, the tool can be used to merge a single record in two different sources. Each widget is a black box with a specific functionality that can be used for integration of information even if the person does not know how the component works internally.
- In the mashup tools **based on pipes**, a "pipe" is used between each of the different data sources to connect them unifying their formats. As with tools based on widgets, these kinds of tools will allow the users with prior knowledge of programming to perform their own data integration using interchangeable components. This set of tools is more powerful, allowing the user to make adjustments, for example, changing the format during data integration or modifying the output structure. As a result, more knowledge is required to use these tools. They can be integrated into web graphics editors (based on widgets) to perform the most important tasks of integration and transformation of information [4].
- Mashups tools **based on spreadsheets** cannot access the real Web content, the information must be inserted directly into spreadsheets since it is the only input

TABLE I. CLASSIFICATION TOOLS: PHASE 1

Class	*Brief description based on the user profile*
Programming by demonstration	Inexperienced users. Pages with a stable structure.
Databases	Inexperienced users. Pages with varying structures.
Widgets	Inexperienced users with little knowledge about technology. Widgets with predefined functions that can be combined to achieve the integration of the data.
Pipes	Users with some prior knowledge of programming. Predefined functions that allow small adjustments using programming such as changes in the output format or in the structure of data integration.
Spreadsheets	Users with extensive knowledge in the use of Spreadsheets. Data input and output is in the spreadsheet where tasks are performed using predefined functions.
Scripting languages	Users with high programming skills. The user must develop the script that will perform data integration.
Automatic Creation	The system is able to obtain the data without human intervention.

format that these tools are able to understand. After processing the data, the results are inserted in the spreadsheet so the user can use them to draw their own conclusions. Their use requires someone with extensive knowledge on the use of spreadsheets, like someone who has studied statistics, for example.

- Mashups tools **based on scripting languages** are quite complex to develop, require a long time to create as well as high programming skills since it is the user who must create the script. That is why, inexperienced users cannot use this set of tools. Their use is recommended for programmers with extensive programming knowledge when they need to implement a very specific function that is not available in the easier-to-use tools.
- **Automatic creation** mashups tools include small components called *mashlets* to perform specific functions like automatically finding and proposing relationships between data without the intervention of human users. This type of tool is very useful when you have a well structured page with high semantic content as in the case of *DBPedia* [9]. Thanks to this technology numerous links between *DBpedia* and *RDF Book Mashup dataset* [10] have been automatically created [1].

After applying the first selection stage, we expect users to be able to find the type of tool that best suits their prior knowledge and with which they will be more comfortable. Table I summarizes the most appropriate set of tools depending on the user's profile. We expect that users will be able to use it to select the set of tools best adapted to their knowledge.

B. Second phase of classification

Within each of the categories listed in Table I we can find numerous tools, so in the second stage of our classification we propose a series of criteria to help the user to select a concrete tool among the ones available. A brief explanation of the selected criteria follows:

- **Autonomy of the tool**: this criterion is related to the ability of the tool to function as a complete program (stand-alone) that is installed on the end user's computer and will be able to function without an Internet connection; a Web tool that does not require installation; or a plug-in that must be installed on the user's browser.
- **Ease of use**: refers to the difficulty that the users will find to create their mashup. Although the users select the type of tool according to their prior knowledge, they may need additional programming skills to use a particular tool, thus preventing inexperienced users from using them. The tools can be easy to use, require prior knowledge of certain technology or require advanced programming skills.
- **Format of the data sources supported**: These tools can be designed to understand: the HTML structure of a Web page; The really easy to understand syndications (RSS) in XML used for sharing data on the Web; the information in various formats such as RDF, XML or CSV (Spreadsheets); or to read the set of subroutines, functions and procedures to facilitate obtaining the information grouped in the application programming interface Web (API).
- **Languages used**: there are many languages to express the content of Web pages that this set of tools can understand or use as output format to provide answers, including: RDF, SPARQL, XML, HTML, RSS, CSV or Atom.
- **License type**: the tools can be free (open source) or proprietary code, in which case it is necessary to purchase them.

The selected criteria can be useful as a guide to locate the right tool even in cases not covered by our work. We also hope that the criteria are clear enough to be understood even by those without experience in the field of computing.

TABLE II. CLASSIFICATION OF TOOLS FOR CREATING MASHUPS

Category	*Tools*
Programming by demonstration	ClipClip, Karma
Databases	Import.io, Yahoo Query Language, MashQL
Widgets	ClickScript, JackBe Presto Wires, Kapow, Lotus Mashups
Pipes	FeedsAPI, WebHookIt, Mulesoft, Huggin
Spreadsheets	Gneiss, StrikeIron SOA Express for Excel & Extensio Excel Extender for Microsoft Excel, AMICO:CALC, Open Refine
Scripting Languages	Web Mashup Scripting Language, WSO2 Application Server
Automatic creation	Revyu, Books@HPClab

IV. APPLYING THE CLASSIFICATION METHOD

Several examples of this technology exist, some of them can be found in Table II. To select these examples an exhaustive search with different keywords has been performed, including the terms: "mashups", "data integration tools" or "building mashups"; in several sources, such as: "Scopus", "Scholar" and "Web of Science". All selected tools are free or have a free trial version. We have focused on those tools with dates after 2012 that are available online for downloading and testing by users. As far as we know, this selection is broad enough to cover most available tools on the web.

Of all the tools available, one of each category described in the first phase has been selected, to which the classification method proposed will be applied. To perform the selection, the most recent date and the availability of an online tutorial to

TABLE III. CRITERIA FOR SELECTING THE MASHUP

Tool	*Category*	*Autonomy of the tool*	*Ease of use*	*Data sources format*	*Languages used*	*License Type*
Karma	Programming by demonstration	Stand-alone	Easy	HTML	HTML	Open Source
Import.io	Databases	Web Tool	Easy	HTML, JSON	CSV	Free
ClickScript	Widgets	Web Tool	Easy	RSS, HTML	JavaScript	Open Source
Huggin	Pipes	Stand-alone	Easy	API	RSS	Open Source
OpenRefine	Spreadsheets	Stand-alone	Easy	Spreadsheets CSV	RDF	Open Source
WMSL	Scripting languages	Web Tool	Advanced programming skills	HTML, metada, Javascript	WSLScripts	Open Source
Revyu	Automatic Creation	Web Tool	Easy	XML, HTML, RDF	HTML, RDF	Free

facilitate the installation and use has been taken into account. A summary of this information can be found in Table III.

Within mashups **based on programming by demonstration** we found: ***Karma*** [11] is a stand-alone, open source tool that allows the user to obtain, model and integrate data easily (Fig. 1) [12]. The user can see the result of the integration at any time during the creation process. This tool suggests predefined tags of its repository that could be helpful for the user to label their own data sets. For the extraction process it uses a Document Object Model (DOM) based on the structure defined by the user.

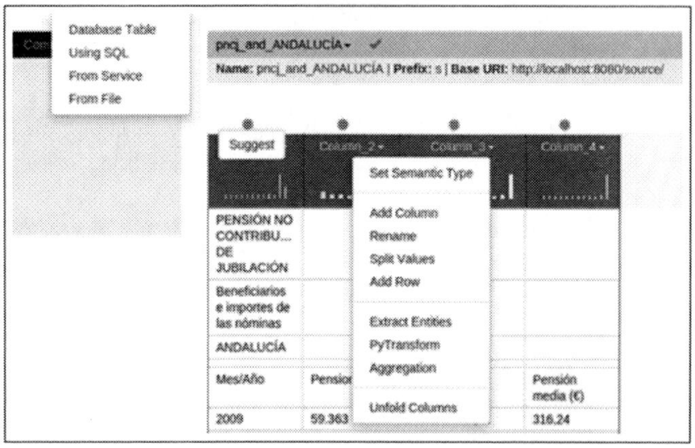

Figure 1. Karma.

As a tool for creating mashups **based on databases** we have: ***Import.io*** [13] is a free Web tool that allows users to obtain information from websites following their HTML structure [14]. It is very easy to use, the users just have to paste the URL that they want to study in the application. In addition, the tool provides a set of sample pages, videos, numerous documents and a forum where users can discuss the problems encountered. The results obtained after the extraction of information can be accessed and modified at any time. Similarly it is possible to add additional information to the data set. The user can choose the structure of integrated data and fill them with the appropriate information manually indicating the sections of the website to use (Fig. 2). Once processed, the data can be downloaded in CSV format.

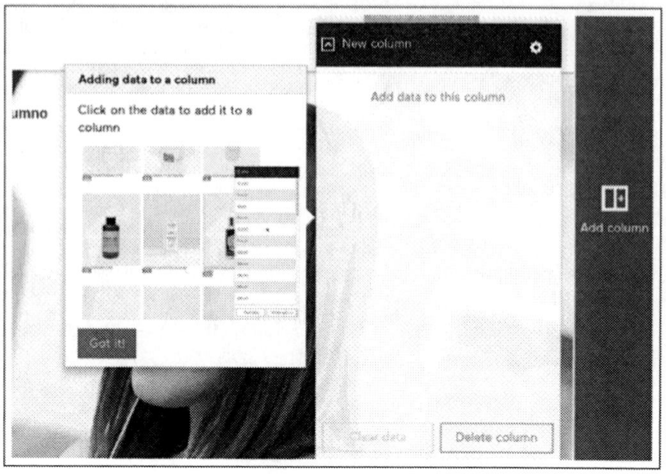

Figure 2. Import.io.

Among the tools **based on widgets** we want to highlight: ***ClickScript*** [15] is a free web tool to obtain data from RSS feeds and Web pages via Javascript functions [16]. The integration of data will be done through the Widgets available in the tool so that users without previous knowledge can use it easily. An example of these widgets can be seen in Fig. 3. The application provides information on the functionality of each widget, the necessary inputs and the outputs it provides.

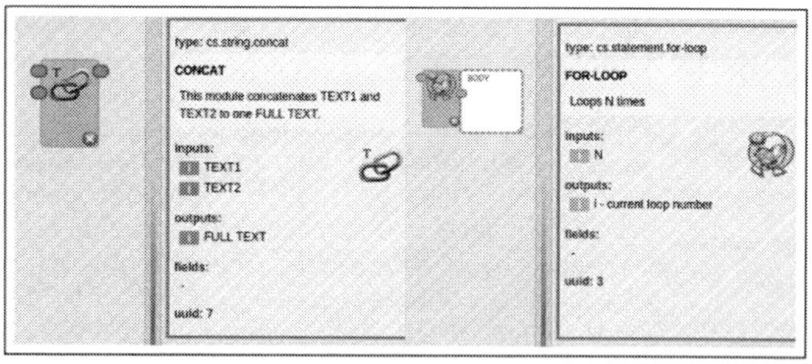

Figure 3. ClickScript.

The most popular example of **mashups based on pipes** was *Yahoo!Pipes*, a tool that was the basis for many other developments such as *DERI Pipes* or *Marmite*. Unfortunately, in 2015 the definitive closure of this tool was announced. As an alternative example we include: ***Huggin*** [17] is a free platform capable of connecting a lot of tools together. It uses the figure of the agent, i.e., a predefined functionality connectable with others. This tool takes advantage of the available APIs to connect applications such as Twitter, Dropbox, Basecamp or JIRA [17]. As an example of the functionality offered we have, among others, an agent capable of detecting changes in a document in Dropbox and sending them by mail; or an agent able to check the weather in a town and send an alert to the user's mobile at a specific time. It is easy to use, the user must follow the instructions described on each agent (see Fig. 4). *Huggin* has a lot of online guides to help users during installation and use. Additionally it has the ability to add functionality by programming directly.

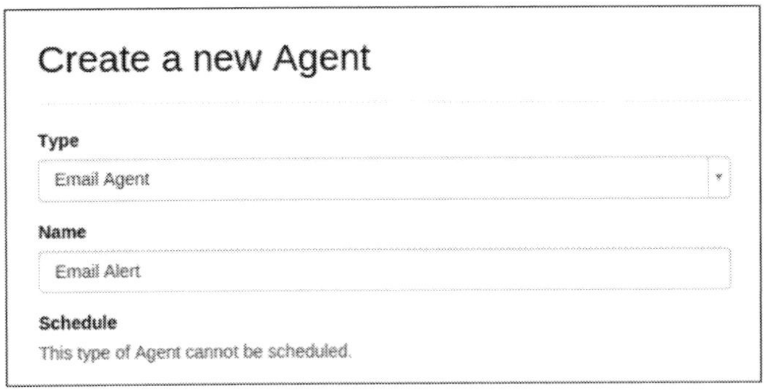

Figure 4. Huggin.

As an example among tools **based on spreadsheets** we found: ***Open Refine*** [18] is a stand-alone, open source tool developed by Google [19]. It adds functionality allowing the integration of information from different sources, such as, from one or more files from the user's computer, from a website via its URL or from a Google Drive document. It supports different formats, including CSV, Excel, XML and JSON. Open Refine also contains default features (Fig. 5) that facilitate management, integration and data filtering. This tool allows the user to add semantic information so data can be integrated in RDF format. The application is easy to use even for inexperienced users with minimal knowledge of spreadsheets.

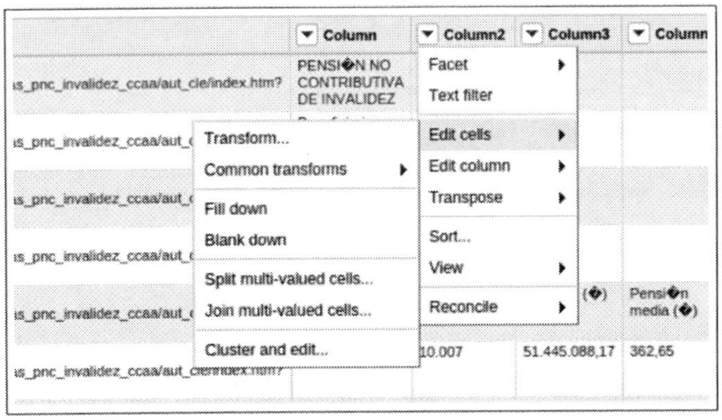

Figure 5. Open Refine.

An example of tools **based on scripting languages** is: ***Web Mashup Scripting Language*** o ***WMSL*** [20] allows end users to work on their browser without additional plug-ins [21]. To create the application the user must develop a page that combines HTML, metadata that describes the mapping relationships and a small piece of code or script, which is why advanced programming skills are required to use it. In the tutorial available online, numerous examples of this language appear (Fig. 6).

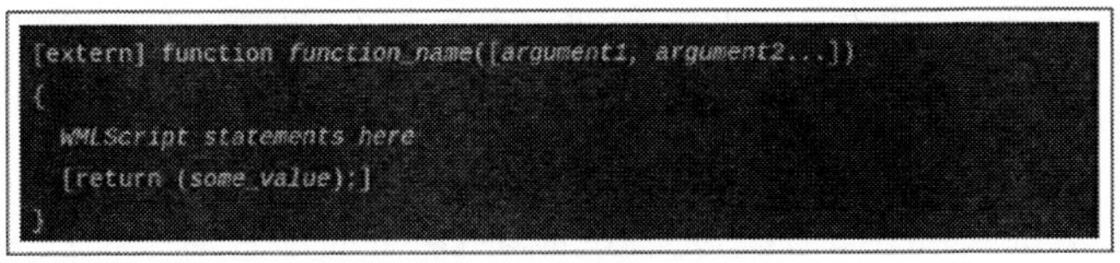

Figure 6. WMSL.

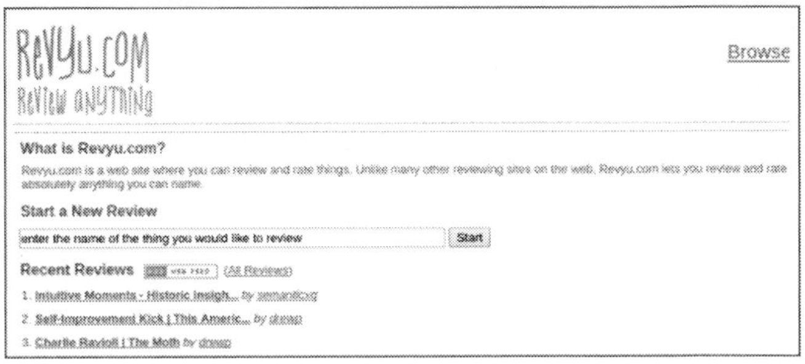

Figure 7. Revyu.

As an example of the tools **based on automatic creation** we have: ***Revyu*** [7] is a web application that allows users to create reusable reviews in RDF without knowledge of semantics being necessary [22]. This tool adds functionality allowing a user without the necessary knowledge to access, compare and query RDF sources. It is free and simple to use, the user must copy the URL of the website that he wants to analyze (Fig. 7). Revyu is able to understand HTML, XML and RDF. The integrated information will be presented to the user in HTML format so it can be easily read and in RDF format so it can be understood by a computer.

V. Global Analysis of the Proposal

Although the tools studied in the previous section can be used depending on the specific needs of users, the selection of the tool based on prior knowledge of the user is recommended. The classification proposal contains two stages:

The first stage classifies tools according to the interface provided. An inexperienced person interested in collecting information on a particular subject on a news website, should choose a mashup tool "based on programming by demonstration" that will allow them to obtain relevant data easily by simply copying and pasting the text from the page. The functionality of this tool is quite limited; however, it is the best technology to start using tools to create mashups. By contrast, people with extensive knowledge of programming who want information on an unknown and very specific topic will select a mashup tool "based on scripting language" that will allow them to develop their own functionality by programming their own script. This tool is quite complex to use and requires the user to know the structure of data to be processed perfectly. Even for expert users, it is recommended using simpler technologies like "based on widgets" for integrating information if the same functionality can be obtained.

The second stage of the classification method provides a set of criteria that will allow the user to select the specific tool within the category. One of the most useful criteria can be the "ease of use" when the user is inexperienced. However, it is possible that within a set of tools of the same category this criterion is not a differentiator. Before choosing the tool, the user must take into account the "type of license". All the tools discussed in Section 4 of our article are free or provide a free trial version. Testing the tool before purcharsing it is recommended, to ensure it provides the proper functionality. Finally, the criterion on "the format of the data sources supported" indicates that the tool is able to understand different languages on the website without requiring the user to have additional knowledge and therefore without additional costs involved. If the tool is easy to use, has the necessary functionality for the integration of data and is able to understand the language in which the website is written, the user can choose any of the tools that meet the criteria.

Tools based on spreadsheets require input data to be inserted into the worksheet and the output will be generated in the same document using the same format. It is for this reason that the functionality may seem more limited when compared to other tools. However, experts in the use of this technology will find the ideal tool within this set.

In recent years more efforts have been made to develop tools that can understand natural language, i.e., the language used by humans to communicate. This language is quite complex to understand by a machine, that is why efforts to add semantics in Web services abound. With the increasing amount of linked data, ontologies and semantic information available on the web, it is likely that new "automatic creation" tools that do not require human intervention appear [23]. Unfortunately, in most cases, the heterogeneity of the sources prevents this automatic integration. Humans must evaluate the decisions taken. This field gradually progresses, however, progress is still not enough [24].

This classification is intended to help users, even those that do not have prior technological knowledge, to choose a tool even in cases not covered by our study. Generally, on the website of the tool users will be able to find the necessary information described in our classification criteria, which will help them to choose a proper tool.

VI. Conclusion and Future Work

This paper presents a classification method to help users choose a proper tool to create mashups. The fundamental criterion, complemented by others, that allows the refining of the choice, and that guides the proposal, is the prior technological knowledge of the user. The interest of a classification system that helps to select a tool is to reduce, the cost of this task for a user unaccustomed to building mashups, as it can become too costly and even frustrating in cases where the selection is wrong.

This classification is a step forward with regards to the ones presented in Section 2 because users, even those completely unaware of technological terminology, will be able to use it to select the right tool. This is clearly an advantage, since the proposed classification method may be used by a wider range of users. Of all classifications previously proposed, only [5] has a similar objective to the one laid out in this article, namely to help end-users choose a tool to create mashups. However, to understand and use our classification, minimal technical knowledge is required. Similarly, we hope that users can use this method of classification as a guide to locate the right tool even in cases not covered by our work: for example, tools that may arise in the future or existing ones that the users are able to locate on their own.

The application of our classification to select a tool is made in two stages, in order to simplify the work of selecting a tool restricting the number of tools to study. Thus, in the second stage the amount of tools will have been reduced to a reasonable number. The first phase classifies tools according to the interface they provide, allowing the users to select the technology they feel more comfortable with. The second phase of selection provides a set of criteria that will allow the user to select the most adequate tool.

Regarding future work, we propose to look into the use of at least a tool of each type of the ones discussed to perform the same task. An example would be: "The acquisition and integration of prices of existing degrees on the different university websites in Spain". To do this, the feasibility to perform the tasks will be studied using the different tools provided in this article.

Once we have ensured the viability to perform a certain task, an experimental study will be performed. Our classification method will be provided to different users in order to select the tool that best suits their prior knowledge. Thus, if after choosing the tool the user, regardless of his technical knowledge, is able to perform the task assigned, the usefulness of the classification method provided for selecting a tool to create mashups will be tested. The test of the classification method with real users will allow further conclusions to be drawn and new data to be generated.

References

[1] L. Yu, A developer's guide to the semantic Web, 2nd ed. Springer Science & Business Media, 2014.

[2] "Neighborhood Search for Home Buyers and Real Estate Investment," 2016, URL: https://www.neighborhoodscout.com/ [accessed: 2016-08-25].

[3] M. Krug, F. Wiedemann, and M. Gaedke, "Smartcomposition: extending web applications to multi-screen mashups," in Rapid Mashup Development Tools. Springer, 2016, pp. 50–62.

[4] J. Yu, B. Benatallah, F. Casati, and F. Daniel, "Understanding mashup development," Internet Computing, IEEE, vol. 12, no. 5, 2008, pp. 44–52.

[5] T. Fischer, F. Bakalov, and A. Nauerz, "An overview of current approaches to mashup generation." in Wissensmanagement. Citeseer, 2009, pp. 254–259.

[6] M. Batty, A. Hudson-Smith, R. Milton, and A. Crooks, "Map mashups, web 2.0 and the gis revolution," Annals of GIS, vol. 16, no. 1, 2010, pp. 1–13.

[7] "Revyu.com - Review anything," 2007, URL: http://revyu.com/ [accessed: 2016-08-25].

[8] S. Aghaee, "End-user development of mashups using live natural language programming," Ph.D. dissertation, Università della Svizzera italiana, 2014.

[9] "DBpedia," 2015, URL: http://wiki.dbpedia.org/ [accessed: 2016-08-25].

[10] "RDF Book Mashup," 2007, URL: http://wifo5-03.informatik.uni-mannheim.de/bizer/bookmashup/ [accessed: 2016-08-25].

[11] "Karma: Information Integration Tool," 2016, URL: https://github.com/usc-isi-i2/Web-Karma [accessed: 2016-08-25].

[12] R. Verborgh et al., "Survey of semantic description of rest apis," in rest: Advanced Research Topics and Practical Applications. Springer, 2014, pp. 69–89.

[13] "Import.io Lightning," 2016, URL: http://lightning.import.io/ [accessed: 2016-08-25].

[14] M. Butcher, "Import.io raises $13m series a for its data extraction platform," Tech Crunch, 2016.

[15] "ClickScript," 2016, URL: https://github.com/lnaef/ClickScript [accessed: 2016-08-25].

[16] R. Kleinfeld, S. Steglich, L. Radziwonowicz, and C. Doukas, "glue. things: a mashup platform for wiring the internet of things with the internet of services," in Proceedings of the 5th International Workshop on Web of Things. ACM, 2014, pp. 16–21.

[17] "Huginn," 2016, URL: https://github.com/cantino/huginn [accessed: 2016-08-25].

[18] "OpenRefine," 2014, URL: http://openrefine.org/ [accessed: 2016-08-25].

[19] R. Verborgh and M. De Wilde, Using OpenRefine. Packt Publishing Ltd, 2013.

[20] "WMLScript," 2016, URL: http://www.developershome.com/wap/wmlscript/ [accessed: 2016-08-25].

[21] B. Endres-Niggemeyer, The mashup ecosystem. Springer, 2013.

[22] A. Mayer, "Linked open data for artistic and cultural resources," Art Documentation, vol. 34, no. 1, 2015, pp. 2–14.

[23] A. K. Kalou and D. A. Koutsomitropoulos, "Towards semantic mashups: Tools, methodologies, and state of the art," International Journal of Information Retrieval Research (IJIRR), vol. 5, no. 2, 2015, pp. 1–25.

[24] R. Guha, D. Brickley, and S. Macbeth, "Schema. org: Evolution of structured data on the web," Communications of the ACM, vol. 59, no. 2, 2016, pp. 44–51.

A Proposal of Quantification Method Describing the Difference between the Meaning of the Terms in the International Standards for Safety

Yohei Ueda
Department of Information Science and Engineering,
Shibaura Institute of Technology,
Tokyo Japan
Email: ma16013@shibaura-it.ac.jp

Masaomi Kimura
Department of Information Science and Engineering
Shibaura Institute of Technology,
Tokyo Japan
Email:masaomi@sic.shibaura-it.ac.jp

Abstract—**International safety standards define and regularize many aspects of product safety during manufacturing processes. However, principles in international standards contain many homographic keywords or words with similar but slightly different meanings, which can cause ambiguity. We propose a method to quantify the differences in the meanings of keywords. We focus on the different meanings of definition statements, different dependency relationship structures, and different tendencies of the dependency relationships.**

Keywords–safety; homograph; international standard; semantics;

I. Introduction

Nowadays, human injury is caused by many daily-use products such as electronic devices, toys, and bicycles. This has recently become a critical situation that requires attention. Injuries are difficult to avoid by only "human attention." Therefore, product manufacturing processes must adhere to established international safety standards. The primary purpose of such standards is to define fundamental safety principles for product creation.

However, the statements of principles often include many homographic keywords, i.e., words that are spelled the same but have different meanings or words with similar but slightly different meanings; thus, their meaning may be ambiguous. Misinterpretation of the meanings of terms may cause difficulty to discuss in the International Organization for Standardization. Moreover, product designers may not adhere to the standards; this may result in manufacturers producing inappropriate products. Certification authorities might authenticate a dangerous product by mistake.

For example, the ISO/IEC Guide 51 safety standard, defines "risk" as a "combination of the probability of occurrence of harm and the severity of that harm." On the other hand, the ISO/IEC Guide73 risk management standard defines "risk" as the "effect of uncertainty on objectives." Clearly, the meaning of "risk" differs in these two standards.

In this study, we introduce a method to quantify the difference in meanings of safety terms based on international standards by using the content of terms and definitions and other elements (e.g., risk assessment and risk reduction). We focus on three types of differences, i.e., the meanings of definition statements, dependency relationship structures, and dependency relationship tendencies.

II. Methods

A. *Difference calculation in definition statements*

In this study, we focused on essential details included in the "Terms and definitions" chapter of international standards. This chapter provides definitions of safety -related terms. Such definitions are very important for quantifying the difference between the meanings of terms in such documents.

We considered the definition statements that contain many important words for characterizing those statements. Because of the role of the "Terms and definitions" chapter, important words must be modified by other words to limit their meanings. In other words, a word with many dependency relationships can be regarded as more important in a sentence than words with fewer dependency relationships. For example, if we compare an "event" and a "harmful event," the latter meaning of "event" can be more stressed than the former; this represents a generic event.

Our method focuses on quantifying differences between the meanings of terms in definition statements. It measures the weights of words by estimating how meanings are limited for reducing ambiguity. In addition, the proposed method calculates a distance d_{def} between two international standards A and B.

To calculate this distance, we define a weight of word importance for a definition statement, v_{ids}.

According to our observations, most definition statements are noun phrases rather than sentences; this contributes to an incorrect dependency analysis. Therefore, to change the noun phrases to sentences, the phrase "this is" was added at the beginning of each definition statement.

We used the Stanford Parser to extract a parse tree based on dependency relationships in sentences. Degree centrality in the parse tree was used to identify the ratio of modifying or modified words to the total number of dependency relationships. Since the degree centrality should be high if a word has many dependency relationships, the word with a high degree centrality is considered as important. Therefore, v_{ids} can be expressed as follows:

$$v_{ids}(w) = \frac{k(w)}{\sum_{w \in W} k(w)}, \quad (1)$$

where $k(w)$ denotes the degree of the node representing the word w in a word set W in the sentence.

Note that from the viewpoint of importance of words, stop words (e.g., "a", "is", "the", and "from") can create noise; thus, stop words were not included in the word set during analyses. In addition, after parsing, the appended phrase "this is" was also not considered. We refer to the obtained words as "word groups."

After obtaining the words with their corresponding v_{ids} values in the word groups from international standards A and B, their distance (d_{def}) values were calculated on the basis of the concept of Levenshtein distance. Levenshtein distance is a well-known measurement of the difference between two strings and is calculated as the minimum number of insertions and deletions of characters required to transform one string into the other. In this study, rather than characters, words in the word groups were replaced. The distance d_{def} is given as follows:

$$d_{def} = \sum_{w \in R} v_{ids}(w), \tag{2}$$

where R is a set of words added or deleted to make the word group for A coincide with that for B. Note that the words $w \in R$ only appear in one standard. Thus, we used the value of $v_{ids}(w)$ calculated in the network where w appeared.

B. Calculation of word meaning difference in body text

The above mentioned method does not cover the case in which words are used differently in the body text of international standards documents but their difference is not clarified in "Terms and definitions."

Therefore, we suggest two quantification methods using the body text of international standards documents. The first method is based on the structure of dependency relationships in the body text. The corresponding quantified value is expressed by $d_\phi = |\phi_A - \phi_B|$. The second method is based on latent semantics appearing in a dependency relationship tendency in the body text. Here, the quantified value is denoted d_{cos}.

1) Quantification of the difference in meaning using a dependency relationship structure: As discussed in Section II-A, the meaning of a word is limited when it is modified by other words, and this may cause a difference in meaning and importance. In other words, if there is a difference between the importance of the same word in different standards, there should also be a difference in meaning.

To extract this difference, we introduce an importance index $\phi(w)$ for a word w in the body text of an international standards document. The index value should be higher, if the word is limited and should be modified by words that are also important and have a high ϕ value. If $\phi_A(w)$ and $\phi_B(w)$ are the ϕ values of w for international standards A and B respectively, $|\phi_A(w) - \phi_B(w)|$ gives the difference in the extent of importance of the word w in the body text of the standards.

First, dependency analysis was applied to extract dependency relationships of the words in the body text of a given standard. Then, each verb was changed to its prototype and stop words were removed. Dependency relationships were represented as edges in a network in order to express the word relationships in the body text. Words in sentences were considered as nodes.

Secondly, after generating the networks, an importance value was assigned to each node using PageRank method. PageRank assigns a higher value to a node linked to many other nodes that have high values. In this study, the PageRank value corresponds to a higher importance value assigned to a word that modifies or is modified by the various and important words. In this paper, we denote the value assigned to word w by PageRank as $\phi(w)$.

Finally, the difference in meaning on the basis of the dependency structure was calculated as $|\phi_A(w) - \phi_B(w)|$. We used d_ϕ as a difference index for $|\phi_A(w) - \phi_B(w)|$.

2) Difference in meaning of the tendency of dependency relationship: Section 2.2.1 showed how to quantify the difference in meaning using the structure of modification. However, if two words are modified by the same number of words, the difference could be low. For example, international standards A and B have dependency networks around the word "train," as shown in Figs. 1 and 2. However, in international standard A, "train" means teaching someone, and in international standard B, "train" means a railway train.

In this case, $|\phi_A(train) - \phi_B(train)|$ could be low because they have the same structure. In this section, we show that the difference between word meanings in international standards A and B are quantified by expressing the frequency tendency of dependency relationships as a matrix, applying latent semantic analysis, and calculating the distance.

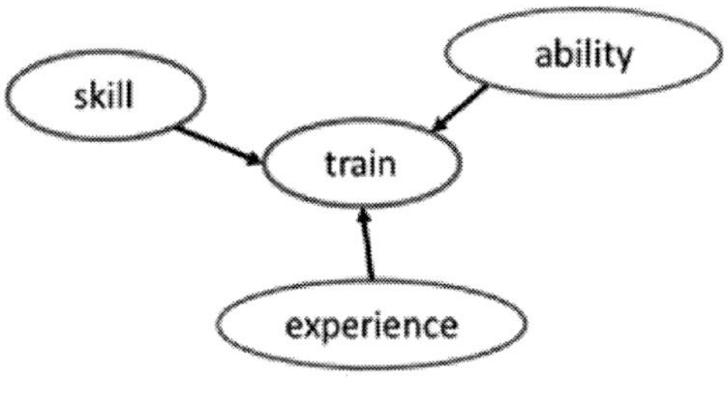

Fig. 1. International Standard A

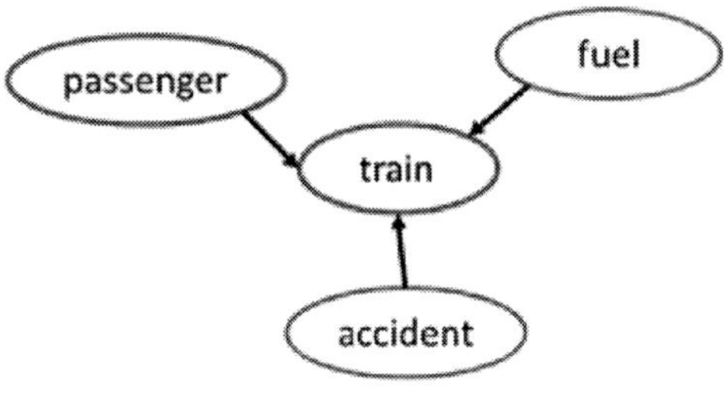

Fig. 2. International Standard B

First, dependency parsing was applied to the sentences in the body text of each standard. Second, a matrix was used to quantitatively express words that have dependency relationships with other words. The matrix M has frequencies of dependency relationships as elements. The rows correspond to modified words that commonly appeared in both standards, and the columns correspond to the modifying words in the standards that are handled separately. For example, if word w modifies word w' with frequency f_{w_A} in international standard A and with f_{w_B} in B, the matrix has a row w', columns w_A (denoting w in A) and w_B (denoting w in B), and elements f_{w_A} and f_{w_B} respectively.

It is convenient to use a vector space model to calculate the semantic similarity of words. To reduce the effect of noise, we employed latent semantic indexing(LSI) with singular- value decomposition. By applying singular- value decomposition, M can be decomposed as follows:

$$M = U \Sigma V^T, \tag{3}$$

where U and V are orthogonal matrices and Σ is a singular value matrix. The column vectors of V gives principal eigenvectors corresponding to the modifying words whose cosine values were used to measure similarity. Let $\vec{v}(w_A)$ and $\vec{v}(w_B)$ denote the principal eigenvectors for w_A and w_B respectively. Then, their cosine value is given as follows:

$$\cos\theta(\vec{v}(w_A), \vec{v}(w_B)) = \frac{\vec{v}(w_A)\cdot\vec{v}(w_B)}{|\vec{v}(w_A)||\vec{v}(w_B)|}, \quad (4)$$

whose value is in the range [0, 1]. However, in this study, we need to use distance rather than similarity. Therefore, we set the distance d_{cos} as follows:

$$d_{cos} = 1 - \cos\theta(\vec{v_a}, \vec{v_b}). \quad (5)$$

We used d_{cos} as a difference index for word meanings based on the tendency of the meaning of words.

C. Quantification of the difference in the meaning of a term

Finally, we merged the above mentioned indices, d_{def}, d_ϕ and d_{cos}. On the basis of the idea that the merged index needs to take a larger value if some or all of the indices have a large value, we designed it to be a linear combination as follows:

$$D = \alpha d_{def} + \beta d_{cos} + \gamma d_\phi, \quad (6)$$

where α,β and γ are coefficients to adjust the ranges of the indices.

To determine α, β and γ, we investigated the ranges of d_{def}, d_ϕ and d_{cos} by calculating them for words that appear in both the ISO/CD Guide51 and ISO12100 standards. We found that the ranges were completely different. Since the average values of d_{def}, d_ϕ and d_{cos} were 0.323, 0.41 and 0.0019, respectively, we set $\alpha = 1.28$, $\beta = 1$ and $\gamma = 250$ such that the product of the average values and the coefficient for each index equaled one. We expected that the coefficients would allow the ranges to be in the same order and confirmed that this method was effective by investigating other document pairs.

III. EXPERIMENTS

We conducted experiments to evaluate the D value by comparing it with each pair in four international standards. The standards used in our experiment. are listed in TABLE I. TABLE II lists the paired standards used in our experiment.

TABLE I. STANDARDS USED IN OUR EXPERIMENT

Standards	Summary
ISO/CD Guide 51	Safety aspects Guidelines for their inclusion in standards
ISO 12100	Safety of machinery
ISO/IEC Guide 50	Safety aspects Guidelines for child safety
ISO 8124	Safety of toys Age determination guidelines

TABLE II. PAIRED STANDARDS IN OUR EXPERIMENTS

	Standard A	Standard B
#1	ISO/CD Guide 51	ISO 12100
#2	ISO/IEC Guide 50	ISO 8124

We observed the D value containing d_{def}, d_{cos} and d_ϕ obtained by our method.

TABLE III. d_{def}, d_{cos}, d_ϕ AND D VALUES BETWEEN ISO/CD GUIDE 51 AND ISO 12100

Words	d_{def}	d_{cos}	d_ϕ	D
harm	0.575	0.502267	0.00010945	1.50713
standard	0	0.504292	0.01577331	4.44761
train	0	0.097685	0.00016153	0.13807

TABLE IV. d_{def}, d_{cos}, d_ϕ AND D VALUES BETWEEN ISO/IEC GUIDE 50 AND ISO 8124

Words	d_{def}	d_{cos}	d_ϕ	D
harm	0.25	0.262754	0.00134539	1.024101
edge	1	0.421634	0.00630093	3.276866
period	0	0.139401	0.00029886	0.214116

TABLE III and TABLE IV show the d_{def}, d_{cos}, d_ϕ and D values for each standard.

As shown in TABLE III, the D value for "standard" was greater than that for "harm" and "train." Clearly, there was a large difference in the meaning of the word "standard" between ISO/CD Guide 51 and ISO 12100. The D value of "train" was smaller than that of "harm" and "standard." The d_{def} value of "harm" was greater than that of "standard" and "train." As shown in TABLE IV, the D value of "edge" was greater than that of "harm" and "period." Clearly, there was a large difference in the meaning of the word "edge" between ISO/IEC Guide 50 and ISO 8124. The D value of the word "period" was smaller than that of "edge" and "harm," and the d_{def} value of "harm" was greater than that of "period" and "edge."

IV. DISCUSSION

A. Comparison of ISO/CD Guide51 and ISO12100

Here, we discuss our index values for the words "harm,"which is defined in "Terms and definitions" in each standard, with "standard" having a large D value and "train" having a small D value.

- **harm** The word "harm" had large d_{def} and d_{cos} values. Definition statements in both standards included the meaning "physical injury or damage to the health of people," while definition statements in Guide51 included "damage to property or the environment." This difference influenced the d_{def} value. TABLE V lists the words modified by "harm" and their frequency in ISO/CD Guide51 and ISO12100.

TABLE V. WORDS WITH A DEPENDENCY RELATIONSHIP WITH "HARM" AND THEIR FREQUENCY

	dependency relationship	Frequency
ISO/CD Guide51	harm → present	4
	harm → eliminate	1
	harm → avoid	4
ISO12100	harm → severity	3
	harm → occurrence	3

As can be seen in TABLE V, there was no common word modified by "harm" in ISO/CD Guide51 and ISO12100; this resulted in high d_{cos} values. No definition statements limited the meaning of "harm;" this resulted in a small ϕ and, therefore, a low value of d_ϕ. Thus, we observed that the values of the indices included in D coincide with the situation related to "harm."

- **standard** The large value of D for "standard" originates in the value of d_ϕ.
TABLE VI shows the total number of words that modify "standard" in Guide51 and ISO12100. As can be seen in Table VI, more words modified "standard" in Guide51 than in ISO12100, i.e., in Guide51, "standard" is limited more by other words than in ISO12100. We believe this is because Guide51 is an introductory safety guideline; thus, "standard" is modified by many other words. This means its modification structures give different ϕ values and high d_ϕ values.

TABLE VI. TOTAL NUMBER OF WORDS THAT MODIFY "STANDARD" IN GUIDE51 AND ISO12100

	Guide51	ISO12100
Total	22	3

- **train** The word "train," which has a small D value, did not have a definition statement in either of the standards. Furthermore, each instance of "train" had few dependency relationships with other words. Regarding d_{cos}, there was a common dependency relationship, i.e., "train $\rightarrow$ skill," between Guide51 and ISO12100. This shows that both standards use "train" to mean "teach." In addition, "train" was not modified in either standard and, thereby, d_ϕ took small values; consequently, d_ϕ took a small value. Therefore, we obtained a small D value.

B. *ISO/IEC Guide50 and ISO 8124*

Words subject to evaluation were "harm," which had definitions in "Terms and definitions" in each standard; "edge," which had a large D value; and "period," which had a small D value.

- **harm**
The word "harm" had different meanings in definition statements, i.e., "physical injury" or "injury." However, there was a common statement "damage to the health of people, or damage to property or the environment." Therefore, we obtained a small d_{def} value. The value of d_ϕ was relatively high. TABLE VII shows the total number of words that modify "harm" in ISO/IEC Guide50 and ISO 8124.

TABLE VII. TOTAL NUMBER OF WORDS THAT MODIFY "HARM" IN ISO/IEC GUIDE50 AND ISO 8124

	Guide50	ISO 8124
Total	9	3

There were more words that modified "harm" in ISO/IEC Guide50 than in ISO 8124, i.e., "harm" in Guide50 is more limited by other words than in ISO 8124, which gave the high d_ϕ value.

- **edge**
The word "edge" had a large d_ϕ value. TABLE VIII shows the total number of words that modify "edge" in ISO/IEC Guide50 and ISO 8124. There are more words that modify "edge" in ISO8124 than in Guide50. In the body of Guide50, "edge" had an abstract meaning, e.g., "corner, end." However, there are many sentences that define "edge" specified with concrete values in ISO8124. Furthermore, the value of d_{def} was 1 because although there was no definition statement for "edge" in Guide51, there was a definition statement for "edge" in ISO8124, i.e., "line, formed at the junction of two surfaces, whose length exceeds 2,0 mm." We considered the case without a definition statement as a definition with "no word." Moreover, we obtained a high d_ϕ value because of the difference in modification structures. Therefore, a large D value was obtained for "edge."

TABLE VIII. TOTAL NUMBER OF WORDS THAT MODIFY "EDGE" IN ISO/IEC GUIDE50 AND ISO 8124

	ISO/IEC Guide50	ISO 8124
Total	5	47

- **period** The word "period" had a small D value, which was primarily because of the small d_ϕ value. TABLE IX shows the words that have a dependency relationship with "period" and their frequencies in ISO/IEC Guide50 and ISO 8124.

TABLE IX. WORDS THAT HAVE DEPENDENCY WITH "PERIOD" AND THEIR FREQUENCIES(ISO/IEC GUIDE50)

	dependency relationship	Frequency
ISO/IEC Guide50	certain $\rightarrow$ period	1
	extend $\rightarrow$ period	1
	long $\rightarrow$ period	1
	time $\rightarrow$ period	2
ISO 8124	h $\rightarrow$ period	1
	time $\rightarrow$ period	1

According to Table IX, the difference in the number of words that modify "period" was 2. There were more words that directly modify "period" in ISO/IEC Guide50. In contrast, the word "h," which is a unit for "hour" in ISO 8124, was modified by many numbers, such as "72." Therefore, there were many words that modify "period" indirectly.
Consequently, the value of d_ϕ was small because the difference of meaning based on limiting a meaning was not large.

V. CONCLUSION

Principles in international standards contain many homographic keywords that may cause ambiguity for readers. Furthermore, previous studies have not quantified the difference in the meanings of words in international standards because this is a difficult task to know it.

In this study, we proposed a method and indices to quantify this difference, on the basis of three types of differences the meanings of definition statements, structure of dependency relationships, and tendency of dependency relationships.

For the first difference, the source of the extent of difference was considered to be the relationships of word modifications in definition sentences, weighting, and calculation of distances. Based on this, we proposed the index d_{def}.

For the second difference, it was considered to the different structures of dependency relationships. The index d_{ϕ} was calculated by creating networks that express the relationships among words in the complete text of the standards and by applying PageRank to the networks.

For the third difference, the idea of a latent semantic index was applied to obtain the trends of word meanings. The value of d_{cos} was computed as the cosine similarity of the obtained characteristic vectors.

Finally, we combined these three indices to obtain an index D to evaluate different word meanings in international safety standards.

Consequently, a high D value was obtained when the number of words with different dependency relationships and the number of different meanings for the definition statements were large and vice versa.

REFERENCES

[1] M. Mukaidono,"The basic concept of safety design", Japanese Standards Association, Tokyo, 2007, ISBN: 4542404056

[2] International Organization for Standardization, COMMITTEE DRAFT ISO/CD Guide51, ISO/TC COPOLCO / SC IEC/ACOS N 49, 2012

[3] Y. Miyazaki; T. Shioi, and K. Hatano, "A Word Sense Disambiguation Method based on Dependency Relations", "Information Science and Technology Forum Proceedings", no. D-021, Aug. 2015, pp.111-112

[4] T. Michishita; K. Nakayama; T. Hara; S. Nishio, and "A Word Sense Disambiguation Method by Using Topics of Documents in Wikipedia," Information Processing Society of Japan Kansai Branch Conference Papers", no. C-12, 2009

[5] International Organization for Standardization, Safety of machinery General principles for design Risk assessment and risk reduction, ISO 12100:2010(E), 2010

[6] M. Ishida, Text mining introductory study in R, Morikita Publishing Co., Ltd., Tokyo, ISBN: 4627848412

[7] H. Toyoda, An introduction to Data mining, Tokyo Tosho Co., Ltd., Tokyo, ISBN: 4489020457

[8] T. Suzuki, Data science to learn in R 8 Network analysis, Kyoritsu Publishing Co., Ltd., Tokyo, ISBN: 4320019288

[9] The Stanford Natural Language Processing Group, The Stanford Parser: A statistical parser, http://nlp.stanford.edu/software/lexparser.shtmlhttp://nlp.stanford.edu/software/lex-parser.shtml/[accessed: 2014-01-12].

[10] International Organization for Standardization, Safety aspects - Guidelines for child safety in standards and other specifications, ISO/IEC Guide50:2014, 2014

[11] International Organization for Standardization, Safety of toys Part 1:Safety aspects related to mechanical and physical properties, ISO 8124-1:2009(E), 2009

[12] International Organization for Standardization, Cycles - Safety requirements for bicycles, ISO 4210:2014, 2014

[13] International Organization for Standardization, Bicycles for young children - Safety requirements and test methods, EN 14765:2005, 2005

Sentiment Analysis on Maltese using Machine Learning

Alexiei Dingli and Nicole Sant

Department of Intelligent Computer Systems
Faculty of ICT
University of Malta
Email: alexiei.dingli@um.edu.mt, nicsant@gmail.com

***Abstract*—Sentiment analysis refers to the task of analysing a piece of text and classifying it according to the overall sentiment of the opinion being expressed. In this paper, we present a novel, supervised context based, machine learning system capable of performing such a task for text written in Maltese. Our system consists of two components both capable of performing classification of Maltese text at a context window level, yet while one follows the more traditional approach where features are hand-crafted and passed on for classification, the other performs unsupervised feature extraction and makes use of a deep learning algorithm. Through experimentation we determined that a Random Forest classifier in conjunction with 80% of our dataset for training and a four word context window achieved the best results, and were successful in achieving an accuracy of 62.3%.**

***Index Terms*—Sentiment Analysis; Maltese; Machine Learning; Deep Learning**

I. Introduction

Given today's easy accessibility to the web, the choice of medium most preferred for individuals who wish to express their opinion about one matter or another is that of online facilities, such as discussion forums or social media websites like Facebook. However, for entities such as companies conducting marketing research about their product, this introduces the problem of having to manually track, study and analyse the vast amount and diversity of people's opinions over the entire web, which requires a great deal of manual labour. The use of a sentiment analysis tool can help shoulder this burden since it can automatically classify any given piece of text, based on the polarity of the opinion expressed towards an entity being discussed within that text.

Due to the fact that in the recent years the Maltese population has adjusted and adapted to the use of online communication for sharing their experiences and opinions, this problem is now faced on a local basis. Motivation for this research stems from the observation that while numerous amounts of solutions have been developed to carry out the task of sentiment analysis for the English language, no studies have ever been carried out in an attempt to design such a system for Maltese. In light of this identified problem, and due to the fact that technology has become a dependable source of communication in our everyday lives, we decided to implement a Maltese based sentiment analysis tool in order to try and minimize the gap between our native language and technology. This system is capable of performing classification at a context window level by means of both traditionally used algorithms for the task at hand, which make use of hand-crafted features extracted from the text, as well as by utilizing a deep learning algorithm. Our main contributions by means of this research were the construction of a unique and novel system capable of performing sentiment analysis for text written in Maltese, as well as the composition of the first Maltese corpus consisting of manually labelled text.

This paper is structured in the following way. Section 2 highlights the aims and objectives behind this paper. The following section provides us with general information about the various approaches used for sentiment analysis. Details on the design and implementation of the artefact can be found in section 4, which is followed by an in-depth explanation of the tests carried out in order to evaluate our system in section 5. Finally, we provide a summary of the work carried out and ideas for possible improvements and future work in section 6.

II. Aims & Objectives

We aim to experiment with a number of different classifiers, particularly those commonly used throughout literature, in order to determine the most suited classification algorithm for Maltese text within our system. This shall be achieved through the design and implementation of a sound methodology, based on state-of-the-art solutions designed for English, consisting of the use of manually designed preprocessing techniques and extraction of hand-crafted features, when necessary, as well as that of third-party algorithms. Furthermore, we aim to establish the optimal parameters used to obtain the highest accuracies possible with our system by evaluating the chosen algorithms using different parameters, including context window size and training set size. Finally, since this is a first attempt at solving this problem, through the preparation and preprocessing of the dataset as well as the evaluation on the aforementioned parameters, we aim to find the best configuration which will help our system surpass a minimum accuracy of 34%, achieved by a random classifier, and possibly reach a target accuracy of 64%, which was obtained through the use of manually designed rules in [1].

III. Related Work

Sentiment analysis refers to the task of classifying a given piece of text, based on the polarity of the opinion expressed by the author within the text itself. This technique can be interpreted as a form of text classification, where the criterion of classification is the attitude expressed in the text rather than the content or topic [2]. The sentiment in question may be the authors overall judgement, mood or evaluation of the topic being discussed in the text [3]. Sentiment analysis is a context sensitive field of study [4] which requires various natural language processing, information retrieval and extraction tasks. It is said to be domain dependent, however generally, the majority of positive and negative opinions expressed by authors maintain a consistent meaning throughout various domains [4].

In order to perform sentiment analysis, we researched both lexicon based approaches as well as machine learning approaches. The former approach, which utilizes sentiment lexicons and scoring methods to perform classification, was used by the likes of Turney in [5] who achieved a 74% accuracy, as well as Dave et al. in [6] who increased this value to 76% with a similar system. The majority of solutions involve the use of machine learning techniques, such as those proposed in [1], [4], [7], and [8]. These systems were built using the traditional machine learning approach involving manual preprocessing and feature extraction methods, as well as algorithms including Naive Bayes, Maximum Entropy, SVMs and Decision Tree algorithms. The highest accuracy amongst these solutions was that of 87.4% achieved in [7] through the use of the Maximum Entropy classifier. Finally, we reviewed machine learning systems which utilize deep learning classifiers. The current state-of-the-art deep learning system is that found in [9], which by means of a Recursive Neural Tensor Network (RNTN) achieved an 88.5% accuracy. This was an improvement over the 85.4% accuracy achieved with the same classifier in [10]. Other researchers opted to use a Deep Belief Network classifier, such as in [11], where a 75.6% accuracy was achieved, while others implemented their own custom deep learning network, as done in [12] and [13].

IV. Methodology

In this section, we shall discuss the overall approach taken towards solving the problem for sentiment analysis in Maltese, as well as go into further detail regarding the system design and the two components which comprise our system.

A. Proposed Approach

As mentioned earlier, our solution is a supervised, machine learning context based system which performs classification at a context window level rather than at sentence or single word level. We opted for a context based approach rather than a Bag-of-Words approach due to the importance of context when determining the sentiment of specific words, since the surrounding words may change the overall polarity of the word itself. We incorporated context into our solution in two ways. Firstly, when required, we applied a Part-of-Speech (POS) tagger to the text as a whole before redundant data is removed, such that each word is assigned a POS tag within the context of its surrounding words. Secondly, we broke down each sentence of each piece of text to be classified into context windows, based on a predefined context window size, and trained our classifiers on these windows. For example, the sentence "Jiena ma rridx niekol il-frott." (Translated to "I do not want to eat the fruit.") and a context window size of three would produce the following context windows:

Jiena ma rridx
ma rridx niekol
rridx niekol il-frott.

The idea behind this decision was to be able to determine the different sentiments expressed within a sentence and classify them within the context of their surrounding words. While other researchers made use of predefined sentiment bearing expressions to identify the presence of an opinion, such as in [14], this was opted against since it would render our approach domain specific, while we are opting for a more general one. Therefore, the use of context windows was adapted from information extraction procedures such as in [15] and our classifiers were trained on a dataset composed of these context windows in order to learn representations of every possible pattern found within a sentence. The use of such a technique complements our idea of a general approach towards sentiment analysis since it is much easier for a classifier to generalise parts of a sentence rather than the sentence as a whole. Such an approach also helps reduce the risks brought about by sparseness and overfitting in the dataset.

B. System Design

Our system is comprised of two components, the Custom Feature Component (CFC) and the Unsupervised Feature Component (UFC). The CFC was designed such that it follows the traditional sentiment analysis process where it extracts hand-crafted features and passes them on to conventionally used algorithms for classification. On the contrary, the UFC was designed to perform unsupervised feature extraction for classification by a deep learning algorithm. The reason for including both components in our approach is to enable us to evaluate how one component fares against the other. The following sections shall provide an insight as to how each component was implemented.

C. Custom Feature Component

The first step within this process consists of parsing the provided dataset entry by entry from an XLSX file and passing each entry on for preprocessing. The preprocessing techniques we employed were chosen due to their success in previous work, such as in [1] [2] [16] [17] [4] [5]. We first tokenized each dataset entry into separate sentences and further passed each sentence on to the POS tagger, as mentioned previously. We made us of the MLSS POS tagger found in [18]. By parsing the POS tagger output we were able to further tokenize each sentence into separate word tokens. Finally, based on the resulting POS tag for each word, we removed uninformative word tokens including numbers, proper nouns, punctuation and determiners.

We next passed on the remaining word tokens for feature extraction, where we extracted four features per token. These are the unigram, the part-of-speech, the negation presence and the stem word. Once again the features used were chosen based on their performance in similar systems, particularly in [7], and include unigram value, that is, the value of the word token itself, the POS tag of the word extracted from the MLSS tagger, negation presence, which is a binary feature indicating whether a verb has been negated or not, and the stem word of each token. We made use of the stemmer found in [19]. Unfortunately, the sentiment was not included since we were unable to include a feature indicative of the sentiment associated with each word token due to the lack of a translator for the Maltese language, rendering us unable to use the SentiWordNet tool. Once all required features were extracted, we compiled the feature vectors in order to perform the final classification step.

As mentioned earlier, classification within our system takes place at a context window level and a feature vector is created to represent each context window within a sentence. To do this, we predefined a context window size and iterated through every sentence of every dataset entry, and built a feature vector for every context window within that sentence. Therefore, since a word token within a sentence is now a quadruple of features, a feature vector for a given context window size will consist of an amount of word tokens, hence an amount of quadruples, equivalent to that predefined context window size, as well as a sentiment value. Due to time restrictions we were unable to have each context window individually labelled by our annotators and so each context window took the sentiment label of its originating dataset entry, introducing a noise value of 33.2% in our approach.

Finally these feature vectors were passed on to classification algorithms for training. We opted to include Naive Bayes, Maximum Entropy, Support Vector Machine (SVM), a Decision Tree and Random Forest classifier. We ran these algorithms by means of the WEKA Explorer GUI. These classifiers were chosen due to their popularity throughout the literature reviewed as well as their successful performance, as can be seen in [4], [7], [3] and [8].

D. Unsupervised Feature Component

In order to implement this component, we made use of the Deep Learning for Java (DL4J) library [20] and based the design of this constituent on an example of sentiment analysis for an English corpus found on the library's website [21].

The first step in the UFC process consists of parsing the provided dataset, tokenizing each dataset entry down to context window level, and storing the resulting windows in a CSV file. Once again, time limitations restricted us from manually labelling each context window and so the 33.2% noise rate was re-introduced, with each context window taking the sentiment label of the overall dataset entry. The resulting dataset, consisting of the labelled context windows, was separated into training and test sets. Since deep learning algorithms handle preprocessing of text automatically, we did not carry out any preprocessing ourselves, but rather we created a data pipeline, which would be used to iterate through the latter dataset and pass on the data directly for feature vector creation. This pipeline, known as a label-aware sentence iterator, simply takes each context window within the dataset, together with its label, and passes it on for feature extraction.

The DL4J implementation of the Word2Vec algorithm was used to perform the unsupervised feature extraction. This algorithm is a neural network which processes text before handing it over to deep learning algorithms for training by creating feature vectors consisting of numerical values to represent the text. This algorithm works by creating a word vector for each individual word based on its context, usage and past appearances. A lookup table of these word vectors is constructed and used to compose feature vectors for phrases by averaging out the vectors of the individual words. The resulting feature vectors are finally passed on to our deep learning algorithm for training.

The algorithm chosen for use within this component is a Deep Belief Network (DBN), which we configured based on the example in [21] and similar networks used throughout literature. Our final configuration states that our DBN consists of three layers, each representing a Restricted Boltzmann Machine and each trained 50 times, as in [11]. We initialized the weights of the network using a uniform distribution, and used the "tanh" function as the activation function for each node within each layer. We also took a number of measures to help the network avoid overfitting. These include constraining the gradient, using AdaGrad (a feature-specific learning rate optimization technique), integrating the L2 Regularization technique (reduces overfitting by adding a complexity penalty to the loss function), and performing Dropout (a bootstrapping technique which forces the network to learn different representations of the data by randomly dropping different features within a feature vector). Finally, we configured the final, output layer where we used the softmax function to produce the final classification. Once the network was completely configured, we used our data pipeline to pass in data from the training dataset in order to train our classifier.

Our initial aim was to also include an RNTN classifier within this component, however the model within the DL4J library was being improved upon at the time of implementation and so we were unable to configure it correctly for use within our research.

V. Evaluation

In this section, we shall discuss the compilation process of the dataset as well as the various tests carried out to evaluate our system and the respective results obtained by each.

A. Compilation of Dataset

In order to compile our dataset, we extracted 900 microblogs written purely in Maltese, as is required by both components of our system, from various online Maltese gazettes, such as the Times of Malta and The Malta Independent amongst others. After collection, we proceeded to spell check each microblog in order for the tools used within our system, such as the POS tagger and the stemmer, to produce the optimal results possible. Finally, manual labelling of the dataset was carried out by three individuals, who were asked to label each microblog as positive, negative or neutral, based on the sentiment, if any, expressed, in an objective manner, irrelevant of their political opinions and by understanding the text in the most literal sense possible. The inter-annotator agreement value was 51.22% and the final distribution of the dataset is as shown in Fig. 1.

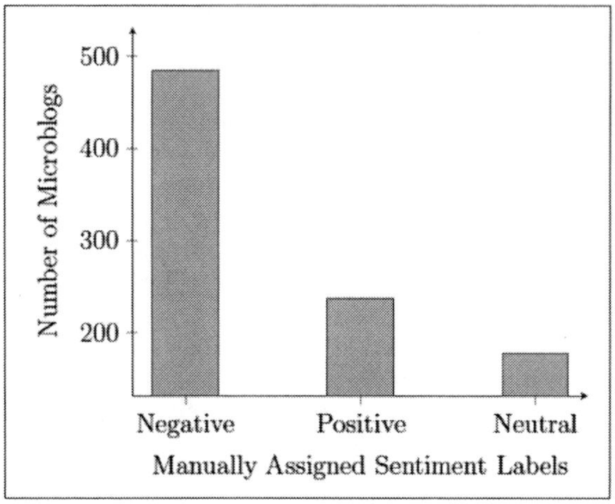

Fig. 1. Dataset Distribution

B. Experiments

In the experiments carried out, we followed the approach taken by [16], [4], [7], [3], and [8], where we evaluated algorithms from both components against each other using standard information retrieval measures, including accuracy, precision, recall and F-measure, also used in the above mentioned literature. Due to the fact that the DL4J library did not permit us to evaluate the deep learning model using the cross-fold validation technique, we used a separate test dataset for evaluation so as to directly compare algorithms in the CFC with that in the UFC. Through experimentation we evaluated our dataset, as well as the effects of increasing both the context window size as well as the training set size, and finally the chosen algorithms.

1) Evaluation on Dataset Distribution: As can be seen in Fig. 1 above, a bias towards the negative class is present within our dataset. We attempted to balance out this distribution by both reducing the amount of negative examples as well as applying the Synthetic Minority Over Sampling Technique (SMOTE) filter, which reduces bias by under-sampling the majority class and over-sampling the minorty class through the use of synthetic examples. We carried out all experiments mentioned above on all three datasets, and concluded that both attempts to reduce bias were futile, since none of the chosen algorithms were able to overcome the bias, and furthermore always performed better when trained using the original dataset. This dataset was therefore used for the remaining tests.

2) Evaluation on Context Window Size: We experimented with a number of different context window sizes in order to determine the effects of including more words, therefore more context, within a context window. We conducted the remaining experiments, that is, those regarding training set size and classifiers, using context window sizes of 3, 4, and 5 words. The results obtained allowed us to come to the conclusion that a context window size of 4 words was the optimal parameter within our system since it achieved the best results in the majority of the remaining tests.

3) Evaluation on Training Dataset Size: The aim of this test was to evaluate whether increasing the size of the training dataset improved performance of the classifiers. We experimented with training dataset sizes of 70, 80 and 90% of our original dataset, in conjunction with the optimal 4 word context window size. Results in Fig. 2 showed that using 80% of our dataset for training yielded the best performance for most classifiers.

Balanced Dataset by SMOTE Filter					
Context Window Size 4		Average Weighted Results			
	Training Set Size	Accuracy	Precision	Recall	F1
Naive Bayes	70	0.440	0.469	0.440	0.449
	80	0.430	0.471	0.430	0.445
	90	0.432	0.461	0.432	0.443
Maximum Entropy	70	0.591	0.349	0.591	0.439
	80	0.603	0.363	0.603	0.453
	90	0.588	0.346	0.588	0.435
SVM	70	0.591	0.349	0.591	0.439
	80	0.603	0.363	0.603	0.453
	90	0.588	0.346	0.588	0.435
Decision Tree	70	0.512	0.459	0.512	0.474
	80	0.552	0.511	0.552	0.522
	90	0.505	0.462	0.505	0.477
Random Forest	70	0.583	0.524	0.583	0.508
	80	0.600	0.542	0.600	0.529
	90	0.595	0.553	0.595	0.525

Fig. 2. Results of Evaluation on Balanced Dataset by the Synthetic Minority Over-Sampling TEchnique (SMOTE) Filter with Context Window Size 4

4) Evaluation on Classifier: In light of the above conclusions drawn, we evaluated the performance of the classifiers based on the results obtained when using 80% of the dataset for training and a 4 word context windows. The results are shown in Table I below.

Compared to their performance throughout literature, the algorithms used within both the CFC and the UFC performed very poorly when trained on a Maltese corpus, and were unsuccessful in overcoming the bias present within the dataset. It was also noticed that algorithms used within the CFC always outperformed our DBN, allowing us to conclude that the algorithms which required hand-crafted features were more successful in classifying Maltese text and therefore more suitable for use within our system. Finally, it was observed that the Random Forest classifier achieved the best results, rendering it the most suited classifier for our corpus with a maximum accuracy of 62.3%, and allowing us to surpass the 34% baseline accuracy while also coming close to reaching the 64% target.

TABLE I. RESULTS OF CLASSIFIERS

Classifier	Accuracy	Precision	Recall	F1
Naive Bayes (NB)	0.603	0.363	0.603	0.453
Maximum Entropy (ME)	0.603	0.363	0.603	0.453
SVM	0.603	0.363	0.603	0.453
Decision Tree (DT)	0.546	0.489	0.546	0.507
Random Forest (RF)	0.623	0.579	0.623	0.547
DBN	0.285	0.200	0.335	0.250

5) Evaluation on Features in CFC: By means of WEKA's attribute evaluator, we were able to determine which features used within the CFC were most helpful during classification for each context window size. From the obtained results, we concluded that unigram and stem word values were the most informative, particularly the value of the last unigram in the window, followed by that of the first word in the window. POS tags and negation presence proved to be uninformative in all cases.

VI. Conclusion & Future Work

In this research, we implemented a novel machine learning, context based system capable of performing sentiment analysis for text written in Maltese. Through experimentation we concluded that a Random Forest classifier was the best classifier for use within our system when used in conjunction with the optimal parameters, that is, a 4 word context window and 80% of our dataset for training. By means of this setup we were able to achieve a maximum accuracy of 62.3%, surpassing the 34% baseline. Future work for this research includes increasing the dataset and manually labelling each context window separately, while also attempting to split sentences on conjunctions rather than in context windows. The incorporation of a feature indicative of a word's sentiment value is also a worthwhile improvement, together with the experimentation of alternative deep learning classifiers, such as an RNTN.

References

[1] E. Spertus, "Smokey: Automatic recognition of hostile messages," in *AAAI/IAAI*, 1997, pp. 1058–1065.

[2] M. Gamon, "Sentiment classification on customer feedback data: noisy data, large feature vectors, and the role of linguistic analysis," in *Proceedings of the 20th international conference on Computational Linguistics*. Association for Computational Linguistics, 2004, p. 841.

[3] J. Khairnar and M. Kinikar, "Machine learning algorithms for opinion mining and sentiment classification," *International Journal of Scientific and Research Publications*, vol. 3, no. 6, pp. 1–6, 2013.

[4] A. Kamal and M. Abulaish, "Statistical features identification for sentiment analysis using machine learning techniques," in *Computational and Business Intelligence (ISCBI), 2013 International Symposium on*. IEEE, 2013, pp. 178–181.

[5] P. D. Turney, "Thumbs up or thumbs down?: semantic orientation applied to unsupervised classification of reviews," in *Proceedings of the 40th annual meeting on association for computational linguistics*. Association for Computational Linguistics, 2002, pp. 417–424.

[6] K. Dave, S. Lawrence, and D. M. Pennock, "Mining the peanut gallery: Opinion extraction and semantic classification of product reviews," in *Proceedings of the 12th international conference on World Wide Web*. ACM, 2003, pp. 519–528.

[7] E. Boiy and M.-F. Moens, "A machine learning approach to sentiment analysis in multilingual web texts," *Information retrieval*, vol. 12, no. 5, pp. 526–558, 2009.

[8] B. Pang, L. Lee, and S. Vaithyanathan, "Thumbs up?: sentiment classification using machine learning techniques," in *Proceedings of the ACL-02 conference on Empirical methods in natural language processing-Volume 10*. Association for Computational Linguistics, 2002, pp. 79–86.

[9] L. Dong, F. Wei, M. Zhou, and K. Xu, "Adaptive multi-compositionality for recursive neural models with applications to sentiment analysis," in *Twenty-Eighth AAAI Conference on Artificial Intelligence*, 2014.

[10] R. e. a. Socher, "Recursive deep models for semantic compositionality over a sentiment treebank," in *Proceedings of the conference on empirical methods in natural language processing (EMNLP)*, vol. 1631. Citeseer, 2013, p. 1642.

[11] D. Tang, B. Qin, T. Liu, and Z. Li, "Learning sentence representation for emotion classification on microblogs," in *Natural Language Processing and Chinese Computing*. Springer, 2013, pp. 212–223.

[12] C. N. dos Santos and M. Gatti, "Deep convolutional neural networks for sentiment analysis of short texts." in *COLING*, 2014, pp. 69–78.

[13] D. Tang, F. Wei, B. Qin, T. Liu, and M. Zhou, "Coooolll: A deep learning system for twitter sentiment classification," in *Proceedings of the 8th International Workshop on Semantic Evaluation (SemEval 2014)*, 2014, pp. 208–212.

[14] J. Ramanathan and R. Ramnath, "Context-assisted sentiment analysis," in *The 25th Annual ACM Symposium on Applied Computing*, 2010, pp. 404–413.

[15] F. Ciravegna, "2, an adaptive algorithm for information extraction from web-related texts," in *In Proceedings of the IJCAI-2001 Workshop on Adaptive Text Extraction and Mining*, 2001, p. organization=Citeseer.

[16] A. Kamal, "Subjectivity classification using machine learning techniques for mining feature-opinion pairs from web opinion sources," *arXiv preprint arXiv:1312.6962*, 2013.

[17] W. Jin, H. H. Ho, and R. K. Srihari, "Opinionminer: a novel machine learning system for web opinion mining and extraction," in *Proceedings of the 15th ACM SIGKDD international conference on Knowledge discovery and data mining*. ACM, 2009, pp. 1195–1204.

[18] U. of Malta, "MLSS: Maltese Language Software Server, Part of Speech Tagger for Maltese," http://metanet4u.research.um.edu.mt/services/MtPOS?wsdl., 2015, [Retrieved: September, 2016].

[19] K.Sultana, "Kurt Sultana - Research: Basic Stemmer for Maltese," http://www.kurtsultana.com/, 2015, [Retrieved: September, 2016].

[20] Skymind, "DL4J - Deep Learning for Java," http://www.deeplearning4j.org/, 2015, [Retrieved: September, 2016].

[21] ——, "Movie Review Sentiment Analysis With Word2Vec, DBNs and RNTNs," http://deeplearning4j.org/sentiment-analysis-word2vec.html, 2015, [Retrieved: September, 2015].

Towards a Common Data Model for the Internet of Things and Its Application in Healthcare Domain

Rıza Cenk Erdur, Özgün Yılmaz, Onurhan Çelik, Anıl Sevici
Department of Computer Engineering
Ege University
İzmir, Turkey
e-mail: cenk.erdur@ege.edu.tr

Olgun Cengiz, Cem Pancar, Tuğçe Kalkavan, Gizem Çelebi, Hasan Basri Akırmak, İlker Eryılmaz, Arda Güreller
Ericsson Turkey
İzmir/İstanbul, Turkey
e-mail: ilker.eryilmaz@ericsson.com

Abstract— **In the Internet of Things (IoT) environment, there exist a lot of devices, such as mobile phones, tablets and sensors, which are connected to each other. Huge amount of data is being generated from those connected devices. One of the challenges in developing IoT platforms and/or IoT applications is the representation and storage of this data. Towards this aim, in this paper, a standards based common data model has been proposed. The proposed data model basically depends on IoT-Architectural Reference Model (IoT-ARM), but is also extended with some concepts coming from the European Telecommunications Standards Institute (ETSI) Machine to Machine (M2M) functional specification. To show its applicability, we have instantiated the data model for the healthcare domain.**

Keywords-internet of things; data model; IoT-ARM; ETSI.

I. Introduction

In the IoT environment, there are a lot of interconnected devices, such as mobile phones, tablets and sensors. Those interconnected devices produce vast amount of data. Representation and storage of that data is one of the hot topics in the IoT area. Accordingly, the main objective of this paper is to define a common data model which is compliant with the current standards in the IoT research area.

There are two main standardization efforts in the IoT area. One of them is the efforts of the ETSI [1] as a result of which a M2M functional architecture specification has been published among many other specifications. The other one is IoT-A (IoT-Architecture), a European Union's Seventh Framework project consortium with several partners both from academia and industry. The objective of IoT-A is to create the architectural foundations of IoT environments as a result of which the IoT-ARM had been released [2]. The common data model presented in this paper basically depends on the IoT-ARM reference model, but is extended with some concepts taken from the ETSI specification.

To show the applicability of the proposed data model, we have instantiated the data model for the healthcare domain. We then mapped that instantiation to MongoDB [3], which is a document oriented NoSQL database.

The rest of the paper is organized as follows. In Section II the IoT-ARM reference model is overviewed to provide a background. Section III explains the IoT-ARM compatible data model which is extended using some concepts taken from the ETSI specification. Section IV discusses the implementation of the data model on MongoDB. Finally, Section V includes conclusion.

II. IoT-Architectural Reference Model

The IoT-A aims to establish an architecture for the Internet of Things. An architectural reference model has been established to form a common ground for developing IoT applications [2]. The layers of this reference model are shown in Fig. 1.

Since the main focus of this paper is to define a common data model, we are interested in the domain and information models.

Part of the IoT domain model is given in Fig. 2. The concepts of service, resource, virtual entity, physical entity and device constitute the main part of the IoT domain model [2] and they are explained in the following paragraphs. Please refer to chapter 7 of [2] for the full UML (Unified Modeling Language) representation and explanation of the IoT domain model.

In the IoT domain model, the physical entity can be any physical object from humans to animals. For example, physical entities can be a kind of flower loaded into a truck for transportation and these flowers are subject to environmental monitoring. Physical entities are used in the digital world as virtual entities [2]. In our model, we have *Virtual Entity* class to include these physical entities.

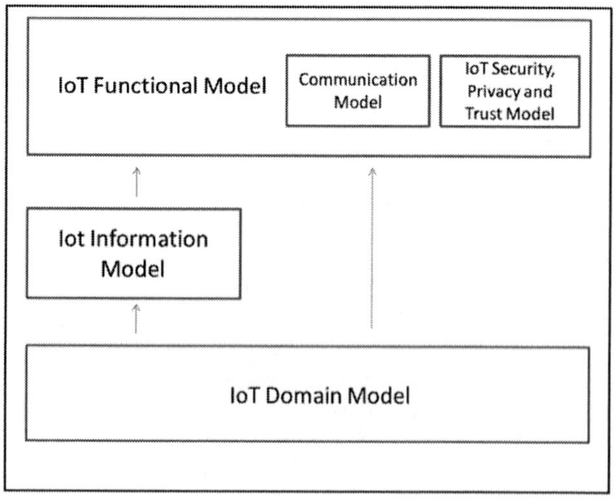

Figure 1. IoT –A Reference Model

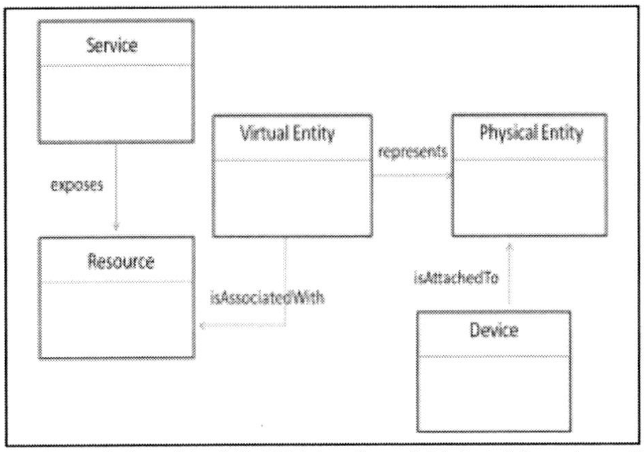

Figure 2. Part of the IoT-ARM domain model (adapted from chapter 7 of [2])

Also, there are devices that can be sensors or actuators in the IoT domain model. They have a relationship with physical entities, and hence with virtual entities [2]. In the example mentioned above, there are sensors that measure the temperature of the truck that carries the flowers (e.g., orchids). Using our data model, which is presented in the next section, the developers can define devices within the sensor list in the *Virtual Entity* class.

Resources are software components that provide data from physical entities. A virtual entity can be associated with resources. IoT domain model also defines service. A service exposes resources and provides a standardized interface to present all of the functionalities for interacting with the resources/devices related with physical entities. For each virtual entity there is an association with different services. These services may provide different functionalities, such as getting information or carrying out the execution of actuation tasks [2].

The information model specifies how the information related with virtual entities is represented. It consists of attributes, their values and meta-data. Please, also refer to chapter 7 of [2] for detailed explanations and UML based representations of IoT information model.

In the following section, the common data model is presented. The data model basically depends on the IoT domain model and is extended with some concepts coming from the ETSI functional specification.

III. The Data Model

The main objective in defining the data model is to form a common data model infrastructure for IoT applications in different domains. For this purpose, open standards in this area, which are IoT-A and ETSI based, have been inspected and a common data model has been defined.

The idea that underlies the process of modeling IoT data is to represent physical entities and the devices (i.e., sensors and actuators) in an abstract way. In the application layer, these abstract entities can be grouped together with the required properties to be used in the form of an upper data model.

The IOT-ARM and ETSI compatible data model that we propose is shown in Fig. 3. *Virtual Entity (VE)*, *Resource* and *Service* tables that exist in the model represent the virtual provisions of the real entities and physical devices in the IoT-A standard.

Subscription, *Registration* and *Group* tables that are provided by the ETSI standard are to help the application layer. These tables are used by applications accessing the services offered by the device.

Subscription represents a request from the application (an actor performing a request) to be notified about the changes made on the parent resource. A subscription resource can also be used as a timer to trigger other actions. In this case, the subscriber is notified at the expiration and receives a timeout reason defined at the subscription resource creation [1].

In order to subscribe to a resource a subscription should be created in the subscriptions collection. The child resource will be notified about the change of the parent resource of the subscriptions resource where the subscription is added [1].

Group table is a representation of the resources that are same or mixed. Manipulation can be made to all members in the group [1].

ETSI M2M adopts a RESTful architecture style. Information is represented by resources that are structured to form a tree. A RESTful architecture provides the transfer of representations of uniquely addressable resources. ETSI M2M standardizes the resource structure that resides on a M2M Service Capability Layer (SCL) by providing each SCL with a resource structure where the information is kept [1].

Resource is a uniquely addressed entity in the RESTful architecture. A resource should be accessed via a Universal Resource Identifier (URI) [1].

Issuer is the actor performing a request. An issuer can be an application or a SCL [1].

As a result of a successful registration of an application with the local SCL, application resource is created. In this scheme, applications should only register to their local SCL [1].

The data model in Fig.3 also illustrates the use of it in the healthcare domain. In the following section, the implementation of this data model on MongoDB is discussed.

IV. Implementation

IoT technologies are suitable for using in e-health systems, because in e-health systems, there is a huge amount of time series data coming from many devices similar to IoT domain.

DataPoint table is the most important table when the data model is mapped to a document oriented database like MongoDB, since data generated by the resources affects this table, and operations on this table are very intensive.

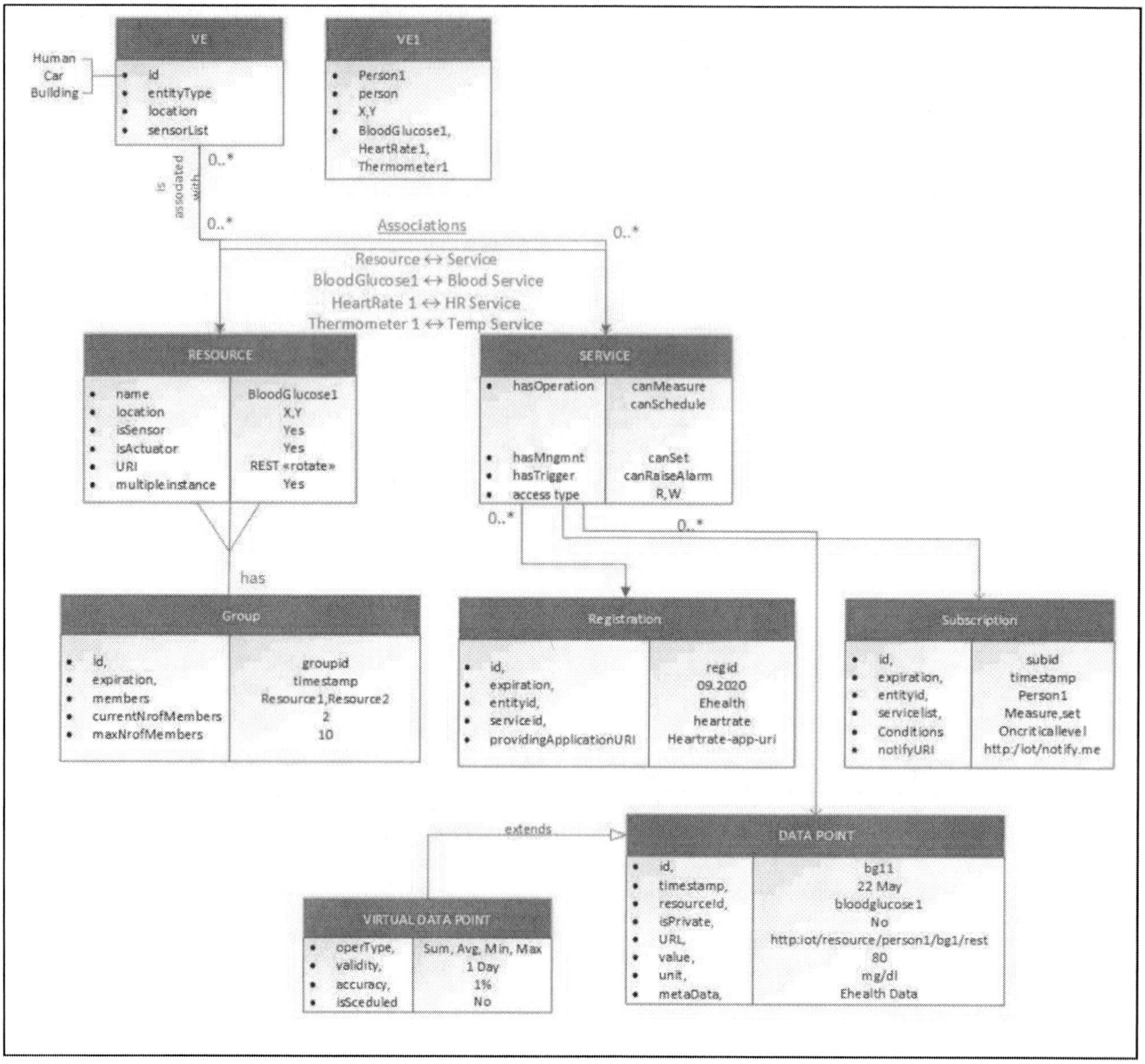

Figure 3. Generic data model which is IOT-ARM and ETSI compatible

Comparing the relational database and non-relational database, collections could be considered analogous to tables and documents analogous to records. The most of the computing is performed on *Data Point* collection in our data model. All data from devices/sensors will be added to this collection directly.

The most important point is how to store that data in an efficient way in terms of both access time and memory space. Hence, *Data Point* collection is designed to meet these constraints.

The data that come from sensors are in the form of time series data. Time series data is a great fit for MongoDB. If we store data in the form of time series, we can obtain high performance.

A row in a relational database management system (RDBMS) is a single data record. On the other hand, in MongoDB a document corresponds to a row. However, we can expand a document with more data records and store them in different formats. Thus, we can design each document to include data in a specified time interval.

Fig. 4 shows how a single data can be held in a single document. The sample data has been formed using the proposed data model.

```
dataPoint(collection)
{
      "_id" : ObjectId("5740a7ee35fe8d03d821bd52"),
      "resourceId" : "thermometer1",
      "timestamp" : ISODate("2016-02-10T23:00:00.000Z"),
      "isPrivate" : "Yes",
      "URL" : " http:iot/resource/human1/thermometer1/rest",
      "metaData" : "Health",
      "unit" : "celsius",
      "values" : "36.2"
}
```

Figure 4. One document storing one data value

The document given in Fig. 4 shows the storage of single data that comes from a resource called "thermometer1" at a certain time. If we use such a document, the document needs to be repeated for all the temperature values coming in a specific time period.

To be more efficient, the design in Fig. 4 needs to be changed. The new model involves all the data values for a specific time period in one document. This document has been shown in Fig. 5. In particular, it includes the data coming from "thermometer1" resource during an interval of one hour, sampled in periods of one second. As shown in Fig. 5, each hour's data has been represented as a different document.

In this way, instead of keeping each second's measured temperature data in a different document, all the data coming from that sensor during a specific period is stored in a single document.

This approach has the following advantages from different perspectives:

- Write performance advantages,
  - The first approach performs 3600 insert operations within the period of one hour. But the second approach performs 1 insert and 3599 update operations.

```
dataPoint(collection)
{
      "_id" : ObjectId("5740a7ee35fe8d03d821bd52"),
      "resourceId" : "thermometer1",
      "timestamp" : ISODate("2016-02-10T23:00:00.000Z"),
      "isPrivate" : "Yes",
      "URL" : " http:iot/resource/human1/thermometer1/rest",
      "metaData" : "Health",
      "unit" : "celsius",
      "values" : {
         0: { 0: 36.1, 1: 36.1, …, 59: 36.2 },
         1: { 0: 36.2, 1: 36.2, …, 59: 36.2 },
         …,
         58: { 0: 37.6, 1: 37.6, …, 59: 37.7 },
         59: { 0: 37.7, 1: 37.7, …, 59: 37.7 }
      }
}
```

Figure 5. Storing time series data

  - By avoiding unnecessary rewriting of the entire document and index entries, less disk I/O is performed. Because field-level updates are much more efficient.
- Read Performance advantages,
  - In the second approach, reads are also much faster. If we need the measurements during a specific hour, using the first approach we need to read 3600 documents. On the other hand, using the second approach we only need to read a single document. Reading fewer documents has the benefit of fewer disk seeks.
- Indexing advantages,
  - Another important advantage is from the indexing perspective. In the first approach, the great number of insert operations increases the size of the index. In the second approach, the size of the index will be reduced significantly due to performing a less number of insert operations.

Also, data can be kept in a document with different time periods. This period can be set depending on the device or sensor. For example, if a sensor/device produces data once per minute, then the document stores 60 data value on an hourly basis.

Sample data for *Data Point* collection is shown in Fig. 6. Two different resources are created with different identity numbers. These devices are blood glucose monitor and thermometer. Each of the devices has different data units and range of values. All of these data are generated randomly.

V. RELATED WORK

In this section, similar studies are reviewed. IPSO Smart Objects provide a common design pattern and an object model for communication between devices and applications. Resources and services in IPSO are used in the same way as the ETSI and IoT-A standards. But IPSO tends to model with RESTful protocol [4].

Resources, devices and services have their own identifier URLs (Uniform Resource Locator). For example, thermometer is a device and it is defined as an object URL. Every object has items that are services. Thermometer has a sensor value and sensor value is an item. Items have their own object URLs. After these definitions, the instance of the object is created and measurements are calculated with the object and the item values.

In our data model, thermometer is a sensor and it is stored in the resource table and it has a defined sensing temperature service in the service table. We also keep data in JSON format like IPSO object model, but there are differences in the definitions of the collections. We have registration and subscription tables originated from the ETSI specification. Resources will be registered to entities and the subscriptions are connected to these registrations. After registration, data streaming will be in the *Data Point* table having all resource data on the same collection.

Bui and Zorzi [5] propose the Internet of Things communication framework as the main enabler for

DATA POINT		
• id,	Human1	Human2
• timestamp,	20 March	2 October
• resourceId,	thermometer1	glucose2
• isPrivate,	Yes	Yes
• URL,	http:iot/resource/human1/thermo1	http:iot/resource/human2/glucose2
• value,	37.7	87
• unit	celsius	mg/dl

Figure 6. Example data for *Data Point* collection

distributed worldwide healthcare applications. The requirements of a unified communication framework are analyzed. Finally, the Internet of Things protocol stack and the advantages it brings to healthcare scenarios in terms of the identified requirements are presented. As for the implementation, this related work contributes to the IoT-A reference model.

De et al. [6] views the functionalities provided by objects of the IoT as 'real-world services' because they provide a near real-time state of the physical world. A semantic modeling approach for different components in an IoT framework is presented in this paper. This paper and the data model presented for modeling the IoT components contributes to the IoT-A reference model. Our data model is also based on the IoT-A reference model.

There are a number of works which use ontologies for representing sensor data. OntoSensor [6][7] defines an ontology-based specification model for sensors by borrowing parts from SensorML [8] descriptions and extending the IEEE Suggested Upper Merged Ontology (SUMO). However, a descriptive model for observation and measurement data is not provided. Reference [9] proposes an ontology-based model for service oriented sensor data and networks. However, representing and interpreting complex sensor data is not described [6]. The SensorData Ontology [10] is built based on Observations & Measurements and SensorML specifications which are defined by the OGC Sensor Web Enablement (SWE) [6][11].

W3C Semantic Sensor Network Incubator Group has constructed an ontology [12] to describe sensors and sensor networks. A high-level schema model is represented by this ontology to describe sensor devices and other related information about these devices. However, modeling aspects for features of interest and units of measurement and domain knowledge about the sensor data is not included. This domain knowledge is needed to be associated with the sensor data in order to support data communication and efficient reasoning [6].

Quwaider and Jararweh [13] discuss that there is a crucial need for efficient and scalable community health awareness in today's health care applications. In this related work, a cloud supported model for efficient community health awareness in the presence of a large scale data generation is presented. The goal is to monitor big data to be available to the end user or to the decision maker in a reliable manner. A system architecture and performance evaluation of the system is provided. But the data model of the system is not presented. So we cannot compare it directly to our system.

VI. CONCLUSION

In the IoT environment, platforms managing data and applications require more flexibility, agility and scalability to meet the requirements of IoT. A huge amount of sensor data which is schemaless, diverse in format and in scale needs to be processed. Thus, NoSQL databases should be the best candidates that can meet these requirements. Relational databases can still be used for structured data and where transaction information is important. For example, relational database systems still fit well for storing billing/charging or customer information. On the other hand, NoSQL databases are good when agility, scalability and heterogeneity are considered.

With all this information given in this paper, a document oriented NoSQL database can be preferred for storing sensor information in IoT environment. Document oriented databases provide flexibility, dynamic or changeable schema or even schemaless documents. New data structures can be added to the system easily.

In this paper, a standards based common data model for the IoT domain has been proposed. The proposed data model is compatible with IoT-A and ETSI M2M standards. Then as a proof of concept, this data model is instantiated for the healthcare domain and mapped to MongoDB. MongoDB is chosen as a document oriented NoSQL database because it provides secure, scalable, flexible solutions for IoT systems, and it is also compatible with cloud architecture.

As a future work, the developed database will be evaluated for its performance by distributing the data on several clusters on a cloud environment. The Yahoo Cloud Serving Benchmark [14] is going to be used in these tests.

REFERENCES

[1] ETSI, Machine-to-Machine communications (M2M); Functional architecture, ETSI TS 102 690 V2.1.1, 2013.

[2] A. Bassi et al., "Enabling Things to Talk", Springer, 2013.

[3] MongoDB, https://www.mongodb.com/ (retrieved: 08, 2016).

[4] J. Jimenez, M. Kostery, and H. Tschofenig, "IPSO Smart Objects", Position Paper for the IoT Semantic Interoperability Workshop 2016.

[5] N. Bui and M. Zorzi, "Health Care Applications: A Solution Based on The Internet of Things", Proceedings of the 4th International Symposium on Applied Sciences in Biomedical and Communication Technologies, pp. 131:1–131:5, 2011.

[6] S. De, P. Barnaghi, M. Bauer, and S. Meissner, "Service Modelling for the Internet of Things", Proceedings of the IEEE 2011 Federated Conference on Computer Science and Information Systems, pp. 949-955, 2011.

[7] D. J. Russomanno, C. Kothari, and O. Thomas, "Sensor ontologies: from shallow to deep models", Proceedings of the Thirty-Seventh Southeastern Symposium on System Theory, pp. 107-112, 2005.

[8] OGC, "OpenGIS Sensor Model Language (SensorML) Implementation Specification", Open Geospatial Consortium, Inc. 2007. http://www.opengeospatial.org/standards/sensorml (retrieved: 08, 2016).

[9] J. H. Kim, K. Kwon, K. D.-H, and S. J. Lee, "Building a service-oriented ontology for wireless sensor networks", Proceedings of the Seventh IEEE/ACIS International Conference on Computer and Information Science, pp. 649-654, 2008.

[10] P. M. Barnaghi, S. Meissner, M. Presser, and K. Moessner, "Sense and sens'ability: Semantic data modelling for sensor networks", Proceedings of the ICT Mobile Summit, 2009.

[11] OGC, "Open Geospatial Consortium (OGC) Sensor Web Enablement: Overview and High Level Architecture", OGC white paper, 2007.

[12] W3C-SSNIG, "W3C SSN Incubator Group Report". 2011. https://www.w3.org/2005/Incubator/ssn/XGR-ssn-20110628/ (retrieved: 08, 2016).

[13] M. Quwaider and Y. Jararweh, "A cloud supported model for efficient community health awareness", Pervasive and Mobile Computing, vol. 28, pp. 35–50, June 2016.

[14] B. F. Cooper, A. Silberstein, E. Tam, R. Ramakrishnan, and R. Sears, "Benchmarking Cloud Serving Systems with YCSB", Proceedings of the 1st ACM symposium on Cloud computing, pp. 143-154, 2010.

Towards Interoperable Ontologies: Blood Test Ontology with FOAF

Emine Sezer, Ozgu Can, Okan Bursa and Murat Osman Unalir
Department of Computer Engineering, Ege University, 35100 Bornova, Izmir, Turkey
e-mail:{emine.sezer, ozgu.can, okan.bursa, murat.osman.unalir}@ege.edu.tr

Abstract— **Healthcare systems around the globe are changing their information systems in order to be able to share and reuse patients' information not only in a department where the information is produced, but also between the departments of an organization and also among the different health organizations or other institutions. For this purpose, lots of data standards and ontologies are developed in the health care domain. `BloodTestOntology`, which is introduced in this work, describes the substances found in the blood to help physicians in making a diagnosis. Friend of a Friend (FOAF), a well-known ontology for defining personal information, is extended to define required relations for the health care domain. `BloodTestOntology` is integrated with extended FOAF ontology in order to create an interoperable treatment system with other information systems. The proposed model can be used for personalized treatment suggestion systems.**

Keywords- BloodTestOntology; Extended FOAF; Healthcare Information Systems; Interperability; Semantic Web.

I. INTRODUCTION

Information technology attempts to meet the demands for all kinds of services from anywhere and at anytime, with the help of today's current technologies and Internet infrastructure. Internet activities like e-commerce, banking, paying taxes, tourism, etc. have become common, as well as the searching for information and using the social media [1]-[5].

Healthcare is a lifelong requirement for any person. The healthcare domain is an area where people, different organizations and various institutions get services, as well as provide services at the same time. To meet the requirements of receiving and delivering health care services with high quality, efficiency and also ensuring continuity, means using resources that are geographically dispersed. Also, more privatized structures have emerged. As a result, the patients' health information has become dispersed and specialized.

Health authorities also began to create health information systems for healthcare services with the successful implementations of information technologies in various domains. The preliminary applications are the systems that record the administrative data like patients' name, surname, address, insurance, etc.

It is desirable to be able to share and reuse the data not only in the system where the data is produced, but also between the systems that need that data. Until recently, it was not reasonable to share a patient's data between the departments of healthcare organizations. Reusing health data of a person in any health organization where he/she is admitted for a health service can accelerate the diagnostic process, while reducing material costs in healthcare.

The Semantic Web is defined as the extension of the current Web where information is given in a well-defined meaning and leads to a better collaboration between computers and humans [6]. The Semantic Web studies focus on developing domain specific ontologies, as well as semantic recommendation systems and decision support systems for defining semantic rules using these ontologies.

In recent years, lots of different ontologies in various domains have been developed with the increasing popularity of the Semantic Web studies. Although interoperability between systems is desired, the developed ontologies must be reusable. When these ontologies are examined, it is seen that the ontology can be used only in the system for which it is developed, whereas it is impossible to share and reuse information between different systems.

Blood is a red liquid that circulates the whole body by vessels. The main task of the blood is to transport the necessary oxygen and nutrients to the cells. When a patient consults a physician with any complaint, after listening to the patient's medical history, the physician requests some medical tests. The priority is always given to the blood tests in order to analyze the substances found in the blood.

`BloodTestOntology`, which is introduced in this work, aims to model the substances measured from the blood during the blood test with the help of the Semantic Web technologies. Blood Test Ontology describes the blood tests being done in the health field, the relationships between these tests, their results and the rules. Thus, developing a knowledge base for a system that can query and reuse the stored information of the personalized test results of blood tests would be provided.

Friend of a Friend (FOAF) is a project that is the most common document to represent the demographical properties of a person. It is represented in RDF (Resource Description Framework) [29]. FOAF is widely used inside various domains to describe personal information [7].

In this work, FOAF is used to describe the patients' information with demographic and dynamic properties and also to describe the personal health information. Connecting FOAF with the `Blood Test Ontology` to use personal information descriptions in FOAF provides an interoperable, personalized and more manageable personal data. A personal health care system needs not only personal information, but also information about the person's parents and/or his/her family. Defining this information with FOAF must support extendable, open and sharable data that could be used as the basic description to create a personalized health information system. By using FOAF, the patient can have full control over his/her data and the system can give a personalized experience to him/her during his/her own treatment.

The paper is organized as follows. Section 2 presents the relevant related work. Section 3 explains the knowledge representation and development of the `BloodTestOntology`. A brief explanation is given for the extended FOAF ontology. Later, the integration of extended FOAF and `BloodTestOntology` is described. Finally, Section 4 concludes and outlines the direction of the future work.

II. RELATED WORK

The healthcare domain is one of the few areas that has a huge amount of domain knowledge. If the ontologies developed in the health care domain are examined, it is seen that the studies focus on defining the medical terms of the domain [8]. Infectious Disease Ontology (IDO) [9] [10], Saliva Ontology (SALO) [11] and Blood Ontology (BLO) [12] are ontologies that are described by formal ontology languages. IDO provides a consistent terminology, taxonomy, and logical representation for the domain of infectious diseases [9]. IDO has 185 concepts, but does not ahve any object properties between these concepts and data properties. IDO covers the terms common for all infectious diseases, but diseases themselves are not defined in the ontology. SALO [11] is defined as a consensus-based controlled vocabulary of terms and relations dedicated to the salivaomics domain and to saliva-related diagnostics. SALO is an ongoing exploratory initiative. BLO is designed to serve as a comprehensive infrastructure to allow the exploration of information relevant to scientific research and to human blood manipulation [12]. It is an ongoing project and the development of the ontology is still a work in progress. BLO describes the structure, diseases and abnormalities of the blood.

FOAF is a vocabulary [30] to define personal information using people-related constructions in a structured data. This personal information includes demographic information such as name, family name and birthday in addition to online information such as mailbox, homepage, URL and much more. FOAF is used in many different applications. In research areas, such as distributed access right management [13], policy and profile integration [14] and Social Web Integration [15], FOAF is widely used to represent personal information in addition to social/friendship networks. Profiling and linking personal information is an important asset for collaborative filtering recommender systems. Film Trust [16] is one of the collaborative recommender systems that use FOAF to represent all kinds of personal information. Moreover, FOAF is used to interview the overall social information [17] and user preferences [18] [19]. Analysis of FOAF documents shows that most used FOAF attribute is `mbox_sha1sum`, which is the unique representation of email address and a necessity for FOAF vocabulary. FOAF is also used to infer characteristics of user habits [20]. All of these applications use FOAF. FOAF is the most used RDF vocabulary due to its simplicity, well documented and easily applied tools, such as FOAF-o-Matic [31] and FOAFpress [32].

III. CONNECTING FOAF WITH BLOOD TEST ONTOLOGY

A. Blood Test Ontology

In the health care domain, blood tests contain information that might be used by any clinic. The same tests are unfortunately performed repeatedly when the patient goes to different clinics in the same hospital or different hospitals. This causes waste of time for the diagnosis of disease as well as an increase in healthcare costs.

Blood tests can be used for the following reasons:

- to analyze the general state of a person's health,
- to confirm the presence of a bacterial or viral infection,
- to see how well certain organs, such as the liver and kidneys, are functioning,
- to screen for certain genetic conditions, such as cystic fibrosis or spinal muscular atrophy,
- to check what medications the person is taking,
- to analyze how well the person's blood is clotting,
- to diagnose diseases and conditions such as cancer, HIV/AIDS, diabetes, and coronary heart disease,
- to find out whether the person has risk factors for heart disease.

The blood test results may fall outside the normal range for many reasons. Abnormal results might be a sign of a disorder or disease. On the other hand, diet, menstrual cycle, physical activity level, alcohol intake, and medications can also cause abnormal results. Many diseases and medical problems can not be diagnosed with blood tests alone. However, blood tests can help the physician to learn more about the patient's health status. Blood tests can also help to find potential problems early, when treatments or lifestyle changes may work best.

`BloodTestOntology`, developed in this work, aims to model the substances measured from the blood during the blood test by using Semantic Web technologies. It describes the blood tests being done in the healthcare domain, the relationships between these tests, the results of these tests and the rules about them according to the related domain.

`BloodTestOntology` provides information about the blood test results to physicians, health workers and patients. In this work, we aim to represent the recent blood test result status with the `BloodTestOntology` and to use it as a part of an information base for the clinical information system. Thus, it could be used to give services to patients and health workers to organize blood information, to support the clinical decision system and to improve the clinical trials. The primary objectives of the `BloodTestOntology` are performing interoperability, sharing information and providing reusability in the healthcare domain.

`BloodTestOntology` has $\mathcal{ALCRIQ(D)}$ DL expressivity with 159 classes, 75 object properties and 35 data properties. The main goal of developing this ontology is using it as an information base for clinical information system. The `BloodTestOntology` is still being developed and extended with new concepts, object and data properties with domain experts from Ege University, Faculty of Medicine [33] according to the Medical Faculty's implementation clinics.

`BloodTestOntology` has a hierarchical structure as seen in Fig. 1. A medical test can be any test that is applied to a patient to assess patient's general state of health. In `BloodTestOntology`, these tests correspond to the human body fluids, such as blood, saliva, stool and urine with the concepts of `BloodTest`, `SalivaTest`, `StoolTest` and `UrineTest`, respectively.

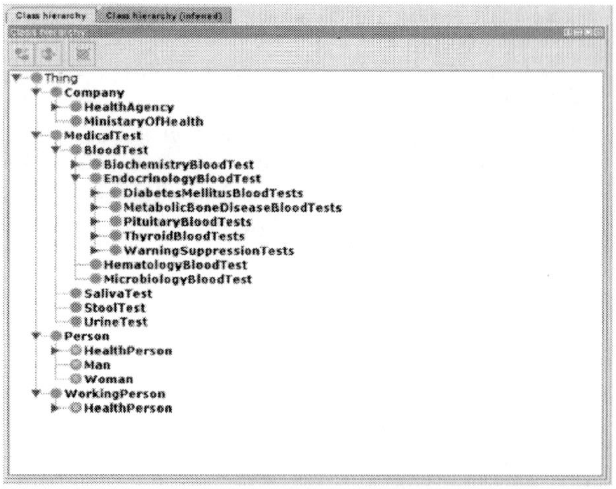

Figure 1. The basic concepts of The `BloodTestOntology`.

In this work, we have focused on the substances of the blood that are measured to analyze a patient's general state of health. The core concepts of a blood test that are defined in `BloodTestOntology` like FT3, FT4, HDL Cholesterol, LDL Cholesterol, etc. do not exist in the current blood ontologies in the literature. In hospitals, the blood is analyzed in four different laboratories that are endocrinology, biochemistry, microbiology and hematology, respectively. By taking these situations into consideration, we classified the blood test concept into four sub-concepts: `EndocrinologyBloodTest`, `BiochemistryBloodTest`, `MicrobiologyBloodTest` and `HematologyBloodTest`. For example, the blood tests like `Hemogram` and `Giemsa` are defined as sub-concepts of `HematologyBloodTest`, blood tests about thyroid like `TSH`, `FT3` and `FT4` are defined as sub-concepts of `EndocrinologyBloodTest`. As the reference values may vary according to the test laboratory, patients' age or gender, the reference values of the substances, which are test concepts, are not defined as data properties.

B. *Integrating Blood Test Ontology and FOAF*

The data can be reused between the systems without changing its given definition in order to provide interoperability. Using ontologies as the information base for the systems, the given definition of data can be provided. However, creating ontologies for the specific domain makes it difficult to get data with its metadata. For this purpose, integrating ontologies with the concepts that have the same meaning presents a useful solution.

Defining personal information as a concept in ontologies is quite familiar (more than 1,000 RDF documents have defined terms containing 'person') [21]. Literature works [22]-[27] provide a vision and various examples of FOAF extensions that can be used to support Web-based information systems. In [28], a comparison of FOAF documents is given.

In this work, FOAF ontology is integrated with the `BloodTestOntology` through the concept "`Person`". First, we extended FOAF ontology with proper data and object properties. The difference between our extended FOAF ontology and the FOAF is given in Table 1. For example, FOAF has only one object property "`knows`". However, in our extended ontology the new object properties, "`has Age`", "`hasIncome`", "`hasOccupation`", etc. are inserted.

Later, the concept "`Person`" in `BloodTestOntology` is imported from the extended FOAF ontology. In this way, data properties like "`firstname`", "`surname`", "`birthday`" and "`agevalue`" can be used in `BloodTestOntology` without describing these properties again. The relation between these ontologies is shown in Fig. 2.

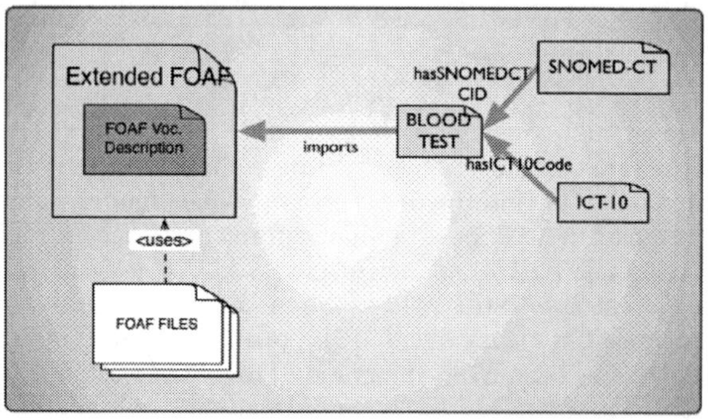

Figure 2. The structure of the integrated model.

As seen in Fig. 2, `BloodTestOntology` also includes the related SNOMED-CT [34] conceptIDs and ICD-10 [35] codes. Thus, when there will be another information system using the SNOMED-CT vocabulary, that system could exchange health information with a clinic information system which is using `BloodTestOntology` as the information base.

TABLE 1. THE EXTENDED FOAF ONTOLOGY.

Class Definition	**Information**	**SubClass/SuperClass**
Income	Income values of a Person/Income Set of a Profile	None
Occupation	Occupation of a Person/Occupation Set of a Profile	None
Age	Age Value of a Person/Age Values Set of a Profiles	None
Object Type Properties	**Domain**	**Range**
hasAge	Person	Age
hasIncome	Person	Income
hasOccupation	Person	Occupation
hasProfiles/isProfileOf	Person/MetaProfile:Profile	MetaProfile:Profile/FOAF:Person
hasPreferences/isPreferenceOf	Person/MetaPreference:Preference	MetaPreference:Preference
preferredDomain	Person	PreferenceVersusDomain
Data Type Properties		
ageValue	Age	xsd:integer
incomeValue	Income	xsd:integer
occupationValue	Occupation	xsd:string
Is	one of{income, Age}	xsd:integer
can-be	Occupation	xsd:string

IV. CONCLUSIONS

In this work, an information base that would be the knowledge base for a treatment system has been created to provide interoperability and to reuse health data. In order to perform this, the health standards ICD-10 codes and SNOMED-CT ConceptID are inserted inside the `BloodTestOntology`. Therefore, if any information system using SNOMED-CT vocabulary or ICD-10 codes that system could exchange health information with a clinic information system that is using `BloodTestOntology` as the information base.

Although blood tests are not sufficient to diagnose diseases, some blood tests named markers can show certain diagnostic results. For example, if a patient's Anti-HCV test is positive, this person can have chronic Hepatitis-C virus infection. Hepatitis-C is usually spread by blood-to-blood contact, so blood transfusion must not be done from these patients. The patient's family and friends can be at risk for this infection. By integrating FOAF ontology with the `BloodTestOntology`, the risk group could be determined easily with the defined rules.

As known, some blood test results have different reference values for genders or ages. Defining domain specific health rules on the integrated extended FOAF with `BloodTestOntology` can also support the creation of personalized treatment suggestions for patients. As taught in medical schools that *there is no illness, there is the patient*; it could be used to give services to patients and health workers to organize blood information, to support the clinical decision system and to improve the clinical trials.

REFERENCES

[1] L. Zhang, M. Zhu, and W. Huang, "A Framework for an Ontology-based E-commerce Product Information Retrieval System", Journal of Computers (JCP), Vol.4/6, pp. 436-443, 2009.

[2] S. Jeong and H. Kim, "Design of Semantically Interoperable Adverse Event Reporting Framework", The Semantic Web - ASWC 2006, First Asian Semantic Web Conference, LNCS, vol. 4185, pp. 588-594, 2006.

[3] M. Austin, M. Kelly, and S. M. Brady, "The benefits of an ontological patient model in clinical decision-support", AAAI'08: Proceedings of the 23rd National Conference on Artificial intelligence, pp. 1774-1775, 2008.

[4] O. Suominen, E. Hyvönen, K. Viljanen, and E. Hukka, "HealthFinland - A national semantic publishing network and portal for health information", J. Web Sem., 7(4), pp. 287-297, 2009.

[5] H. Cheng, Y. Lu, and C. Sheu, "An ontology-based business intelligence application in a financial knowledge management system", Expert Systems with Applications: An International Journal, v.36 n.2, pp. 3614-3622, March, 2009.

[6] T. Berners-Lee, J. Hendler, and O. Lassila, "The semantic web". Scientific American, 284 (5), pp. 34-43, 2001.

[7] FOAF, The friend of a friend project, http://www.foaf-project.org/. [Retrieved: September, 2016]

[8] D. M. Lopez and B. Blobel, "A development framework for semantically interoperable health information systems". I. J. Medical Informatics, 78(2), pp. 83-103, 2009.

[9] A. Goldfain, B. Smith, and L. G. Cowell, "Dispositions and the Infectious Disease Ontology", FOIS 2010, pp. 400–413, 2010.

[10] L. G. Cowell and B. Smith, "Infectious Disease Ontology", In: Infectious Disease Informatics, pp. 373–395, 2010.

[11] J. Ai, B. Smith, and D. T. Wong, "Saliva Ontology: An ontology-based framework for a Salivaomics Knowledge Base", BMC Bioinformatics 11, pp. 302, 2010.

[12] M. B. Almeida, A. B. Freitas, C. Proietti, C. Ai, and B. Smith, "The Blood Ontology: An Ontology in the Domain of Hematology", In: Int. Conf. on Biomedical Ontologies,

Working with Multiple Biomedical Ontologies Workshop, Vol. 833 of CEUR Workshop Proceedings, CEUR-WS.org, 2011.

[13] S. R. Kruk, S. Grzonkowski, A. Gzella, T. Woroniecki and H. C. Choi, "D-FOAF: Distributed Identity Management with Access Rights Delegation", in Riichiro Mizoguchi; Zhongzhi Shi & Fausto Giunchiglia, ed., 'ASWC' , Springer, pp. 140-154, 2006.

[14] Ö. Can, O. Bursa and M. O. Ünalır, "Personalizable Ontology Based Access Control", Gazi University Journal Of Science, 23(4), pp. 465-474, 2010. ISSN 2147-1762. Available at: http://gujs.gazi.edu.tr/article/view/1060000078. [Retrieved: September, 2016]

[15] J.Golbeck and M. Rothstein, "Linking social networks on the web with FOAF: a semantic web case study", In Proceedings of the 23rd national conference on Artificial intelligence - Volume 2 (AAAI'08), Anthony Cohn (Ed.), AAAI Press, Vol. 2, pp. 1138-1143, 2008.

[16] J. Golbeck and J. Hendler, "Filmtrust: Movie recommendations using trust in web-based social networks", Proceedings of the IEEE Consumer communications and networking conference, Vol. 96, pp. 282-286, 2006.

[17] F. Abel, N. Henze, E. Herder, and D. Krause, "Interweaving public user profiles on the web", In Proceedings of the 18th international conference on User Modeling, Adaptation, and Personalization (UMAP'10), Paul Bra, Alfred Kobsa, and David Chin (Eds.), Springer-Verlag, Berlin, Heidelberg, pp. 16-27, 2010. DOI=http://dx.doi.org/10.1007/978-3-642-13470-8_4

[18] Ò. Celma, M. Ramírez, and P. Herrera, "Foafing the music: A music recommendation system based on rss feeds and user preferences", IN ISMIR, pp. 464-467, 2005.

[19] O. Bursa, E. Sezer, O. Can, and M. O. Unalir, "Using FOAF for Interoperable and Privacy Protected Healthcare Information Systems", Research Conference on Metadata and Semantics, Springer International Publishing, pp. 154-161, 2014.

[20] G. A. Grimnes, P. Edwards, and A. Preece, "Learning Meta-descriptions of the FOAF Network", The Semantic Web - ISWC 2004, Lecture Notes in Computer Science, Vol. 3298, pp. 152-165, 2004.

[21] L. Ding, T. Finin, A. Joshi, R. Pan, R. S. Cost, Y. Peng, P. Reddivari, V. C. Doshi, and J. Sachs, "Swoogle: A search and metadata engine for the semantic web," in Proceedings of the Thirteenth ACM Conference on Information and Knowledge Management, pp. 652-659, 2004.

[22] L. A. Adamic, O. Buyukkokten, and E. Adar, "A social network caught in the web," First Monday, Vol. 8, No. 6, Electronic Edition: http://firstmonday.org/ojs/index.php/fm/article/view/1057, June 2003 [Retrieved: September, 2016]

[23] E. Dumbill, "Finding friends with xml and rdf," IBM's XML Watch, http://www-106.ibm.com/developerworks/xml/library/x-foaf.html, June 2002. [Retrieved: September, 2016]

[24] E. Dumbill, "Support online communities with foaf: How the friend-of-a-friend vocabulary addresses issues of accountability and privacy," IBM's XML Watch, http://www-106.ibm.com/developerworks/xml/library/x-foaf2.html, August 2002. [Retrieved: September, 2016]

[25] E. Dumbill, "Tracking provenance of rdf data," IBM's XML Watch, http://www-106.ibm.com/developerworks/xml/library/x-rdfprov.html, July 2003. [Retrieved: September, 2016]

[26] G. A. Grimnes, P. Edwards, and A. Preece, "Learning meta-descriptions of the foaf network", In Proceedings of International Semantic Web Conference, Vol. 3298, pp. 152-165, 2004.

[27] J. Golbeck, B. Parsia, and J. Hendler, "Trust networks on the semantic web", In Proceedings of Cooperative Intelligent Agents, Vol. 2782, pp. 238-249, 2003.

[28] L. Ding, L. Zhou, T. Finin, and A. Joshi, "How the Semantic Web is Being Used: An Analysis of FOAF Documents", In Proceedings of the Proceedings of the 38th Annual Hawaii International Conference on System Sciences (HICSS'05), IEEE Computer Society, Washington, DC, USA, Track 4 - Volume 04, Page 113.3, 2005. DOI=http://dx.doi.org/ 10.1109/HICSS.2005.299

[29] RDF, http://www.w3.org/RDF (accessed September 2016)

[30] FOAF Vocabulary Specification, http://xmlns.com/foaf/spec (accessed September 2016)

[31] FOAF-a-Matic, http://www.ldodds.com/foaf/foaf-a-matic. (accessed September 2016)

[32] FOAFpress, http://foafpress.org (accessed September 2016)

[33] Edge University, Faculty of Medicine, http://www.med.ege.edu.tr (accessed September 2016)

[34] SNOMED-CT, http://www.ihtsdo.org/snomed-ct (accessed September 2016)

[35] ICD-10, http://www.who.int/classifications/ icd/en (accessed September 2016)

Electronic Health Records for Smoking Cessation With a Web Based Software

Gül Eda Aydemir
Dept. of Computer Engineering
Dokuz Eylul University
Izmır, Turkey
e-mail: guledaaydemir@yahoo.com

Tuna Kut
Semafor Technology
Izmir, Turkey
e-mail: tuna.kut@hotmail.com

Alp Kut
Dept. of Computer Engineering
Dokuz Eylul University
Izmır, Turkey
e-mail: alp.kut@ceng.deu.edu.tr

Vildan Mevsim
Dept. of Family Medicine
Dokuz Eylul University
Izmir, Turkey
e-mail: vildan.mevsim@deu.edu.tr

Reyat Yılmaz
Dept. of Electrical and Electronic Engineering
Dokuz Eylul University
Izmır, Turkey
e-mail: reyat.yilmaz@ceng.deu.edu.tr

***Abstract*- Cigarette smoking is the leading preventable cause of mortality. Smokers who quit smoking reduce their risk of developing and dying from tobacco-related diseases. Smoking cessation outpatient clinics play an important role for cessation of smoking. Health information systems such as Electronic Health Records (EHRs), computerized decision support systems, and electronic prescribing are increasingly identified as potentially valuable components to improve the quality and efficiency of patient care. The paper-based methods which are used in Smoking Cessation Outpatient Clinics (SCOCs) are time and resource expensive and unlikely to be performed consistently. EHRs provide a systematic mechanism to improve patient care. In this study, a Web based software is developed for use of primary health care physicians and other health workers to implement smoking cessation for addicts. The system which was developed will be used for recording therapy, following up with the patient and evaluating the quitting process of smokers. Electronic health records computerized decision support systems are potentially valuable components to improve the quality and efficiency of clinical interventions for tobacco use. This software is developed with Microsoft Visual Studio 2015 C# programming language as a Web application.**

Keywords- smoking cessation, electronic health records, decision support systems,

I. Introduction

It is a known fact that both active and passive smoking are damaging to human health and have associated economic costs. Cigarette smoking is the cause of many preventable diseases, leads to premature deaths, and accounts for a significant proportion of many health inequalities. The World Health Organization currently estimates that each year smoking accounts for about ~6 million deaths worldwide and causes about half a trillion dollars in economic damage annually [2]. This number of smoking-attributable deaths is expected to rise to 7 million by 2020 and to more than 8 million a year by 2030 if the current rate of smoking continues unabated [3].

Health information systems such as Electronic Health Records [1], computerized decision support systems, and electronic prescribing are increasingly identified as potentially valuable components to improve the quality and efficiency of patient care. EHRs are also very likely to disseminate rapidly, at least in developed countries, as healthcare systems modernize away from paper records [4].

In this study, a Web based software is developed for use of primary health care physicians and other health workers to implement smoking cessation for addicts. The idea is to combine the power of the Web based environment with primary health care specialists. With these approaches, dependent patients will not only use a computer program, they will also communicate with their physicians for several problems in a easy to use environment. Currently, there is no computer application used by physicians for managing patients in Smoking Cessation Outpatient Clinics. For that reason, it is impossible to retrieve patient's records online since the information is currently stored in paper environment. On the other hand, to analyze patient records is very difficult and having reports about several patients is almost impossible.

Our software is developed with intensive aids of primary care physicians. During the development phase, first of all, the Smoking Cessation process is observed for several patients. After that, each case is discussed with related physicians, then the application program screens are developed for modelling processes. Finally, the beta version of the software is completed for test usage.

II. Background

In 2012, an estimated 31.1% of men and 6.2% of women worldwide were daily smokers [5]. Although daily smoking has been reduced among men and women, population growth has led to a significant increase in the number of smokers around the world [5]. Tobacco use currently kills more than five million people each year and this number is expected to increase substantially [6]. Even if prevalence rates remain unchanged, an estimated 500 million people will die as a direct result of tobacco usage over the next fifty years [7]. The healthcare setting remains an underused venue to provide cessation assistance to tobacco users, particularly in developing countries.

Evidence-based clinical practice guidelines for tobacco cessation support recommend systematic identification and intervention for tobacco use. Changes in health systems operations that institutionalize the identification and clinical treatment of patients using tobacco are a particularly promising way to take advantage of the primary care visit to help patients quit tobacco use [8]. A system level change that might increase the frequency of effective cessation delivery is to take advantage of the electronic medical record for clinician reminders, linking patients to cessation services, monitoring performance, and providing feedback.

Treatment for tobacco use in a healthcare setting first requires an assessment of tobacco use and patient willingness to stop using tobacco [9]. Healthcare clinician advice has a small effect on cessation - leading to approximately three to six per cent of patients stopping using tobacco [10]. However, higher rates of cessation are achieved when a coordinated system within the healthcare setting facilitates evidence-based actions such as cessation counselling and use of cessation medications [8]. In the absence of electronic records, a stamp or similar visual aid in a paper chart can serve as a clinician reminder to discuss tobacco use, to provide treatment, and to facilitate referrals. Chart audits by hand can also provide performance measure information needed for quality improvement. However, these paper-based methods are time and resource expensive and unlikely to be performed consistently. EHRs provide a systematic mechanism to improve the fidelity of following clinical practice guidelines consistently [11].

In many countries, a large investment is being made in technology to computerize patient medical records. One potential of electronic health records is that they could be used to remind doctors and other clinic staff to record tobacco use, to give brief advice to quit, to prescribe medications and to refer to stop smoking counselling. They could also help refer people to these services and be used to measure how well a clinic was doing. EHRs could also help make the delivery of tobacco use treatments standard practice by providing electronic referrals for additional treatment services (e.g., referral to a telephone tobacco quit line). Specifically, documentation of tobacco uses and referral to cessation counselling appear to increase following EHR changes [3].

Edward G. Feil et al. developed a cessation Web site and examined recruitment approaches on a short time evolution. They proposed a therapy from Internet and observed the results were encouraging however, outcomes were assessed only by self-report for that reason. They cannot conclude that quitting smoking was a function of their Web site [12].

Victor J. Strecher et al. proposed smoking-cessation interventions should be generalized to other cessation interventions. They demonstrated the importance of tailoring for smoking cessation program. They also used a novel fractional factorial design for examining the aims of their study. The aims of the study identifying active psychosocial and communications elements of a web-based smoking-cessation intervention and testing the impact of tailoring depth on smoking cessation [13].

The World Health Organization proposed specific obligations concerning smoking dependence and cessation. The obligations are listed below, as follows:

a) Designing effective smoking cessation program in locations such as educational institutions, health care centers, workplaces and sporting environments.

b) Including diagnosis and treatment of smoking cessation programs in national health and education programs.

c) Establishing programs for diagnosing and treating smoking cessation in health care facibilities and rehabilitation centres.

d) Collabrating with other parties such as pharmaceutical products (14).

Freedom from Smoking Online software is a Web based software for adult smokers. This software is for users who have regular access to a computer and are comfortable with others through online environment [15].

Stop Smoking Center is a Web based software developed in 2000. The software is still enhancing through methodologies from their clinical advisers, technology experts and other program members [16].

III. Material and Methods

B. Software Environment

This software is developed with Microsoft Visual Studio 2015 C# programming language as a Web application. A master page template is used for designing the pages. Microsoft SQL server application is used as a database server. We used a XEON processor server with 32 GB for publishing our software.

C. Methods of Our Software

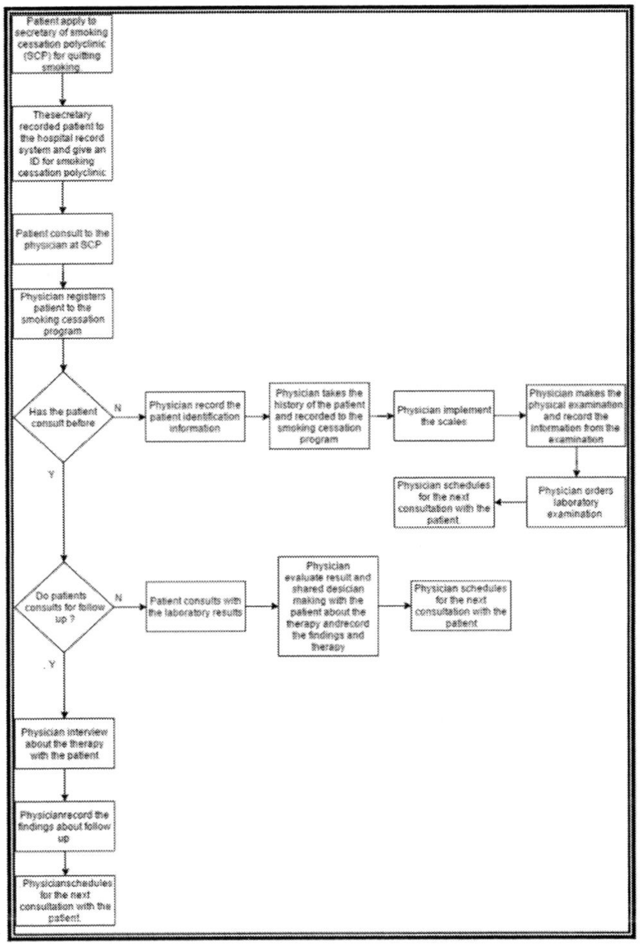

Figure 1. All Steps of our software

Figure 1. shows all steps of Smoking Cessation Process in SCOC. In the first case, the patient visits the outpatient clinic for first time. Patients records are stored the system for future use. In the second case, the patient comes with laboratory and other results. The physician gives related materials and/or therapy. In the last case, after a period of time, the physician checks the patient's current status and physician should request a new laboratory examination if necessary.

- Users of our Software
  There are two types of users: Physicians and Clinic Secretary. To start, the patients first records are entered into the system by the secretary. If the patient comes again, it will not be necessary to enter the same information into the system. The secretary will only find the related records of the patient before treatment. Finally, the physicians will continue the treatment using related Web pages. Figure 2. shows the data entry page of the software.

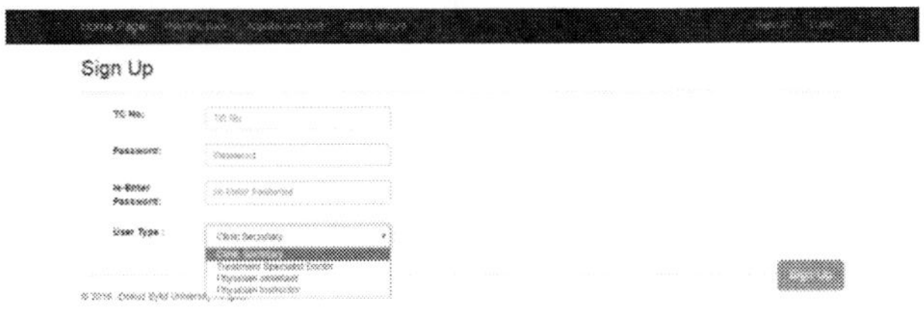

Figure 2. Enterance Web Page

- Functions of our Software
  There are three types of physicians: Treatment Specialist Doctor, Physician Assistant and Physician Instructor. In our software, three different parts exist for each of them. In addition, three types of patient's visits exist: for first time patients our software has a section for having personal information and background data collected, as shown in Figure 3. For patients with laboratory examination results, there is another section. Finally, for follow up patients, there is another page to record current situations.

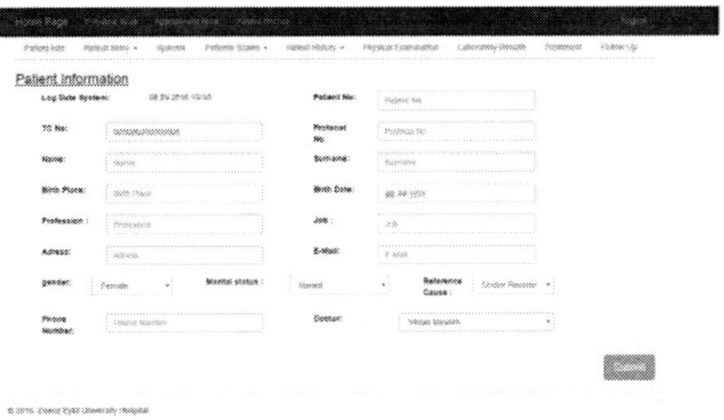

Figure 3. First time patient record page.

- Query and Reports of our Software
  There are two ways for accessing stored information. In the first case, using patient's ID, it is possible to have all the information of the related patient. In the second case, it is possible to have patient's information summary by selecting the date, as shown in Figure 4. In the second case, it is also possible to select one patient for accessing detailed information.

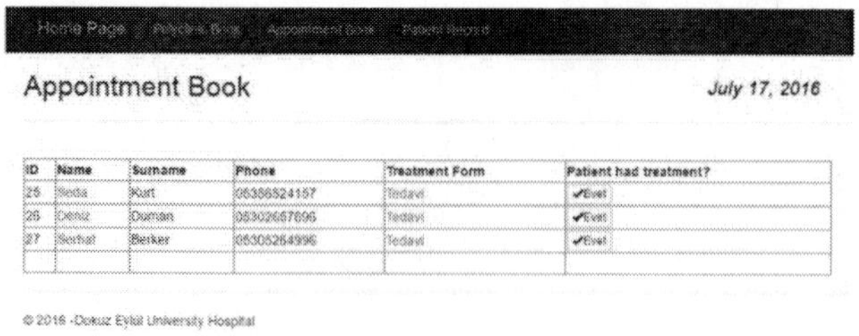

Figure 4. List of patients in a specific day.

IV. Conclusion and Future Work

Because smoking is one of the most important health issues in the world, smoking cessation treatments are intensively studied areas in medicine. Electronic health records are considered for every aspect of health, such as patient registration, patient follow up, etc. A smoking health record system that can be used in SCOC will influence the treatments success. Firstly, the application is programmed as a recording system and allows easy usage for the physicians. Secondly, clinical decisions can be used in accordance with clinical guidelines for the treatment of patients is the first step in the creation of support systems. Additionally, collected patient data will consist of data banks and will allow the emergence of new therapies and new approaches to smoking cessation.

As a future work, collected patient records will be analyzed by machine learning techniques for implementing a Decision Support System. With this system, common characteristics of smokers will be discovered and also treatment methods should be customized for related patient clusters.

References

[1] Boyle R, Solberg L, Fiore M. Use of electronic health records to support smoking cessation. Cochrane Database of Systematic Reviews 2014, Issue 12. Art. No.: CD008743.DOI: 10.1002/14651858.CD008743.pub3.

[2] World Health Organization . WHO report on the global tobacco epidemic: enforcing bans on tobacco advertising, promotion and sponsorship. Geneva, Switzerland: 2013.

[3] Shafey O, Eriksen M, Ross H, Mackay J. The Tobacco Atlas. 4th ed. American Cancer Society; Atlanta: 2012.

[4] Agaku IT, Ayo-Yusuf OA, Vardavas CI. A comparison of cessation counseling received by current smokers at US dental and physician offices during 2010-2011. *American Journal of Public Health* 2014;104(8):e67–75.

[5] Ng M, Freeman MK, Fleming TD, Robinson M, DwyerlindgrenL, Thomson B, et al. Smoking prevalence andcigarette consumption in 187 countries, 1980-2112. *JAMA* 2014;311:183–192.

[6] WHO. WHO Report on the Global Tobacco Epidemic. Geneva, Switzerland: WHO, 2009.

[7] WHO. *The Tobacco Atlas. 1st Edition.* Geneva, Switzerland: WHO, 2002.

[8] Fiore MC, Jaén CR, Baker TB, Bailey WC, Benowitz NL, Curry SJ, et al. Treating Tobacco Use and Dependence: 2008 Update U.S. Public Health Service Clinical Practice Guideline. *Treating Tobacco Use and Dependence: 2008 Update Clinical Practice Guideline.* Rockville, MD: US Department of Health and Human Services, 2008.

[9] Fiore MC. The New Vital Sign. *JAMA* 1991;**266**:3183–84.

[10] Stead LF, Buitrago D, Preciado N, Sanchez G, Hartmann-Boyce J, Lancaster T. Physician advice for smoking cessation. *Cochrane Database of Systematic Reviews* 2013, Issue 5. [DOI: 10.1002/14651858.CD000165.pub4]

[11] Hesse BW. Time to reboot: resetting healthcare to support tobacco dependency treatment services. *American Journal of Preventive Medicine* 2010;**39**(6S1):S85–S87.

[12] Edward G. Feil, John Noell, Ed Lichtenstein, Shawn M. Boles, H. Garth McKay [Received 17 January 2002; accepted 6 August 2002] "Evaluation of an Internet-based smoking cessation program: Lessons learned from a pilot study",

[13] Victor J. Strecher, Jennifer B. McClure, Gwen L. Alexander, Bibhas Chakraborty, Vijay N. Nair, Janine M. Konkel, Sarah M. Greene, Linda M. Collins, Carola C. Carlier, Cheryl J. Wiese, Roderick J. Little, Published in final edited form as: Am J Prev Med. 2008 May ; 34(5): 373–381. doi:10.1016/j.amepre.2007.12.024, "Web-Based Smoking-Cessation Programs.Results of a Randomized Trial", Article in American Journal of Preventive Medicine · June 2008,

[14] "WHO European Strategy for Smoking Cessation Policy", Revision 2004 ,

[15] http://www.ffsonline.org/ (27.08.2016 – 5:00 PM)

[16] http://www.stopsmokingcenter.net/ (27.08.2016 – 5:00 PM)

Intensive Care Unit – Clinical Decision Support System

Seçil Bayrak
Dept. of Computer Engineering
Dokuz Eylul University
Izmır, Turkey
e-mail: bayraksecil@gmail.com

Yunus Doğan
Dept. of Computer Engineering
Dokuz Eylul University
Izmır, Turkey
e-mail: yunus@cs.deu.edu.tr

Reyat Yılmaz
Dept. of Electrical and Electronic Engineering
Dokuz Eylul University
Izmır, Turkey
e-mail: reyat.yilmaz@ceng.deu.edu.tr

Alp Kut
Dept. of Computer Engineering
Dokuz Eylul University
Izmır, Turkey
e-mail: alp.kut@ceng.deu.edu.tr

***Abstract*- The Intensive Care Unit Automation System and Clinical Decision Support System (ICU-CDSS) were developed in the scope of our project as a multi-disciplined study within 1507-TUBITAK. ICU-CDSS software collects vital information from medical equipment and makes it available for the needs of the medical doctors and the nurses of the Intensive Care Unit (ICU) via Web based and mobile interfaces. Collected data could also be easily accessed immediately, using the query tools for research purposes by the authorized physicians. The forms which were formerly filled manually will be able to get reported digitally. Also, data mining assisted decision support system is developed and used. Decision Support System will be able to make suggestions to the physicians for detecting critical states before they happen. The appropriate size ICU automation devices will be sterilized and will allow easy data input by the side of the patient bed. Doctors and nurses will be able to use the system within the authorities granted to their roles. The performed operations will also be registered in log records. ICU-CDSS will be tested and used primarily in Dokuz Eylul University ICU Clinic.**

Keywords- Data Mining; Hospital Information Systems; Web Services; Decision Support System; Vital Risk Scoring.

I. INTRODUCTION

The aim of the project is to create an easy to use intensive care unit automation software and decision support system. The software also has capabilities for integrating ICU medical devices and Hospital Information System (HIS).

All of the brands that work intensively in this market in Turkey are foreign companies. Major brands; GE, Siemens, EvoluCare, Drager, IMD (MetaVision) are companies. All of them are serving only 10% of intensive care units in our country. The automation is not available by 90% of the intensive care unit because of the high price of the products and the stipulating of the firms to use their own brands.

The outline of this project could be summarized as follows:

-An electronic data collection device is used for collecting data from the Hospital's Intensive Care (IC) Division.

-A Web Based Software is implemented for Automation. Apachi, Sofa, Rifle Scoring Techniques are implemented for monitoring current status of IC Division Patients.

-Clustering and Classification Techniques are used for predicting patient's future state.

-A mobile Web application was developed for providing mobile access to our system.

The software will use vital patient information, such as the one obtained from mechanical ventilator, etc., for clinical research and also will collect information for future data mining analysis.

Using digitally collected data will decrease errors instead of using manually entered data. Intensive Care Unit staff physicians and nurses will be able to access the database which contains fresh information gathered from related devices.

Through Risk Identification and Data Mining Decision Support System, which use techniques to gather information prior to a possible critical situation, physicians are informed on and can be guided in their type of treatment based on these Vıtal Operations. Because of this, it is a positive development in the patient's health status.

II. RELATED WORK

The main reference projects related to our work are described below.

Artificial Neural Networks, which are one example of the Data Mining algorithms, showed successful results in the ICU [1]. The ICU data center stores in the database clean and reliable data for medical studies. The Multi-parameter Intelligent Monitoring in Intensive Care II (MIMIC-II) study consisted of almost 25,000 intensive care unit stays. It established a resource for research, supporting a diverse range of analytic studies, clinical decision-rule development, and electronic tool development [2].

Intensive Care Information System Impacts (ICSI) enable intensive care physicians and staff to use the system in a more meaningful way for better patient care. This study provides a better understanding and greater insight into the effectiveness of ICIS in improving patient care and decreasing health care expense [3].

The PDMS innovation has been selected in 2003 has been configured in 2004 and has been in use since 2005 [4]. Large-scale employees are held daily in intensive care units due to the workload required to carry out the regular work plan. It has been observed that a lot of time is wasted for other administrative work. Therefore, we emphasize the importance of a data management system that is easy to control [5].

Successful results for intensive care unit have been observed in real-time by using of the support vector regression algorithm in this study. The implemented interfaces are also included in the study and shed light on our project [6].

Business planning, management, monitoring, and decision support systems in Intensive Care have provided successful results [7].

The results have been obtained for renovation forecasting with data from the ICU data mining algorithms (Decision Tree Learning, First Order Random Forests, Naive Bayesian networks and Tree-Augmented Naive Bayesian networks) and also, they have been compared [8].

Consisting of clean data from the device and formed by the continuous flow of current data, intensive care unit's data-intensive data mining and artificial intelligence algorithms constitute an important input to yield successful results. This study has highlighted that the use of these algorithms in the intensive care unit of a smart system appears to play an important role in the quality of patient care observed [9].

The study SANDS_A demonstrates the feasibility of the architecture, which is a Service-oriented Architecture for the National Health Information Networks for clinical decision support. Service-oriented Architecture is used for the Decision Support System [10].

This article shows that the information platform assists in the presentation of user queries from the services in order to form individualized suggestions. A service-oriented architecture model is used that calculates asynchronous duties, modularity and flexibility. It is shown that this study is used to discover and process data in Web for transforming into knowledge [11].

In another study, a service-oriented architecture is used for communication with each other; XML, Service-Oriented Architecture Protocol and Web-Service Description Language communication protocols are used for supplying Web services functionalities. This paper gives a comprehensive account on improving the software system for Clinical Decision Support by using Health Level Seven. By means of this architecture, the implementation of rule based CDSS will be developed [12].

III. BACKGROUND

Requirements Analysis, Functional and non-functional requirements were determined. The requirements analysis report has been prepared in accordance with the IEEE 830 standard. The design modeling part of the "Unified Modeling Language" has been using. The design modeled User Scenarios (Use-Case diagram) and class / object diagrams have been drawn. To create the database, we designed the Entity Relationship Diagram. SOA (service-oriented / based architecture) was drawn on the diagram.

A. Device Integration

The serial interface of the Ethernet enables a conversion between the hardware units developed in this project. To use in intensive care units, a device that transfers data to the snapshot automation software is developed and designed. This data can be accessed instantly via any mobile or fixed devices. Our software is based on the V model process and collects this data for the decision support system. The patients are able to start the required device sterilization process with the appropriate touch interface.

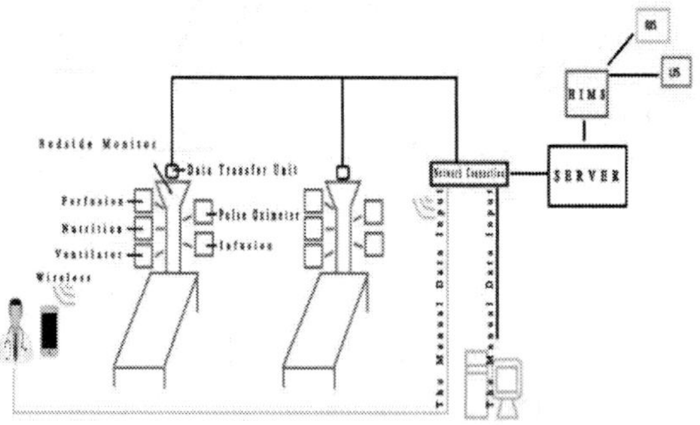

Figure 1. Hospital System View

This unit supports more than one medical device connection and has a buffer against communication failure (Figure 1).

B. ICA-DSS Operation Steps

- *Requirements Analysis-* At this stage, all standards and requirements (interfaces, security and performance requirements) were defined by physicians in team meetings.

The documentation with the standards defined and all the requirements has been prepared.

- *Data Transferred to The Intensive Care Device-* This module's task is to obtain real-time data transfer to the database through the front of the devices formed in the design stage.

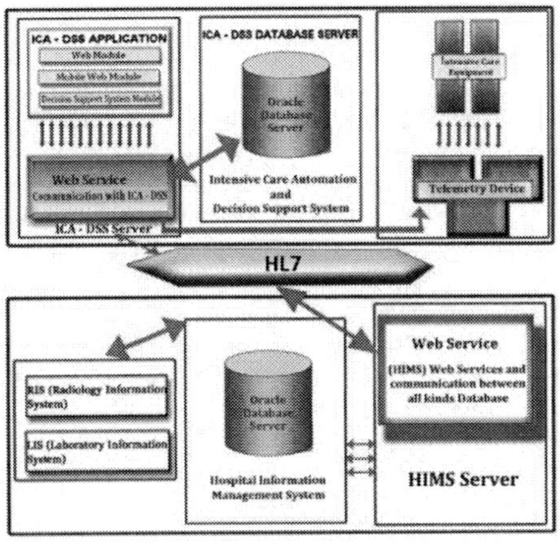

Figure 2. Interaction Modules

- *Development of Intensive Care Patient Tracking Application Process-* Patient registration and other patient medical information are connected by Web-Based Software. This service is used with both the Web-Based Software Module and Mobile Web Module. It increases the security of the system and provides the ability to support the new platform.

- *Risk Identification and Development of Decision Support System-* It includes patient demographics, laboratory results, diagnostic and treatment data, such as results formed an important part of parameters to be investigated. Subsequently, data mining literature review on the use of algorithms provided a vision for the work to be done.

- *Development of Mobile Web Applications-* The main task was to improve the visual interface on the stage of the Mobile Web application. Therefore, we considered the ease of use of mobile devices and requirements analysis to provide all of the components obtained at the design stage.

- *Integration and Testing of Software Modules-* The project team worked together in an integrated process, analyzing the potential problems and testing again

- *Pilot Application and User Tests-* The project team worked together in the testing process, analyzing the potential problems and testing again.

IV. PROPOSED SOLUTION

Our project provides the ability for medical devices used in a system to instantly record patient data from the intensive care unit. Patient data from intensive care units in Turkey is not stored in the electronic media. It is a big disadvantage in terms of operation and clinical research. Patient data can be often taken automatically by the system software modules. Data from patients participating in clinical trials can be accessed in batches, in seconds.

ICA-DSS hospital is the primary recording system "Hospital Information Management System" able to communicate with the HL7 protocol. Another factor is that it enables private cloud computing innovation of our project (Private Cloud Computing) to be used.

The goals of our project are listed as the following list;

- decreasing the error accrued by reducing the manual entry of the patient records
- storing the data obtained from the medical instruments automatically.
- creating a new database which is capable for clinical researches.
- reducing the diagnosis and treatment time
- reducing the duration of hospitalization in intensive care unit
- reducing the mortality and morbidity rates.

There are 8 parameters for diagnosis Sepsis. A clinical decision support system is introduced by analyzing data with these parameters. By using this system the mortility rate is predicted to be reduced by 50%.

The project, Knowledge Discovery in Databases (Knowledge Discovery in Databases - KDD) steps (Problem Definition, Data Processing, Data Mining and Information Report) was monitored.

Clustering, Data Mining Association Rules such as classification and analysis methods were used. Neural network classification algorithms, decision trees and Bayesian, Association Rules Apriori and Fp-Growth for the analysis, clustering algorithm was also planned to be used as SOM and K-means ++. APACHE, SOFA, ICU and RIFLE were used as scoring standards. In addition, Decision Support Systems for solving complex problems of ensuring the effective use of data and models were created. Thus, this system was able to identify situations that could occur in advance, use instant analysis capabilities and provide advanced communications capabilities.

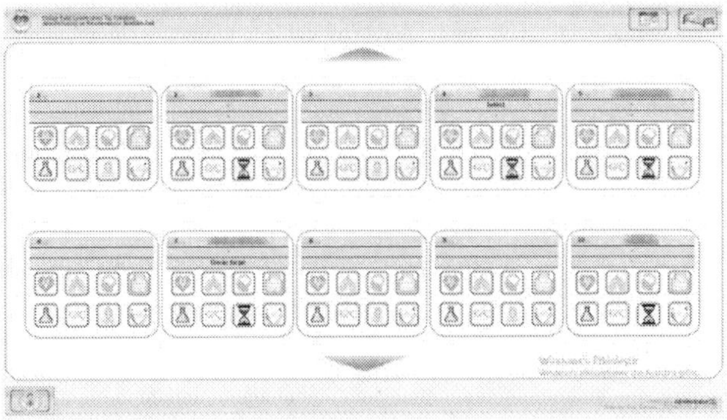

Figure 3. An example interface of ICU-CDSS

Hygiene, Activity, Excretion, Security, Infusion, Neurovascular, Rubbing and Scratching, Vital, Ventilator, Neurology and other topics are elaborated in our project. Figure 3 shows an example interface for all patients with the status of these topics.

V. Conclusion and Future Work

In our country, healthcare cost takes up a good part of our country's budget because of the importance of human health. Another important fact is that there is too much dependence on foreign countries for medical expenses. In addition to the software, hospital devices also come from abroad. The software does not contain any Data Mining algorithms for Decision Support Systems which help physicians and the nurses.

ICU-CDSS is developed in the scope of our project as a multi-disciplined study. Using digitally collected data will help decrease errors compared to using manually entered data. Intensive Care Unit staff physicians and nurses will be able to access the database which contains recent information gathered from related devices. Thus, our country will have a large data warehouse for future medical research.

ICU-CDSS software collects vital information from the medical equipment and makes it available for the needs of medical doctors and the nurses of the ICU via Web based and mobile interfaces. The collected data could also be easily accessed immediately, using the query tools for research purposes by the authorized physicians. The forms which were formerly filled manually are archived and will be able to get reported digitally. Also, a data mining assisted decision support system is developed and used. The Decision Support System will enable the users to make suggestions to the physicians in order to detect critical states before they happen. The appropriate sizes ICU Automation devices will be sterilized and will allow easy data input by the side of the patient bed. Doctors and nurses will be able to use the system within the authorities granted to their roles.

VI. Acknowledgement

Thanks to Prof. Dr. Necati Gökmen who supervised and allowed us to work at ICU in Dokuz Eylül University Hospital.

References

[1] Castellanos, I., Schüttler, J., Prokosch, H.,U., Bürkle, T., Does introduction of a Patient Data Management System (PDMS) improve the financial situation of an intensive care unit? (2013).

[2] Saeed M., Villarroel M., Reisner, A.,T., Clifford G., Lehman L.,W., Moody, G., Heldt T., Kyaw, T., H., Moody, B., Mark, R.,G., "Multiparameter Intelligent Monitoring in Intensive Care II (MIMIC-II)", A public-Access Intensive Care Unit Database, 2011

[3] Ehteshami A., Sadoughi, F., Ahmadi, M., Kashefi, P.,Intensive Care Information System Impacts, 2013.

[4] Nelwan, SP., Dam, TB.,V., Meij, SH., Putten, NHJJ V.,D., "Implementation and Use of a Patient Data Management System in the Intensive Care Unit", A Two-Year Experience, 2007.

[5] Matlakala, M.,C., Bezuidenhout, M.,C., Botha, A.,D.,H., Challenges encountered by critical care unit managers in the large intensive care units, 2014.

[6] Huang G., He, J., Cao, J., Qiao, Z., Steyn, M., Taraporewalla, K., A Real-Time Abnormality Detection System for Intensive Care Management, 2013.

[7] Lundgrén-Lainel, H., Kontio, E., Perttilä, J., Korvenranta, J., Forsström, J., Salanterä, S., "Managing daily intensive care activities", An observational study concerning ad hoc decision making of charge nurses and intensivists, 2011.

[8] Guiza, F., Fierens, D., Ramon, J., Blockeel, H., Bruynooghe, M., Meyfroid, G., Berghe, G.,V.,D., Predictive Data Mining in Intensive Care, 2006.

[9] Hanson, C.,W., Marshall, B.,E., Artificial intelligence applications in the intensive care unit, 2001.

[10] J BioInf - SANDS_A service-oriented architecture for clinical decision support in a National Health Information Network, 2008.

[11] Wanner, Leo, Harald Bosch, Nadjet Bouayad-Agha, Gerard Casamayor, Thomas Ertl, Désirée Hilbring, and others, 'Getting the Environmental Information across: From the Web to the User', 2014.

[12] Fehre, K, and K P Adlassing, Service Oriented Arden-Syntax-Based Clinical Decision Support. Ehealth 2011, Health Informatics, 2011

Semantic Web Technogies for IoT-Based Health Care Information Systems

Emine Sezer, Okan Bursa, Ozgu Can and Murat Osman Unalir
Department of Computer Engineering, Ege University, 35100 Bornova, Izmir, Turkey
e-mail:{emine.sezer, okan.bursa, ozgu.can, murat.osman.unalir}@ege.edu.tr

***Abstract*— The IoT (Internet of Things), as the most popular trend in the next generation Internet technologies, has a variety of application domains, including health care. The healthcare domain is a big and significant area where people, different organizations and various institutions get services as well as provide services at the same time. It is one of the few areas that have a huge amount of domain knowledge. A significant part of this knowledge is composed of the data that is produced by the medical devices and sensors. This health data can be processed to monitor the health status of any person. In this paper, a semantic Web approach for IoT-based health care information systems is proposed. To transfer health data collected from IoT devices to smart devices and then from smart devices to the cloud platform without changing its meaning, the ontologies developed for medical devices and the health domain should describe this data. This way, health care services for the clinical domain can process the data according to the defined rules with the help of semantic rules and inference engines.**

Keywords- Internet of Things (IoT); Healthcare Information Systems; Healthcare; Semantic Web; Ontology.

I. INTRODUCTION

The improvement in Internet technologies allows people, devices, services and systems to be interconnected 24/7. Thereby, due to the rapid increase of the interaction between users and computer technologies with the advances in information and communication systems, intelligent ecosystems are needed. Internet of Things – IoT, which can be thought as one of these ecosystems, is a concept reflecting a connected set of anyone, anything, any place, any service, and any network [1]. IoT aims to exchange the data between all connected "things" to provide full automation with lots of benefits. Getting any data from anywhere at any time supports the analysis of different types of collected data in real-time, as well as over time. The first samples began to develop for IoT applications, such as smart cities, smart traffic control systems, waste management, security, emergency services, logistics and health care [2]-[6].

Health information systems are important application areas where IoT technologies can be used to provide more effective solutions. The healthcare domain is a significant domain, where people, different organizations and various institutions get services as well as provide services at the same time. It is one of the few areas that need a huge amount of domain knowledge. The important part of this knowledge is composed by the information that is gathered by the medical devices.

Remote patient monitoring activities can be carried out in a dynamic way as a result of analyzing the collected patient data from different devices so that many health care applications like monitoring of chronic diseases, elderly care, wellness and fitness programs can be followed and managed for sustainability. Regarding this aspect, medical, diagnostic and imaging devices and sensors which are used effectively for diagnosing, treatment and medication constitute the objects of IoT health care ecosystem. Blood pressure monitor, blood glucose meter, thermometer, and heart rate sensors can be given as examples for IoT in health care. The storage, querying and analyzing this health data, which is collected from these devices, can also be used to define required alarms with defining rules under certain conditions. These applications create IoT-based health care services that are expected to reduce costs, increase the quality of life with guiding the patient's experience, and also reduce the time spent from the perspective of health care providers.

In this context, ensuring consistency in the related terminology, sharing the data between devices and systems, and data exchange without losing its meaning during this sharing are extremely important elements that have to be provided by IoT ecosystems. For this purpose, the semantic Web technologies can be used to define the data that is collected from the IoT health care devices and sensors and also to define rules about IoT-based health care services.

In this work, the use of semantics and ontologies to share large amounts of distributed medical information is described to support interoperability between IoT-based health care information systems. In Section 2, the proposed model is introduced. Lastly, in Section 3, a brief conclusion is given with future works.

II. SEMANTIC WEB AND IOT-BASED HEALTH CARE INFORMATION SYSTEMS

Semantic Web is defined as the extension of the current Web where information is given in a well-defined meaning and leads to better collaboration between computers and people [7]. In semantic Web, the data about each real world concept as well as the data about concept relationships are described. So that, an information network is developed and by using this network, interoperability between systems, services, computer, and people can be achieved.

Ontologies are very important for interoperability between systems. To provide full interoperability, the semantics of information have to be the same for all systems. Ontology presents format as an explicit specification of a conceptualization [8]. An ontology can be handled by machines and describes the definitions of these concepts and restrictions on possible interpretations between these terms to create a structure on the domain and how these concepts are related with each other [9]. In a certain domain, ontologies which represent the knowledge of that domain provide interoperability to be connected with other networks.

There is a huge amount of information and data in the health care domain. In order to reuse health data for various purposes, it should be shared between systems and services. For that reason, ontologies are used as information bases for a common framework in health information systems.

IoT is the most popular trend of the next generation Internet applications with the promise of sharing the information from everywhere continuously and accurately in today's information systems. The current applications in this area are quite new. Health care is a domain that is expected to give personalized services with huge amount of data. Therefore, different opinions are available for developing IoT-based health care information systems which collect the heath related data from medical devices and sensors like blood pressure monitor, blood glucose meter, thermometer, oximeter and heart rate sensors that are used personally at their home on IoT platforms. The main purpose of these opinions is transferring the data form medical devices to smart devices and form smart devices to cloud without changing its definition, and in a secure way.

In the health domain, compared with the other domains, any new application or technology should be carried out very carefully to prevent mortal or permanent disability results. Thus, it is quite important to collect data in the most proper way, to store and to transfer this data in the most accurate and secure way while ensuring the patient privacy, to analyze this health data to help the health care providers to monitor the patient's status, and also to respond by giving proper alarms in emergency cases for quick and effective intervention.

IoT technologies are expected to be implemented to support each health service which offer different solutions for various health care applications. In the scope of the health domain, there is no standard that is currently developed to define the IoT-based health care services. However, there are some cases where the service cannot be separated objectively from a particular solution or application. Therefore, a service has a general level due to its structure and has a potential to be a building block for some solutions and applications. In addition, some changes for general services and protocols required in IoT frameworks may be needed in order to be functioning properly in health care scenarios. These include notification services, resource sharing services, Internet services, cross-link protocols for heterogeneous devices and link protocols for the main connections. Simple, safe and low power devices and services can be added to this list [10].

In Fig. 1, we show a model for an IoT-based health care information system which is supported with ontologies. Health data is collected from IoT medical devices and sensors and defined inside ontologies. Nowadays, with the rapid changes in advancing technology, there are small and practical medical devices that measure blood pressure, fever, blood glucose level, and etc. Transfer of this data collected from medical devices to smart phones, tablets or other smart devices and to the cloud platform by using the current Internet infrastructure is also another important research and application area [11]-[15].

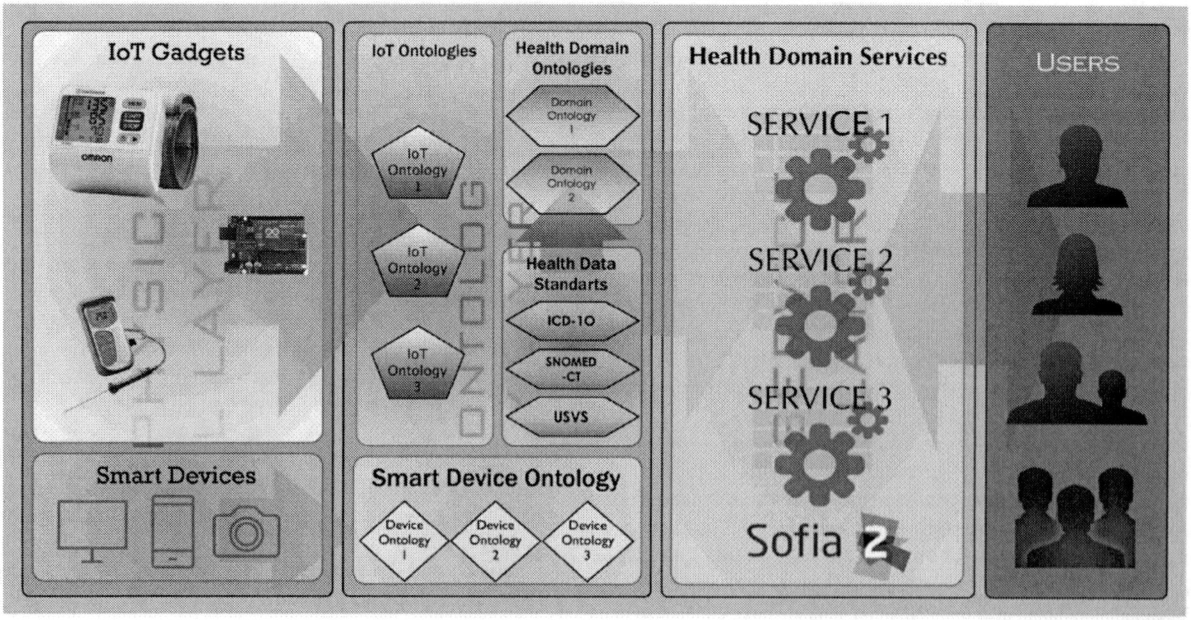

Figure 1. The proposed semantic web model for IoT-based health care information system.

Proper patient care can be done by reliable health data. To transfer the health data without losing its semantics, we are proposing to define health data with ontologies. For this purpose, first of all, ontologies for medical devices and sensors that produce health data have to be developed. Ontologies developed for these IoT devices describe the data not only by its measurement value, but also its relationships with the other data sources and also with descriptive properties like where and when it is produced.

The described health care data should be related with the clinical domain knowledge where it is needed to monitor the patient's health situation. In that case, the specific health domain ontologies like Vaccine Ontology, Infectious Disease Ontology or Blood Test Ontology are needed to process collected health data [16]. Also, to be able to share data between different health information systems, in other words in order to reuse the health data, the health data standards like SNOMED-CT [17] and ICD 10 [18] should be supported by these health domain ontologies. The interoperability between information systems is achieved by using general information descriptions and describing data with its semantics.

After the data is transferred to the cloud, the health care services can provide proper information or services by using the inference and role engines that are offered by semantic Web technologies to the health care providers and clinics.

To describe the overall system interaction, a sample scenario is given. A person who had a heart attack is discharged from the hospital and his responsible physician is supposed to measure his blood pressure twice a day. His physician also defines some limiting values and rules for his measurements. If a measurement exceeds the defined limit, the system requests to make measurements more frequently, such as once an hour. However, if the measurements reach the alarm levels, the system should give an alert. The physician is informed quickly with a message or a call, and also with the health institute that is the nearest one to the patient's location. If the patient specified a person to be informed in emergency situations for himself, the system should also give information to that person. The system should be adaptable and self-driven to different situations.

III. Conclusions and Future Works

In this work, we propose an IoT-based health care information system model which uses semantic Web technologies to describe the domain and device data and also to define rules to make proper inferences to execute health care services. In this model, the health data collected from any medical device or clinic is meant to be reused and shared not only at the point where it was produced, but also on other authorized services, devices and people by using semantic Web technologies. Thus, interoperability between information systems can be achieved.

To implement the proposed model, an application domain area from the health care is determined, primarily. The medical devices, sensors, diagnostic and monitoring devices used in that domain are determined as IoT objects. For the application domain, the health care services are determined and then the information needed for these services is defined. With the goal of interoperable devices and systems and also reusable health care data, IoT device ontologies and specific health domain ontologies should be developed. The developed ontologies will be integrated with Sofia 2 platform. Sofia 2 (Smart Objects for Intelligent Applications) was developed as R&D Artemis project by 19 stakeholders such as companies like Nokia, Philips, Fiat and Acciona from the European Union [19]. It is widely used in IoT applications, works on Eclipse platform [20] and is an open source platform. Sofia 2 platform is defined as a layer that provides seamless interoperability between different devices and systems. The data handled from IoT devices will be stored on Sofia 2 platform that offers big data storage by describing the defined ontologies.

References

[1] S. M. R. Islam, D. Kwak, M.D. H. Kabir, M. Hossain and K. S. Kwak, "The Internet of Things for Health Care: A Comprehensive Survey", IEEE Access, Vol. 3, pp. 678-704, 2015.

[2] J. Höller, V. Tsiatsis, C. Mulligan, S. Karnouskos, S. Avesand, and D. Boyle, "From Machine-to-Machine to the Internet of Things: Introduction to a New Age of Intelligence", Amsterdam, The Netherlands: Elsevier, 2014.

[3] G. Kortuem, F. Kawsar, D. Fitton, and V. Sundramoorthy, "Smart objects as building blocks for the Internet of Things", IEEE Internet Computing, 14(1), pp. 44-51, 2010.

[4] K. Romer, B. Ostermaier, F. Mattern, M. Fahrmair, M., and W. Kellerer, "Real-time search for real-world entities: A survey", Proc. of IEEE, 98(11), pp. 1887-1902, 2010.

[5] D. Guinard, V. Trifa, V., and E. Wilde, "A resource oriented architecture for the Web of Things", in Proc. Internet Things (IOT), pp. 1-8, 2010.

[6] L. Tan, and N. Wang, "Future Internet: The Internet of Things", in Proc. 3rd Int. Conf. Adv. Comput. Theory Eng. (ICACTE), Vol. 5., pp. 375-380, 2010.

[7] T. Berners-Lee, J. Hendler, O. Lassila, "The semantic web". Scientific American, 284 (5), pp. 34-43, 2001.

[8] T. Gruber, "Toward principles for the design of ontologies used for knowledge sharing", Technical Report KSL93-04, Knowledge Systems Laboratory, Stanford University, 1993.

[9] M. Uschold, "Knowledge level modelling: Concepts and terminology", Knowledge Engineering Review, 13(1), pp. 5–29, 1998.

[10] K. Vasanth and J. Sbert. Creating solutions for health through technology innovation. Texas Instruments. [Online]. Available: http://www.ti.com/lit/wp/sszy006/sszy006.pdf. [Retrieved: September, 2016]

[11] S. Imadali, A. Karanasiou, A. Petrescu, I. Sifniadis, V. Veque, and P. Angelidis, "eHealth service support in IPv6 vehicular networks", in Proc. IEEE Int. Conf. Wireless Mobile Comput., Netw. Commun. (WiMob), pp. 579-585, 2012.

[12] A. J. Jara, M. A. Zamora, and A. F. Skarmeta, "Knowledge acquisition and management architecture for mobile and personal health environments based on the Internet of

Things", in Proc. IEEE Int. Conf. Trust, Security Privacy Comput. Commun. (TrustCom), pp. 1811-1818, 2012.

[13] P. Lopez, D. Fernandez, A. J. Jara, and A. F. Skarmeta, "Survey of Internet of Things technologies for clinical environments", in Proc. 27th Int. Conf. Adv. Inf. Netw. Appl. Workshops (WAINA), pp. 1349-1354, 2013.

[14] L. Atzori, A. Iera, and G. Morabito, "The Internet of Things: A survey", *Computer Networks,* 54(15), pp. 2787-2805, 2010.

[15] M. Hassanalieragh, A. Page, T. Soyata, G. Sharma, M. Aktas, G. Mateos, B.Kantarci, and S. Andreescu, "Health Monitorin and Management Using Internet-of-Things (IoT) Sensing with Cloud-Based Processing: Opportunities and Challenges": In Proceedings of the 2015 IEEE International Conference on Services Computing (SCC'15). IEEE Computer Society, Washington, DC, USA, pp. 285-292, 2015.

[16] O. Bursa, E. Sezer, O. Can, M. O. Unalir, "Using FOAF for Interoperable and Privacy Protected Healthcare Information Systems", Research Conference on Metadata and Semantics, Springer International Publishing, pp.154 - 161, 2014.

[17] SNOMED-CT, http://www.ihtsdo.org/snomed-ct [Retrieved: September, 2016]

[18] ICD 10, http://www.who.int/classifications/icd/en [Retrieved: September, 2016]

[19] Sofia2, SOFIA2 IoT Platform: Technical View, [Online]. Available: http://sofia2.com/docs/SOFIA2%20-%20 Technical%20-%20IoT%20Platform%20(oct%202014).pdf [Retrieved: September, 2016]

[20] Eclipse, https://eclipse.org/ [Retrieved: September, 2016]

Knowledge BasedRecommendation onOptimal Spectral and Spatial RecordingStrategy of Physical Cultural Heritage Objects

Ashish Karmacharya, Stefanie Wefers, Frank Boochs
i3mainz – Institute for Spatial Information and Surveying Technology, Mainz University of Applied Sciences
e-mail: {ashish.karmacharya, stefanie.wefers, frank.boochs}@hs-mainz.de

Abstract—**Ontologies have traditionally been used to represent knowledge of a specific domain. They are also used to provide a base to infer the knowledge present inside them. However, the applications of ontologies within the Cultural Heritage (CH) community have been restricted to providing standard documentation for significant heritage objects. E.g., widely used ontology within CH disciplines, International Committee for Documentation Conceptual Reference Model(CIDOC CRM) is designed to provide standards in documenting archival information of physical CH object. There has been hardly any work relating the objects to their documentation purposes. In this paper, we present the Colour and Space in Cultural Heritage Knowledge Representation (= COSCH^{KR}) ontology – a multi-faceted ontology. With COSCH^{KR}, we present a system that infers inter-woven descriptive semantics of different involved CH disciplines in recording CH objects to recommend optimal spatial and spectral technical solutions to humanities experts and guide through the underlying complexities while recording their objects. It takes numbers of facts into consideration including physical characteristics of the CH objects, the characteristics of their surroundings and even other relevant facts such as budget or staff competence to infer against the characteristics of the technologies for a proper recommendation. In contrast to a typical Recommender System, which does the same for web-based content through stochastic methods, we use descriptive semantics at the concept level.**

Keywords-Ontology development; Description Logics; Humanities;Cultural Heritage; 3D Data;Spectral Data; Descriptive Semantics;Inference

I. INTRODUCTION

In the last decade digital 3D and spectral recording of physical cultural heritage (CH) objects is getting more and more common. The digital representations are not only seen as support for CH expert's tasks (e.g., research studies, monitoring, and documentation) but as useful items especially for dissemination. A wide audience can be addressed, e.g., through websitesand interactive digital applications. For this tasks appropriate data are needed optimally supporting the researcher and/or user.To achieve this, the 3D or spectral data recording, its subsequent data processing, analysis and visualisation has to involve experts from multiple disciplines: (a) CH experts responsible for the knowledge about the constraints given by the CH object itself (e.g., research question, conservation condition, light sensitivity, transportation possibilities); (b) recording experts preparing and executing a digitisation strategy (e.g., recording device needs specific amount of space, limitations of sensors, suitable data accuracy and resolution); (c) IT experts applying proper algorithms on the generated data (e.g., point cloud registration) to allow data analysis; and (d) 3D modellers and communication experts visualising the data for different audiences. All these parameters influence each other. Which digitisation strategy meets the requirements of the CH application (A CH application is connected to CH research questions which can be answered through the generated data – they are a tool illustrating the significance about the existence and significance of CH objects w.r.t. the history of mankind)depends on (1) the parameters of the physical CH object (appearance, size etc.), (2) the limitations and abilities of the devices and methods,and (3) the impact of the data processing tasks. Altogether, the elaboration of a digitisation strategy is a complex collaborative and interdisciplinary task.

The COST Action [34] TD1201: Colour and Space in Cultural Heritage (COSCH) [2] [3] contributes to the conservation and preservation of cultural heritage (CH) by enhancing this mutual understanding among the experts from various disciplines. COSCH is a forum for communication and interdisciplinary networking. Bridging the gap between professionals involved in the recording of physical CH objects through discussions and publications such as guides to good practice, the COSCH community decided to go one step further by developing the knowledge model COSCH^{KR} orthe COSCH Knowledge Representation. COSCH^{KR} is an OWL 2 XML-serialised ontology based model currently under development. It expresses and structures the knowledge of the disciplines involved in CH object recording. The main intention of COSCH^{KR} is to guide CH experts by inferring the optimal spatial and spectral technologies for the recording of their specific physical CH object based on facts on its physical characteristics and the purpose behind the recording.It is therefore comparable to a recommender system in a sense that it identifies and provides recommendations on optimal technologies. A typical recommender system works on available data to develop recommendation algorithms based on stochastic methods [31]. However in our case, we do not have abundant data from successfully completed CH applications for the development of algorithms that filter the recommendations. Instead, we rely on experience and knowledge from experts to create the entire recommendation process and reasoning system within COSCH^{KR}.

The challenge in the development of such an ontology lies in capturing expert's decisions of spatial and spectral recording. It needs to capture the core essence of inter-disciplinary dialogues and activities across multi-disciplinary platforms to achieve common goal in a CH documentation project. The ontology, therefore, needs to describe inter-disciplinary dependencies that echo the real world dependencies across disciplines in such a project. Various disciplines have to work together to answer common research questions of CH applications.

Interpretations and observations on issues and vocabularies vary across the discipline. The ontology needs to fill in these gaps in communication as well. At the core, the ontology needs to address what is required and how to get it. To elaborate, any CH application requires a digital surrogate of the concerned physical CH object providing answers to CH research questions. The nature of digital surrogates depends on the application and its requirements. The requirements for answering the research questions thrown by a CH application dictate what the digital data should contain. Thisrequirements on digitaldata in turn influence theselection technology(ies). These digital data and their nature form a bridge connecting requirements from CH applications and possibilities from recording technologies. We use axis *"Applications – Data – Technologies"*(see Fig. 1) to illustrate this further.

COSCH^{KR} is a knowledge model developed through capturing and structuring knowledge of involved disciplines inside CH recordings. The discipline inherent knowledge-otherwise independent - is interlinked through the description logic (DL) concept constructors, which define descriptive semantics of the concepts inside the ontology [16] (restriction axioms inside the ontology). The descriptive semantics are extensively used to 1) bind different heterogeneous conceptual axioms and theorems inside the ontology and 2) infer the results from the queries. The base axis *"Applications – Data – Technologies"* is supported through other axes that define the underlying semantics of objects and/or other factors that have significant influences on the model and its inference system. Technical process is deterministic to the real world considerations when generating data: technologies applied to a CH object generate data with specific data nature and data content under specific external influences that may be coming from CH objects themselves or other conditions influencing the technologies or CH objects. These considerations have to be logically described and are described through descriptive semantics of the relevant classes inside the ontology. Due to a variety of technologies and their underlying instruments and recording strategies, the importance of expert knowledge on them is further justified while recommending the best suited process. A first attempt to give a structured view on characteristics of spatial recording techniques has been presented in [15].

The descriptive semantics binding technologies parameters to object characteristics should take respective views of involved disciplines into account.CH applications and their conditions on the requirement on data are also described inside the ontology through relevant descriptive semantics. The CH applications that ask for specific data content intercede all these inter-linking descriptive semantics for inferring and navigating through optimal recording techniques.

COSCH^{KR} provides a base for expressing common knowledge on technologies, CH objects and CH applications. The ontology will be exploited through an interactive web based application (COSCH^{KR} platform), which will have interactive Graphical User Interfaces (GUIs) for users to assert their queries through a guided mechanism. The platform will apply those asserted queries to the COSCH^{KR} ontological model to infer recommendationsfor a recording device, strategy, and process, which will support the CH expert to receive spectral and/or spatial data with sufficient content and quality to answer the underlying research questions.

The successful creation of such a platform needs to be based on mutual understanding of experts from the involved fields. It has to start with the consolidation of a common vocabulary with unambiguous terms, continue with the formalisation of domain inherent knowledge, and end with the connection of this formalised knowledge. A special challenge is the content capture and its formalisation. For example, humanities research questions are often directly linked to a specific CH object and domain inherent research question. Moreover, the same physical CH object might be connected to different research questions which ask for differing data requirements. This makes the formalisation of decisive factors in humanities research question a sensible task, which has a strong impact on the identification of the best suitable recording strategy. With this paper, we present our hands-on experiences in developing the ontology COSCH^{KR} and the challenges during data capturing and structuring process. We also present how the descriptive semantics inside the ontology lay the necessary foundation for inferring the recommendations of the optimal technical strategy(ies) in spatial and spectral CH documentation.

The structure of the paper is as follows. In section 2, the state of art, we present the use of semantic and knowledge technologies in CH. We also present the existing stochastic methods based recommendation systems. In section 3, we present our approach, illustrating the purpose and scope and then methodology and principles behind it. We also present an example use case to demonstrate our approach within this section. Lastly, section 4 concludes the paper summarizing the actual state and what is the future outlook.

II. State of Art

Ontologies have evolved as computational artifacts that provide conceptual and computational models of any particular domain of interest. Ontologies populated with concepts are agreed generally to follow the states of uniform knowledge representation and provide a computational model of a particular domain of interest [8] [4] [19]. The main motivation behind ontologies is that they allow for sharing and reuse of knowledge bodies in computational form [20]. Ontologies have become a popular research topic within the communities of the Semantic Web due to the fact that they promise a shared and common understanding of inter-communicable domains, the primary objective of the Semantic Web. The role of ontologies in the Semantic Web and the gradual evolution of Web Ontology Language [35] are discussed in the research paper [21] [23].

A. Description Language Inferences

The Web Ontology Language is a Description Logic based ontology language for the Semantic Web [23]. There are effective reasoning algorithms for Description Logics that can reason with OWL ontologies. Existing DL Reasoners, such as FaCT++ [24], use these algorithms and are quite efficient. A DL comprises of ABoxes and TBoxes where a TBox describes the terminologies expressed through concepts and roles and ABox contains the assertions about the instances of the concepts described through TBoxes. Most OWL ontology based systems apply TBox and ABox inferences for the rightful categorizations and relationships. The application of these inferences for building up possible components of DL ontologies is presented in [25]. The work describes standard and nonstandard inferences.

- A standard inference uses the TBox inference provided through the concept descriptions to subsume the individuals in the ABox. This facilitates computation of hierarchies and internal instance relationships.
- A nonstandard inference uses the semantic descriptions of individuals in ABox to first create, categorize and populate themselves into respected bottom level concepts. Afterwards, with the least common subsumer (lcs) of these bottom level concepts, their super-concepts are defined and created. The practice continues until the final top concepts are created. The concept descriptions of each level are defined in the process with having individuals as building blocks.

With both TBox inference and ABox inference, the inferences are used to build on DL based knowledge representation.

B. Ontologies and their types

Applications of ontologies are required to play a role in analyzing, modeling and implementing domain knowledge and influence problem solving knowledge [20]. Ontologies can generally be classified for intentions of capturing and modeling static and problem solving knowledge.

Static ontologies do not internally reason about the knowledge, but use it for processing natural language [26], achieving interoperability within heterogeneous datasets [12], which facilitate communication, such as in E-commerce. Ontologies within this category fall under Reference Ontologies, whose main inclination is toward realism [27].

Problem solving ontologies areintended for problem solving knowledge and provide views that could be used for reasoning. They are Application ontologies with computational sublogic of full first order logic. The usage of ontologies in the Semantic Web can be found in both categories: the former with core Semantic Web applications like Linked Open Data applications (LOD) and the later with Semantic Web Service Discovery.

Application ontologies combine task/method ontologies (containing terms and reasoning mechanisms of problem solving methods) together with the domain ontologies (containing descriptions of domains of disclosures) to provide overall interpretationof the problem and attempt to provide answers. Such ontologies are preferred in a Recommender System.

C. Ontologies in Recommender Systems

Recommender Systems (RSs) are software tools and techniques providing suggestions for items to be of use to a user [32] [33]. $COSCH^{KR}$recommends solutions through prior knowledge represented inside its ontology and not through analyzing huge amount of data through statistical methods as a Recommender System does. Recommender Systems are highly influenced by stochastic methods such as machine learning. However, ontologies are routinely used in recommender systems in combination with machine learning and other stochastic methods. Middleton and colleagues presented a recommender system that recommends on-line academic research papers through the profile descriptions of the readers [28]. The system uses classical machine learning algorithms with an ontology based approach to design a recommender algorithm. The inference mechanism is highly influenced by the amount and quality of data for high end results. Similarly, other recommender systems such as [29] extract data from music ontology within LinkedBrainz (A Linked Open Data platform to publish music database) through its SPARQL end points, and then matches results with customized management of user profiles (according to personal preferences). The use of ontologies in Recommender System to use prior knowledge on the resources (academic paper as in [28] and music as in [29]) along with understanding the behavior of the users (through) stochastic methods to provide recommendations to them.

D. Development of ontologies

While developing multi-faceted ontologies any basic metaphors cut across a number of domains [30]. Developments of multi-faceted ontologies are common today both in scientific and commercial communities. Lim and a colleague presented the Multi-faceted product family ontology (MFPFO) that manages the complexity in relationships between physical components with their semantic orientations, such as manufacturing, materials and marketing [17]. The relationships between different facets should be clearly described in such ontology. These knowledge-intensive ontologies need to keep harmony across the people, disciplines and the applications in which they are involved [18] to maintain semantic consistency inside it. Hence, the development issues become much crucial in their development.

Though there is collective experience in designing, developing and using ontologies, there is no common agreed methodology for building ontologies. Different methodologies exist and have been proposed over the years [9] [11] [14] [20] [22]. The commonality among all these propositions is that the ontology should satisfy the purpose of its creation and should not attempt to model the world, should be coherent and extendible and should provide minimum ontological commitment. Another commonality among them is that they prescribe step wise workflow based methodological guidance for ontology engineering. The NeOn methodology presents a different approach through suggesting different pathways for developing ontologies [37]. It presents nine different scenarios covering commonly occurring situations while developing ontologies whereCOSCH^{KR}loosely complies with the first scenario.COSCH^{KR} ontology represents experts' knowledge through inter-linking descriptive knowledge in spatial and spectral CH documentation that could be extended to other technologies and/or other discipline such as architecture as well. The COSCH umbrella provides a base to include experts from different domains to evaluate coherency of ontology and its underlying theorems and axioms through domain specific semantic consistency.

E. Existing domain ontologies

Ontologies for CH disciplines such as CIDOC-CRM [1] are generally designed as standards for stakeholders such as museums who archive CH objects. Though the terminologies used within CIDOC-CRM are of interest for our research and we actually refer to CIDOC-CRM inside our ontology, the intention and application of COSCH^{KR} differs considerably from CIDOC-CRM. Moreover, CIDOC-CRM does not provide a class structure for detailed information about the recording of CH objects. The CARARE 2.0 metadata schema [7] prepared within the frame of the 3D ICONS project provides compatibility to the structure of CIDOC-CRM. The schema is based on CH standards such as MIDAS (English Heritage 2012), an XML based harvesting schema LIDO [6], and EDM-EuropeanaData Model [5]. It harvests meta-, para-, and provenance data of 2D and 3D data of CH objects into Europeana (Europeana Professional). The CARARE 2.0 metadata schema extends the class including technical para- and meta-data of recording strategies. However, it is meant to harvest the content into open knowledge hubs for linking data. The schema does not have provisions to reason itself for choosing optimal para- and metadata from the existing ones when new cases arise. The development of CARARE 2.0 metadata schema thus follows a pattern that is necessary for ontologies managing and harvesting contents. All in all, the core group worked out to develop a new common ontology, not integrating existing domain ontologies since 1) not all involved disciplines have their own well accepted ontology (CH has CIDOC-CRM, but for spatial and spectral technology there is no widely accepted one such as OPPRA cannot be considered as common ontology for spectral domain or no ontology at all as in spatial domain) and 2) ontologies are designed for different purposes and scopes (e.g., CIDOC-CRM is designed for providing standards for museums archiving physical CH objects [1] or OPPRA.owl is designed for 20th century paint conservation [13]) and harmonizing them through inference rules is a long and tedious task.

III. APPROACH

An ontology base system that recommends the optimal spatial/spectral technologies for a CH documentation application requires:

- ontology consisting of descriptive semantics of
    - involved spatial and spectral technologies and data
    - CH object and CH applications
- a recommendation mechanism that infersdescriptive semantics of CH objects, their respective applications against those of technologies

COSCH^{KR} intends to provide recommendations (on spatial and spectral technologies for the CH applications) from the conceptual level and not from the data level through their analysis as no database exists to be used for the purpose. Therefore, there is no possibility of ABox inference inside. This negates any possibilities of implementing any external stochastic mechanisms within inference system. The system hence has to work on pre-defined expert knowledge at schema level to do reasoning. Consequently, it becomes prominent that existing state of art solutions have limited implementations on COSCH^{KR} as

- the inference on knowledge model needs to use the descriptive semantics at concept level for inference and not at data or individual level
- the intention is not to classify the assertions as conventional reasoners in the Semantic Web technologies are meant to but to infer right

relations between technologies and applications through data

- till date, there is no ontology on spatial and spectral technologies that could be used for the case. This limits the assessments of physical objects through the semantics of technologies within an ontology based system
- the existing CH ontology is based for documenting biographical information of the CH objects and has limited scope to define descriptive semantics of concerned object that trigger the technological selection process.

Through COST action we have the leverage of technical and humanities expertise in their respected fields. $COSCH^{KR}$ represents their knowledge and experiences inside within one common framework. They are semantically encoded through DL axioms and theorems.$COSCH^{KR}$ reasoning engine (used for recommendations) reasons these axioms and theorems at TBox level and do not assert any individuals inside. Additionally, the engine distances itself from using any stochastic methods to carry out reasoning.It is solely based on the concepts' descriptive semantics (defined through DL concept constructors), which represent the knowledge and experiences of the domain experts.

A. Purpose and Scope

$COSCH^{KR}$ isa system that guides CH experts by inferring the optimal spatial and spectral technologies for the recording of a specific physical CH object based on facts about the physical CH object and the CH application. The purpose is to help the CH end users to answer their competency questions querying for the optimal technical solutions. An example of such questions could be *"What is the right technical solution to record my CH object (a Roman coin) for the CH application determining its origin and time period".* Such a purpose was discussed and agreed on within the COSCH community and through this the scope of involved domains was madeclear: CH domains (archaeology, conservation, art history etc.), spatial technology domains (surveying, computer vision, photogrammetry etc.), spectral technology domains (multi- and hyperspectral imaging etc.), and IT domains (algorithms, data processing etc.). In meantime a core group comprising experts from semantic, spatial and spectral and CH domain responsible for designing the top-level ontology was agreed on, for evaluation of different approaches in knowledge collection, for guidance in knowledge collection, and for regular updating of the entire expert group.

B. $COSCH^{KR}$ontology

$COSCH^{KR}$ontology represents inter-disciplinary knowledge ofCH recording. It is designed and developed and woven together through rules.

Fig. 1 illustrates the five top level classes of $COSCH^{KR}$. These top level classes and their specializations are defined through 1) a logical taxonomical structure based on shared concepts 2) the relationships between them and 3) their existence defined through the conditions. The green boxes are classes related to CH domains, the orange box is a class related to spectral and spatial recording domains and the blue box is a class related to data processing domains. The five top-level classes are linked through different properties displayed as arrows.

The intention is to maintain and support the base of the conceptual axis: *"Application – Data – Technologies"* (see grey strip in Fig. 1). We first define the classes under this major axis. Class *"Technologies"* encompasses the technical methods, procedures, tools and their setups to generate or process the generated data. They are presented through specializations of the class where each specialization contains semantic descriptions that describe their best practice, limitations through their characteristics. These specializations generate data which are stored under specializations of class *"Data"*. We can illustrate this with a simple example: *"Photography"* is a technology that generates photos. Therefore *"Photography"* will be a specialization of class *"Technologies"*. Photos are 2D images i.e., 2D Data – and hence specialization of class *"Data"*. The class also includes the capabilities and limitations of instruments that are used to generate data. For instance: *"Photography"* with a mobile camera can have different quality on photo than that with a high end DSLR camera.

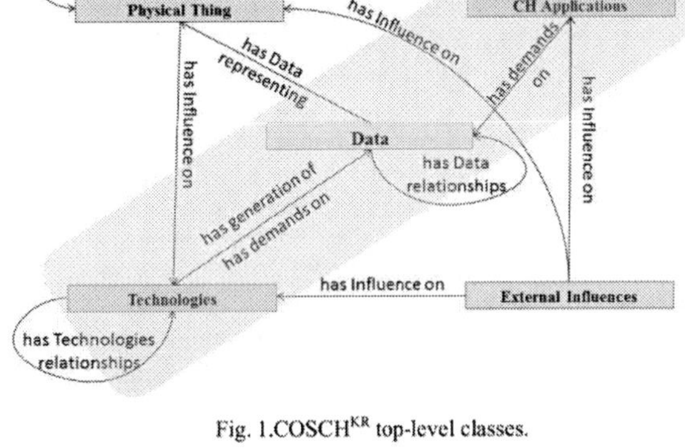

Fig. 1.$COSCH^{KR}$ top-level classes.

The first obvious outlet of class *"Technologies"* is data represented through class *"Data"*. This is bridged through the statement *"Technologies generate Data"* which is expressed through the DL concept constructors inside the ontology (see (1)). This bridging statement provides a conceptual crossover between two.

$$\text{Technologies} \equiv \exists \text{hasGenerationOnData.Data} \quad (1)$$

TheseDL concept constructors are ourbase for *inference rules* becausethey will be combined and translated as rules for inferring the content inside $COSCH^{KR}$ system. These DL constructors are defined and formulated in close collaboration with experts in technical fields of spatial and spectral technologies.

Moving on, the purposes and reasons behind the acquiring the data are represented within class "Application". It is a class that determines the nature and quality of data that needs to be acquired and lies on the other side of the axis "*Application – Data – Technologies*". The specializations are again defined through the descriptive semantics through DL concept constructors. They link to data through the expressions of what kind of data is required (see (2)).

$$\text{Applications} \equiv \exists \text{hasRequirementOnData.Data} \quad (2)$$

Let us continue taking example of "Photography" to illustrate our example on applications. We can think of two simple applications of photos here: printingfor i.)a billboardand ii.) a travel album. Even though both require photos as the main product, the qualities required of them differ a lot. The photos needed for the billboard need to have high resolution photos with different degree of sharpness while the same should not holdtrue for the photos for the travel albums. They have impacts on the concerned technology acquiring the photos. The billboard photos should be taken with high end DSLR camera and needs some post- processing while those for travel album can be taken with simple digital cameras or mobile cameras.

The classes outside this axis are equally important in terms that they affect the technologies. Class "*Physical Thing*" represents the main subject to be measured (in our case it is CH Physical Objects). COSCH^{KR} does not define these objects as their real world counterparts. They are defined through the physical characteristics of which they are built-up. For example: churches do not have pseudo representation with class "Church" inside the class "*Physical Thing*". Therefore, they cannot be asserted as "Church". They need to be asserted as composite objects (under sub-class "*CompositeObjects*") built-up with different individual objects (under class "*IndividualObjects*"). These composite/individual objects have certain characteristics like in case of church, they are big in size. COSCH^{KR} therefore does not differentiate between a church or a building. The main reason is: it is not important to know what are being digitized (in terms of how they are called in real world), but important to know whether the physical characteristics of object support or deny its digitization process when certain technology is being used. The core mantra is "the physical characteristics of the objects decide how any technology should be used to digitize them and not objects themselves". Let us roll back to the example of "*Photography*" and its product "Photos". The possibility of "*Close-range Photography*" has high dependency on the size of the object. It cannot photograph big sized objects (see (3)) because it cannot capture entire object in one photo shooting action. So a church cannot be photographed with close range photography.

$$\exists \text{hasSuitabilitiesFor.}(\text{Physical-Thing} \sqcap \forall \text{hasSize.}(\neg \text{Big})) \quad (3)$$

The class "ExternalInfluences" has similar technical implications to that of class "*Physical Thing*". It defines constraining semantics that effect the recommendations of the technologies. They include constraints deriving from the project limitations such as budget, human resource or from the surroundings of the measured objects like available space, lights, access and so on. These factors play major roles in technical solution and need to be defined inside the ontology.

C. Content capture

At the very beginning of development of the ontology, the COSCH community established a core group responsible to collect, manage and structure knowledge from the relevant expert groups. The core group was also responsible to define common vocabulary. It developed theoretical concepts on the basis of the collected unstructured knowledge through: 1) questionnaire; 2) discussion. These theoretical concepts were represented through respective axioms and theorems.

To be able to get an overview of expert's knowledge within the COSCH community, a questionnaire was designed, which has the intention to ask for spectral and spatial recording approaches and technical details applied in various humanities projects. For each group of physical CH objects, which were recorded within a humanities project, one questionnaire requires to be completed, where a group is mainly defined through the purpose of the spectral or spatial recording. The actual version of the questionnaire consists of twelve main questions with subordinate questions asking primarily for technical details [36]. The completed questionnaires are supporting the analysis to structure the content, to define work areas through the determination of relevant terms and vocabularies, and to identify contact persons having a specific expertise and being available for discussions and feedback. All in all, it should be highlighted that this tool cannot have the intention to collect knowledge, which is already structured and ready for the integration into the ontology (see below). In contrast, the specific content related to one physical CH object and application, which is described within the completed questionnaires, gives evidence for structuring theoretical concepts included in the ontology.

D. Case Study example

The analysis of the completed questionnaires led to the following strategy: the ontology will be developed using case studies as framework since it provides concrete facts for a discussion with experts from different domains. These facts on the one hand are the basis for a common understanding and on the other hand are helpful to stay focused. Furthermore, a case study provides added advantage important for the development of theoretical concepts: the case study discussion can be expanded easily by fact modifications even after it has been included through theoretical concepts inside the ontology. For example, if the original case study was related to small physical CH objects a fact modification could be to imagine the physical CH object being very large. Depending on the facts under discussion this approach helps to extend branches of the ontology.

The first selected case study dealt with waterlogged wood as through unavoidable conservation treatment the shape and volume of these objects is modified. To be able to measure the influence of various conservation treatments a high number of samples of waterlogged wood were recorded in 3D before and after conservation. And through a comparison of the two 3D models representing one sample changes could be evaluated giving information on the influence of the conservation on the shape and volume of the objects [10].

The physical CH objects of interest are samples from different time periods having a minimum size of 100 x 60 x 60 cubic mm (Fig.2 CH Object Size "small"). The material condition of the samples before conservation treatment was an important issue as the archaeological waterlogged wood samples had a dark brown to black appearance and were partly shiny. The translucent and reflective surface of the untreated samples had impact on the data quality. However, this impact was reduced to a minimum through careful toweling of the samples before recording (Fig.2 CH Object Reflectivity "low"). After conservation the appearance of the samples sometimes changed immensely as the water inside the wood is gone and conservation materials stabilized the object causing sometimes a colour change to light brown. However, all sample surfaces were dry after treatment which means they were not reflective anymore (Fig.2 CH Object Reflectivity "low"). A crucial factor was the high number of samples: All in all 777 objects were recorded before and after treatment (Fig.2 CH Object Number "large") why an industrial recording device – a structured light scanner – was chosen as selected processing steps could be automated and controlled through scripts of associated software (Fig. 2 Workflow Method "Automated, semi-automated"). The workflow control was applied for quality management of the required data and accuracy (Fig. 2 "3D" and "high"). Due to this the operating staff of the structured light scanner could be changed without major impact on the workflow and data quality as the number of possible error sources was reduced to a minimum (Fig.2 technical competence "low"). However, the varying operating staff needed supervision by a 3D recording expert. Especially the above mentioned workflow control possibilities determined the choice of the 3D recording technique.

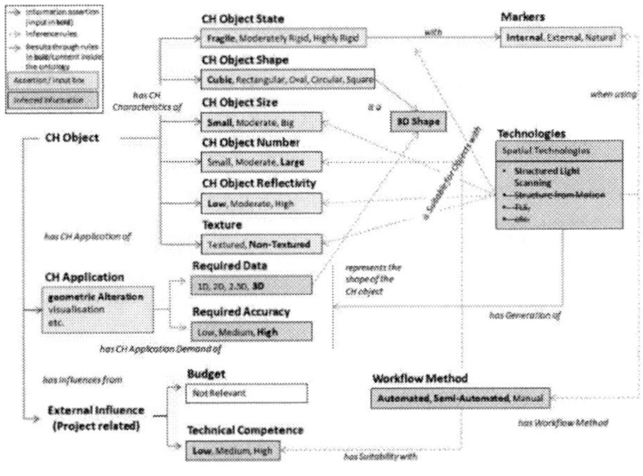

Fig.2.Simulation of a GUI for the case study "conservation of waterlogged wood". The red boxes represent the user input and the grey boxes represent the inferred information.

$$\text{Applications} \sqcap \geq 2\ \text{hasRequirementOnData.(Data} \sqcap (\leq 1\ \text{hasRepresentationOf.PhysicalObjects)} \quad (4)$$

The CH application in this case study is to compare the deformation of geometry (Fig.2 CH Application "geometric Alteration"). This CH application requires high level of accuracy to detect any changes, which also means it requires high resolution datasets for the comparison. This needs to be explicit while describing semantics of the class representing the CH Application Geometric Alteration (class *"Deformation Analysis"* – a specialization to top level class *CH Application*). Through these descriptive semantics (see below), we relate and compare different classes to derive suitable answer.

Going back to our *"Applications – Data – Technology"* (see Fig. 1) conceptual axis, the CH application *"Deformation Analysis"* demands for data representing the objects with high accuracy e.g. depending on their size. *"Deformation Analysis"* is an immediate sub-class of *ChangeDetection* (again a specialization of class *CH Applications*), defined through the descriptive semantics stating that at least two dataset of the same object is required (see (4)).

Besides inheriting these descriptive semantics encoded in DL class constructors of parent classes, *"Deformation Analysis"* describes the semantics of required data such as nature (3D) and accuracy (high) (see (5)).

$$\text{ChangeDetection} \sqcap \exists \text{hasRequirementOn-Data.(Data} \sqcap \exists\ \text{hasRepresentationOf.(PhysicalObjects} \sqcap \exists \text{has-ObjectShape.Shapes)} \sqcap \exists \text{hasSpatialAccuracy.High)} \quad (5)$$

Once the requirement on data is known in the axis Applications – Data – Technologies, COSCH^{KR}uses these semantic descriptors to infer right technology(ies). In this case, the descriptive semantics of measurement method *StructuredLightScanning*, which is a specialized class under *MeasurementMethods*(specialization of class *Technology)*is inferred as the recommended because

1) nature of data and accuracy it can generate with

$$\exists \text{hasGenerationOnData.}(\text{3D\_Data} \sqcap \exists \text{hasSpatialAccuracy.High}) \quad (6)$$

2) evaluating the technology against the object characteristics

a) Size/volume

$$\exists \text{hasSuitabilitiesFor.}(\text{PhysicalObjects} \sqcap (\exists \text{hasObjectSize.2DSize\_Small} \sqcup \exists \text{hasObjectVolume.3DVolume\_Small})) \quad (7)$$

b) textured: non textured

$$\exists \text{hasSuitabilitiesFor.}(\text{PhysicalObjects} \sqcap (\exists \text{hasObjectTexture.NonTextured}) \quad (8)$$

c) number of objects: large with 777 samples

In order to determine the effectiveness of the technology to manage large number of objects, the technology should provide automated or semi-automated work flow. Therefore, semantic description of the technology (Structured Light Scanning) is semantically described through the workflow and number of objects with a single DL statement (see (9)).

$$(\exists \text{hasSuitabilitiesFor.}(\text{PhysicalObjects} \sqcap (\exists \text{hasObjectQuantity.LargeNumber})) \sqcap (\exists \text{hasWorkflowMethod.}(\text{SemiAutomatedWorkflow} \sqcup \text{AutomatedWorkflow}) \quad (9)$$

d) reflectivity: low

$$(\exists \text{hasGenerationOnData.}(\text{3D\_Data} \sqcap \exists \text{hasSpatialAccuracy.High})) \sqcap (\exists \text{hasSuitabilitiesFor.}(\text{PhysicalObjects} \sqcap \exists \text{hasObjectReflectance.Low\_Reflectivity})) \quad (10)$$

The initial reflectivity of the waterlogged wooden samples was high because of the higher reflectance of water. COSCH^{KR}in such a case does not provide any technology to generate high accuracy data with the highly reflected objects. Therefore, the ontology does not provide any technical solutions for highly reflected wooden samples and checks with the user if the reflectance could be lowered. In our case, the sample could be wiped to lower the reflectance. This again infers *StructuredLightScanning*as right technology.

e) fragile: no possibilities to put markers

This again gives no results. The standard setup of the technology (Structured Light Scanning) represented through class *MeasurementSetups*(a specialization of class Technology) will check whether one can stick any markers into the object. If the answer is yes then the rule of high accurate 3D data will be possible with the structured light scanning. The standard setup of the method is described through class StandardStrcturedLightScanning-Setups (specialization of class *MeasurementSetups*with relation to class *MeasurementMethods*) .

$$(\exists \text{hasGenerationOnData.}(\text{3D\_Data} \sqcap (\exists \text{hasSpatialAccuracy.High})) \sqcap (\geq 1 \text{hasImplementingInstruments.}(\text{InternalMarkers} \sqcup \text{NaturalInternalMarker}) \quad (11)$$

3) evaluating technology against external influencing characteristics

Technical competence is the characteristics of the project influences. In this case the technical competence among operating staff is low. The case resembles the case of ii.c. Therefore, the technical competence depends on the kind of workflow the technology provides. If it provides automated workflow like in this case, the technology will only require operating staff with low competence. We defined this inside the class of *StructuredLightScanning*

$$(\exists \text{hasOperatingProject.}(\text{ProjectInfluences} \sqcap (\exists \text{hasOperatingStaffCompetence.}(\text{Competence\_Medium} \sqcup \text{Competence\_Low}))) \sqcap (\exists \text{hasWorkflowMethod.}(\text{SemiAutomatedWorkflow} \sqcup \text{AutomatedWorkflow}) \quad (12)$$

Here class *ProjectInfluences*is specialization of top-level class *ExternalInfluences*.

This summarises that the Structured Light Scanning is the optimal recommended technology for scanning wooden samples in order to estimate deformation. The technologies are sorted out while the ontology processes knowledge inside to infer at different level. For example, at the very beginning when the requirement was 3D data, the ontology suggested all technologies that generate 3D data including Terrestrial Laser Scanning (TLS), Structure from Motion (SFM) and so on. As more semantic constraints were applied, technologies were filtered out. E.g., when the requirement was highly accurate data SFM was ignored, and when the object size was asserted "small" TLS was ignored. All technologies are semantically defined to support or deny the conditions they will be inferred against. At the end, semantically defined rules of Structured Light Scanning supported all the asserted conditions so the system recommended the technology.

Different technology might be recommended if and when the situation changes or other different constraints are added into. The knowledge model will alter the parameters of this case study to simulate other situations, e.g., instead of a high number of physical CH objects a low number is assumed, to identify why and how the recording strategy would have changed.

We are working with two other case studies. They are still under development and not yet integrated in COSCH^{KR}.They concentrate on a CH application related to the spectral recording and visualization domains (www.cosch.info/case-studies). Through these two case studies the better part of the technical classes could be developed. One of the most important reasons choosing the case study related to the spatial recording was the fact that the spatial recording expert was personally available for face-to-face. The development of a common understanding might be a longer iterating exchange of views and content, the number of iterations increases with the distance between the science fields, why for matter of convergence it is proposed to use face-to-face discussions. All in all, it is recommended to center the discussions around a case study in a process-related manner to stay focused and to create a common understanding between the different experts. The aim of the discussion is to develop theoretical concepts, which could be integrated into the ontology as formal axioms presenting the descriptive semantics and which finally display the case study as theoretical concepts addressing and linking all top-classes within the ontology. After the integration of both case studies as theoretical concepts in the ontology further identified work areas will be approached through discussions with other experts creating theoretical concepts related to other case studies.

IV. Conclusions

CH is arguably one of the most multi-disciplinary areas of research where disciplines from highly diverse disciplines (incl. human science, technologies and even pure science like chemistry) are actively involved. Developing ontology that not only smoothen the communication problems but also provides inter-disciplinary understandings to support recommendation on the best possible technical approach for a CH application requires a platform where experts from individual respective domain are open to exchange inter-disciplinary discussions. COSCH – the COST Action TD1201 provides such a platform where experts from spatial and spectral technologies discuss on specific CH research questions with humanities experts to suggest on best usages of the technologies for answering them. The underlying knowledge from those discussions are captured and encapsulated within ontology COSCH^{KR}.

In this paper, we have presented the experiences we gained in developing COSCH^{KR}. With COSCH^{KR} we intend to address issues relevant in the area of CH, spatial and spectral technologies and the Semantic Web technology itself. The usage of semantics within CH communities is mostly limited to knowledge management and rarely to knowledge processing. They are mostly used to capture, document and re-use information on CH objects through knowledge management technologies.We see huge potential in using semantics to go beyond knowledge management; they can be used for knowledge processing with their in-built reasoning capabilities.

COSCH^{KR} exploits Description Logics reasoning capabilities by encoding knowledge already at concept level. This has an added benefit against conventional recommender systems. We use experts with prior knowledge and experience in CH documentation that can be already encoded inside the knowledge model and not rely on stochastic on huge amount of data at data level. These encoded knowledge sets can then be exploited by any interpreting systems to infer the right recommendations. In addition, the existing databases and knowledge hubs with para-, meta- and provenance information could benefit from COSCH^{KR} for evaluating their own data.

COSCH^{KR} is developed within the conceptual axis of requirement on data by CH application – generation of data by technologies. Other concepts are woven around this axis. Though we use the concept with the application field of CH, it could be applied in other domains as well. We are currently working on a mechanism that interprets descriptive semantics encoded through DL concept constructors into inferencing rules. These descriptive semantics will be parsed into rule based statements that could be reasoned by existing reasoning engines to provide the recommendations.

ACKNOWLEDGMENT

This work was partly supported by COST under Action TD1201: Colour and Space in Cultural Heritage (COSCH). Furthermore, we would like to thank Dipl.-Ing. (FH) Guido Heinz M.Eng., Uwe Herz (both RGZM), Marcello Picollo, Tatiana Vitorino (both IFAC-CNR), Dr. Julio del Hoyo Melendez (The National Museum in Krakow) and Christian Degrigny (HE-Arc) for discussions and support in developing the classes and rules.

REFERENCES

[1] P.L. Boeuf, M. Doerr, C.E. Ore, and S. Stead, Definition of the CIDOC Conceptual Reference Model. ICOM/CIDOC CRM Special Interest Group, 2013.

[2] F. Boochs, "COSCH - Colour and Space in Cultural Heritage, A New COST Action starts". The 4th International Conference of EuroMed 2012. Ioannides M., Fritsch D., Leissner J., Davies R., Remondino F. and Caffo R. eds., pp. 865-873, 2012. Limassol, Cyprus: LNCS.

[3] F. Boochs et al., "Towards Optimal Spectral and Spatial Documentation of Cultural Heritage. COSCH – An Interdisciplinary Action in the COST Framework".XXIV International CIPA Symposium. Strasbourg: International Archives of the Photogrammetry, Remote Sensing and Spatial Information Sciences, pp. 109-113, 2013.

[4] C. Brewster and K. O'Hara, "Knowledge representation with ontologies: Present challenges - Future possibilities".International Journal of Human-Computer Studiesm vol. 65, no. 7. pp. 563-568, 2007.

[5] V. Charles, "Introduction to the Europeana data model". 17th International Conference on Theory and Practice of Digital Libraries. Malta: International Conference on Theory and Practice of Digital Libraries, 2013.

[6] E. Coburn and R. Stein, *LIDO*. [Online] Avaliable from:http://network.icom.museum/cidoc/working-groups/lido/. [retrieved: November, 2015]

[7] K. Fernie, D. Gaverilis, and S. Angeli, TheCARARE meta data schema v2.0. Europeana Carare project, 2013.

[8] G. Jakus, V. Milutinovic, S. Omerovic, and S. Tomazic,"Concepts, Ontologies and Knowledge Representation". SpringerBriefs in Computer Science, 2013.

[9] D. B. Lenat and R. V. Guha,Building large knowledge-based systems: Representation and inference in the cyc project. Boston: Addison-Wesley Longman Publishing Co., Inc, 1989.

[10] C. Mazzola, "What to do with "Large Quantity Finds in Archaeological Collections" - A KUR-project". News in Conservation 6 (December 2009).

[11] T.R. Gruber,"A Translation Approach to Portable Ontology Specifications". Knowledge Acqusitionvol. 5 no. 2,pp. 199-220, 1993.

[12] A. Młka, B.Kryza, and J. Kitowski,"Integration of heterogeneous data sources in an ontological knowledge base".Computing and Informaticsvol. 31, no. 1.pp. 189-223, 2014

[13] S.A. Odat, A Semantic e-Science Platform for 20th Century Paint Conservation, PhD dthesis. University of Queensland, Australia, 2014.

[14] M. Uschold andM. Gruninger,"Ontologies: Principles, methods and applications". Knowledge Engineering Review, pp. 93-136, 1996.

[15] A.-K. Wieman, S. Wefers, A. Karmacharya, and F. Boochs, "Characterisation of Spatial Techniques for Optimised Use in Cultural Heritage Documentation".M. Ioannides, N. Mageanat-Thalmann, E. Fink, R. Zarnic, A. Yen, E. Quak, eds. Digital Heritage,Lecture Notes in Computer Science, pp. 374-386, 2014.

[16] I. Horrocks, P. F. Patel-Schneider, D. L. McGuinness, and C.A. Welty, OWL: a Description Logic Based Ontology Language for the Semantic Web, 2004.

[17] S. Lim, Y. Liu, and W. B. Lee, "A methodology for building a semantically annotated multi-faceted ontology for product family modelling". Advanced Engineering Informatics, vo. 12, no. 2, pp. 147-161, 2011.

[18] Y. Sure, J. Angele, and S. Staab, "OntoEdit: Multifaceted Inferencing for Ontology Engineering". Journal on Data Semantics, 2003, pp. 128-152, 2003.

[19] S. Grimm, P. Hitzler, and A. Abecker, "Knowledge Representation and Ontologies: Logic, Ontologies and Semantic Web Languages". R. Studer, S. Grimm and A. eds.,Semantic Web Services. Springer Link, pp 51-105, 2007.

[20] R. Studer, V. R. Benjamins,and D. Fensel, Knowledge Engineering: Principles and Methods, Karlsruhe, 1998.

[21] S. Grimm, A. Abecker, J. Völker,and R. Studer, "Ontologies and the Semantic Web". J. Domingue, D. Fensel,and J. A. Hendler, eds., Handbook of Semantic Web Technologies, Springer, pp. 507-579, 2011.

[22] X. Wang, J. Almeida,and A. Oliviera, "Ontology Design Principles and Normalization Techniques in the Web".Data Integration in the Life Sciences, 5th International Workshop, DILS 2008, Evry, France, Springer Berlin Heidelberg, pp 28-43, 2008.

[23] I. Horrocks, D. Patel-Schneider, D. L. McGuinness, and C. A. Welty, "OWL: a Description Logic Based Ontology Language for the Semantic Web". F. Baader, D. Calvanese, D. McGuinness, D. Nardi,and P. F. Schneider, eds, The Description Logic Handbook: Theory, Implementation, and Applications (2nd Edition), Cambridge University Press, 2007.

[24] D. Tsarkov and I. Horrocks, "FaCT++ Description Logic Reasoner: System Description".Automated Reasoning, Bd. 4130, Nr. LNCS, pp. 292-297, 2006.

[25] F. Baader and R. Küsters, "Nonstandard Inferences in Description Logics: The Story So Far".Mathematical Problems from Applied LogicI, Bd. 4, Springer New York, pp. 1-75, 2006.

[26] D. Estival, C. Nowak,and A. Zschorn, "Towards Ontology-Based Natural Language Processing".The Workshop on NLP and XML (NLPXML-2004): RDF/RDFS and OWL in Language Technology, Strousburg, Association for Computational Linguistics, pp 59-66, 2004.

[27] C. Menzel, "Reference Ontologies - Application Ontologies: Either/Or or Both/And?"The KI2003 Workshop on Reference Ontologies and Application Ontologies, 2003.

[28] S. E. Middleton, D. D. Roure,and N. R. Shadbolt, "Ontology-Based Recommender Systems".Handbook on Ontologies, Springer, pp. 779-796, 2009.

[29] M. Á. Rodrígues-García, L. O. Mendoza, R. Valencia-García, A. Lopez-Lorca,and G. Beydoun, "Ontology-Based Music Recommender System, Distributed Computing and Artificial Intelligence". 12th International Conference of the series Advances in Intelligent Systems and Computing, Vol. 373, Springer International Publishing, pp. 39-46, 2015.

[30] G. Lakoff and M. Johnson, Metaphors We Live By. The University of Chicago Press, 1980.

[31] F. Ricci, L. Rokrach,and B. Shapira, "Introduction to Recommender Systems Handbook".Recommender Systems Handbook, Springer, pp. 1-35, 2010.

[32] R. Burke, "Hybrid web recommender systems".The Adaptive Web, Springer Berlin / Heidelberg, pp. 377-408, 2007.

[33] P. Resnick and H. R. Varian, "Recommender systems". Communications of the ACM vol. 40, no. 3, pp. 56-58, 1997.

[34] COST, COST Action, *COST European Cooperation in Science and Technology.* [Online] Available fromhttp://www.cost.eu/COST_Actions, 7 July 2015. [retrieved: July, 2016]

[35] S. Bechhofer, F. v. Harmelen, J. Hendler, I. Horrocks, D. L. McGuinness, P. F. Patel-Schneider, and L. A. Stein, "OWL Web Ontology Language". *W3C Recommendation.* [Online]Available from http://www.w3.org/TR/owl-ref/ [retrieved: September, 2016]

[36] COSCH, COSCH^{KR}, *Colour and Space in Cultural Heritage.*[Online] Available from www.cosch.info/coschkr [retrieved: July 2016]

[37] M. C. Suárez-Figueroa, A. Gómez-Pérez, and M. Fernandez-Lopez. "The NeOn Methodology framework: A scenario-based methodology for ontology development." *Applied Ontology* 10, no. 2,pp. 107-145, 2015.

Word Sense Disambiguation Using Active Learning with Pseudo Examples

Minoru Sasaki, Katsumune Terauchi, Kanako Komiya, Hiroyuki Shinnou
Dept. of Computer and Information Sciences
Faculty of Engineering, Ibaraki University
4-12-1, Nakanarusawa, Hitachi, Ibaraki, Japan
Email: {minoru.sasaki.01, 16nm717f, kanako.komiya.nlp, hiroyuki.shinnou.0828}@vc.ibaraki.ac.jp

Abstract*—In recent years, there have been attempts to apply active learning for Word sense disambiguation (WSD). This active learning technique selects the most informative unlabeled examples that were most difficult to disambiguate. The most commonly addressed problem has been the extraction of relevant information, where the system constructs a better classification model to identify the appropriate sense of the target word. Previous research reported that it is effective to create negative examples artificially (i.e., pseudo negative examples). However, this method works only for words that appear in a small number of topics (e.g., technical terms) because the evaluation set is strongly biased. For common noun or verb words, it is hard to apply this system so that problems still remain in the active learning with pseudo negative examples for WSD. In this paper, to solve this problem, we propose a novel WSD system based on active learning with pseudo examples for any words. This proposed method is to learn WSD models constructed from training corpus by adding pseudo examples during the active learning process. To evaluate the effectiveness of the proposed method, we perform some experiments to compare it with the result of the previous methods. The results of the experiments show that the proposed method achieves the highest precision of all systems and can extract more effective pseudo examples for WSD.

***Keywords*-word sense disambiguation; active learning; uncertainty sampling; pseudo examples; reliable confidence score.**

I. Introduction

Word sense disambiguation (WSD) is one of the major tasks in natural language processing (NLP). WSD is the process of removing ambiguities and identifying the most appropriate sense for a polysemous word in context. This technique is crucial in many application in other areas of NLP, such as machine translation [16], information retrieval [17], question answering [1], information extraction [2], text summarization [13], and so on.

One of the successful approaches to WSD is based on applying corpus-based learning [6] [11]. In this approach, machine learning (ML) or statistical algorithms have been applied to learn classifiers from corpora in order to perform WSD. WSD approaches based on the ML are classified into two categories, supervised and unsupervised approaches. The supervised learning method is used to learn the rules that correctly classify documents for a given classification algorithm. The unsupervised learning method is used to cluster word contexts into some sets which indicate the same meaning. A variety of techniques for supervised learning algorithms have demonstrated good performance for WSD, when we have enough labeled training data for learning. However, the supervised WSD methods require a large sense-tagged corpus which is expensive to obtain by manual annotation.

In recent years, there have been attempts to apply active learning for WSD [3] [18]. This active learning technique selects the most informative unlabeled examples that were most difficult to disambiguate. Previous research reported that the active learning methods with supervised learning methods could effectively reduce the amount of human labeling effort and can be helpful to improve the WSD models. For example, in the previous research [14], it is realized by automatically extracting pseudo negative examples that have reliable confidence score from unlabeled examples for WSD in Web mining. This method achieves high accuracy compared to the method with manually extracted negative examples for World Wide Web data. However, this method works only for words that appear in a small number of topics (e.g., technical terms) because the evaluation set is strongly biased. For common noun or verb words, it is hard to apply this system so that problems still remain in the active learning with pseudo negative examples for WSD.

In this paper, to solve this problem, we propose a novel WSD system based on active learning with pseudo examples for any words. This proposed method aims at learning WSD models constructed from training corpus by adding pseudo examples during the active learning process. The contribution of our work is three-fold,

- By using active learning with pseudo examples, the proposed WSD system can compute the effective semantic distribution of each sense of words.
- The proposed WSD system can be effective for common noun or verb words by using a new calculation method of confidence score.
- The proposed WSD system adopts support vector machine (SVM) as classifier, which can extract more effective pseudo examples than the previous system.

A series of experiments shows that our method effectively contributes to WSD precision.

The rest of this paper is organized as follows. Section II is devoted to the introduction of the related work in the literature. Section III describes the proposed WSD system based on active learning with pseudo examples. In Section IV, we describe an outline of experiments and experimental results. Finally, Section V concludes the paper.

II. Related Works

This paper proposes a WSD method using active learning with pseudo examples. In this section, some previous research using active learning for WSD will be compared with our proposed method.

Active learning is the study of machine learning systems that select the data from the data pool and get the labeled data to reduce the amount of labeling efforts. One intuitive approach in pool-based active learning is called uncertainty sampling [10]. This approach selects example for which the classifier is most uncertain. Chan and Ng (2007) propose to combine active learning method with domain adaptation for word sense disambiguation system [3]. This method estimates the reliable confidence score with the prior probability of the target sense to select the most informative data, whereas our method does not consider the prior probability of sense to calculate the reliable confidence score.

Zhu and Hovy (2007) analyzed the effect of resampling techniques, under-sampling and over-sampling with active learning for the WSD imbalanced learning problem [18]. This method uses labeled training data set that includes the positive and negative examples as the input. However, our method of active learning starts with the small positive examples and the pool of unlabeled examples.

Takayama et al. (2009) propose a method of active learning to artificially create negative examples (i.e., pseudo negative examples). This method achieves high accuracy compared to the method with manually extracted negative examples for search results. Our method artificially creates positive and negative examples (i.e., pseudo examples) to improve the WSD performance for common noun or verb words.

III. Active Learning Method with Pseudo Examples for WSD

In this section, we describe the details of the proposed WSD system based on active learning with pseudo examples. The proposed method employs uncertainty sampling active learning strategy.

A. Classifier

In our experiment, to classify the sense label to unlabeled example, we use support vector machine (SVM) as classifier [5]. The SVM is one of the most popular machine learning algorithms. The SVM computes a hyperplane with the largest margin separating the training examples into two classes. A test example is classified depending on the side of the hyperplane. In order to deal with the multi-class problem, we can reduce this problem to a set of binary classification problems by using one-versus-one [7] or one-versus-rest [15] strategy. Therefore, SVM has been successfully applied to many natural language processing problems.

function Active-Learning-with-Pseudo-Examples (D,s,S,k);
Input : Data set with positive training examples and unlabeled examples D; Sense label of the target word s; Set of sense labels S; Total number of labeled examples that are required k
Output: Labeled training data set L
$P \leftarrow$ training examples with label s;
$N \leftarrow \{\}$;
$PP \leftarrow \{\}$;
$PN \leftarrow \{\}$;
repeat
  foreach d *in D-P-N* **do**
    $c(d,s) \leftarrow$ reliable confidence score for d that has the sense s;
    $c(d,\bar{s}) \leftarrow$ reliable confidence score for d that doesn't have the sense s;
    diff $\leftarrow c(d,\bar{s}) - c(d,s)$;
    if diff $\geq \tau$ **then**
      if $s = \arg\max_{s_i \in S} c(d,s_i)$ **then**
        $PP \leftarrow PP \cup d$;
      else
        $PN \leftarrow PN \cup d$;
      end
    end
  end
  Construct classifier M using $(P+PP, N+PN)$;
  $c_{min} \leftarrow \infty$;
  foreach d *in D-P-N* **do**
    $s' \leftarrow$ sense label that d is classified into, using the WSD model M;
    $c(d,s') \leftarrow$ reliable confidence score for d that has the sense s';
    if $c(d,s') < c_{min}$ **then**
      $c_{min} \leftarrow c(d,s'), d_{min} \leftarrow d$;
    end
  end
  $s_m \leftarrow$ sense label that is manually annotated to d_{min};
  if $s_m = s$ **then**
    $P \leftarrow P \cup d_{min}$;
  else
    $N \leftarrow N \cup d_{min}$;
  end
until *the number of labeled examples is equal to k*;

Figure 1. Algorithm of active learning with pseudo examples

To perform our sense label classifier, we convert an example to features. In this paper, we use the following five types of features.

f_1 : Content words (noun, verb, adverb) in the sentence that the target word appears(i.e., current sentence) and also in the previous and the next sentence.

- f_2 : The previous content word of target word in the same Japanese phrasal unit (bunsetsu).
- f_3 : The next content word of target word in the same Japanese phrasal unit.
- f_4 : Unit phrase that depends on the unit the target word appears.
- f_5 : Unit phrase the target word depends on.

These above features were used in previous research [14]. This research reports that the WSD system using these features gives good results. In this paper, to compare with the previous method, we employ the same five types of features in our experiments.

B. Active Learning Method

We describe the proposed active learning method for WSD. This proposed method is based on uncertainty sampling that selects unlabeled examples that were most difficult to disambiguate. By using this method, we can construct a better classifier for active learning because we can obtain pseudo negative examples with high confidence and pseudo positive examples that are near a decision boundary of SVM.

Algorithm 1 shows the proposed active learning method with pseudo examples. This active learning function receives four inputs D, s, S and k. D is a data set with positive training examples and unlabeled examples: s is a sense label of the target word. S is a set of sense labels of the target word and k is the total number of labeled examples that are obtained by active learning.

Firstly, the proposed method generates pseudo examples to construct a classifier M. For each unlabeled example d in $D-P-N$, reliable confidence scores $c(d,s)$ for the sense s and $c(d,\bar{s})$ for the other sense $\bar{s}$ are calculated using the following formula:

$$c(d,s) = \sum_{j=1}^{5} \log p(f_j|s). \quad (1)$$

In the previous research [3] [14], the reliable confidence score is calculated using a different formula, as follows:

$$c(d,s) = \log p(s) \sum_{j=1}^{5} \log p(f_j|s). \quad (2)$$

Here, $p(s)$ represents the prior probability of the sense s. In the experiments from the [14], target words are almost proper nouns such as product name and personal name so that the prior probability $p(s)$ of each word is effective for the reliable confidence score. However, when we use general words such as common noun or verb words as the target word, the prior probability $p(s)$ is not so effective for the reliable confidence score. This reason is that the prior probability $p(s)$ of proper nouns in search result document set is heavily biased. Therefore, we use (2) to calculate the reliable confidence score using the same value of the prior probability value.

For the obtained two reliable confidence scores $c(d,s)$ and $c(d,\bar{s})$, the difference of these scores $diff$ is calculated. When the $diff$ value is not less than the threshold value τ, the example d is added to the pseudo positive example set PP if the sense with the highest reliable confidence score is equal to the sense label s, otherwise the example d is added to the pseudo negative example set PN. If the sense with the highest reliable confidence score is the positive sense label s, the example d is likely to be positive example that is near a decision boundary. It is important to obtain such examples to construct a better decision boundary, If the $diff$ value of the another sense label is the highest, the example d is an almost negative example. In this experiment, the threshold parameter τ which predicted a significant difference between the target sense and the other is set to be 1.0.

Next, we construct the sense label classifier M using SVM from the training set with the pseudo examples $(P+PP, N+PN)$. We use LIBSVM as the implementation of the SVM for our experiments [4]. In the previous research [14], naive bayes classifier is used to develop the classifier. However, we obtain high classification precision using SVM so that we use the SVM as the classifier. For each unlabeled example d in $D-P-N$, d is classified into the sense s' by using the classifier M. Then we calculate the reliable confidence score $c(d,s')$ and extract the example d_{min} that minimize the reliable confidence score $c(d,s')$. For the obtained example d_{min}, sense label s_m is provided manually and the example d_{min} is added to the positive example set P if the sense s_m is equal to the sense label s, otherwise the example d_{min} is added to the negative example set N.

This process is repeated until the number of labeled examples is equal to k. In this experiment, k is set to be 50.

IV. Experiments

To evaluate the effectiveness of the proposed method of active learning with pseudo examples for WSD, we perform some experiments and compare the results of the previous method. In this section, we describe an outline of the experiments.

A. Data

To evaluate our active learning method, we used the Semeval-2010 Japanese WSD task data set, which includes 50 target words comprising 22 nouns, 23 verbs, and 5 adjectives from the BCCWJ corpus [12]. In this data set, there are 50 training and 50 test examples for each target word. One example in the training and test set is the sentence where the target word appears in.

In the experiments of this paper, we use randomly selected 10 words (2 nouns and 8 verbs) in the Semeval-2010 Japanese WSD task data set. For each sense of the target word, as the input data of the system, we use some labeled data that were randomly selected from the training examples and the other examples in the data set as unlabeled data. For the input data, the system extracts the previous and next sentences of each example and extracts noun, verb and adverb words from these sentences by using Japanese morphological analysis tool MeCab [9] to obtain the features f_1, f_2 and f_3. Moreover, the system uses the dependency analysis tool Cabocha [8] to obtain the features f_4 and f_5. Table I shows the number of the initial training examples for each sense of the target word and Table II shows the number of test examples for each sense of the target word, where the $s_i (i = 1, \cdots, 7)$ indicates the i-th sense of the word in the Iwanami Japanese Dictionary.

TABLE I: The number of the initial training examples for each sense of the target word

Words	s1	s2	s3	s4	s5	s6	s7
ageru	5	5	2	5	5	1	1
ataeru	5	5	5	-	-	-	-
imi	5	5	5	-	-	-	-
kodomo	5	5	-	-	-	-	-
suru	5	5	2	2	3	-	-
dasu	5	5	3	1	-	-	-
deru	5	5	2	-	-	-	-
toru	3	5	4	5	3	1	1
noru	5	2	4	5	-	-	-
motsu	5	5	2	-	-	-	-

TABLE II: The number of test examples for each sense of the target word

Words	s1	s2	s3	s4	s5	s6	s7
ageru	10	10	4	10	10	2	2
ataeru	10	10	10	-	-	-	-
imi	10	10	10	-	-	-	-
kodomo	10	10	-	-	-	-	-
suru	10	10	4	3	5	-	-
dasu	10	10	5	2	-	-	-
deru	10	10	5	-	-	-	-
toru	7	10	8	10	7	2	2
noru	9	5	9	10	-	-	-
motsu	10	10	2	-	-	-	-

B. Experiment on Active Learning for WSD

To evaluate the results of the proposed method for the test examples, we compare the four systems as follows:

System 1:
Active learning with pseudo negative examples using naive bayes classifier and the original reliable confidence score in the equation (2) (baseline).

System 2:
Active learning with pseudo negative examples using SVM classifier and the proposed reliable confidence score in the equation (1).

System 3:
Active learning with pseudo examples using SVM classifier and the original reliable confidence score in the equation (2).

System 4:
Active learning with pseudo examples using SVM classifier and the proposed reliable confidence score in the equation (1) (proposed method).

We obtain the precision value of each system and analyze the average performance of systems.

C. Experimental Results

In this section, we present the experimental results on the WSD system using active learning with pseudo examples. Table III shows the precision for each of the target words by using each WSD system.

TABLE III: Precision of the each WSD system for target words

Words	System1	System2	System3	System4
ageru	14.6%	**44.8%**	14.6%	33.3%
ataeru	40.0%	56.7%	40.0%	**60.0%**
imi	26.7%	53.3%	26.7%	**60.0%**
kodomo	5.0%	60.0%	5.0%	**95.0%**
suru	15.6%	18,8%	15.6%	**59.4%**
dasu	7.4%	14.8%	7.4%	**77.8%**
deru	40.0%	20.0%	40.0%	**60.0%**
toru	6.5%	15.2%	6.5%	**58.7%**
noru	17.6%	**64.7%**	20.6%	47.1%
motsu	36.4%	27.3%	36.4%	**50.0%**

As shown in the Table III, the proposed method achieves the highest precision of all systems for the eight target words. For the target word "kodomo (子供; child)", although the precision of the system 1 and 3 is very low, the precision is 95% by using the proposed system. For the word "suru (する; do, play ...)", "dasu (出す; put out, appear, ...)" and "toru (取る; take, catch, ...)", despite these words have many senses, the proposed system obtains the highest precision. Therefore, the proposed active learning method can extract more effective pseudo examples for WSD.

The baseline system (system 1) and system 3 give almost the same results in this WSD experiment. Using these systems, precision of WSD is low in comparison with the proposed systems. Hence, these systems are not effective to estimate an appropriate word sense for common words. Moreover, these results show that it is not so effective to append pseudo examples to the training data by using the reliable confidence score with the prior probability.

System 2 obtains higher precision than the system using the reliable confidence score with the prior probability for the eight target words (except for the words "deru" and "motsu"). For the target words "ageru (あげる; give, get up, ...)" and "noru (のる; ride, go into gear, ...)", this system also obtains higher precision than the proposed system. However, for the other target words, the precision is less than 50% so that system 2 did not obtain high precision. This result shows that it is effective for WSD system to append pseudo examples to the training data by using the reliable confidence score without the prior probability.

V. Conclusion

In this paper, we propose a novel WSD system based on active learning with pseudo examples for any words. This proposed method is to learn WSD models constructed from training corpus by adding pseudo examples during the active learning process. To evaluate the effectiveness of the proposed active learning method, we perform some experiments and compare the results with the results of the previous method. The results of the experiments show that the proposed WSD system can be effective for common noun or verb words by using a new calculation method of confidence score. Moreover, the proposed method achieves the highest precision of all systems and can extract more effective pseudo examples for WSD. However, by using the reliable confidence score with the prior probability, it is not so effective to append pseudo examples to the training data. Therefore, the proposed WSD system can compute the effective semantic distribution of each sense of words.

Further work would be required to consider some additional features such as thesaurus information and add more unlabeled data to obtain more meaningful examples by active learning to improve the performance of word sense disambiguation.

REFERENCES

[1] S. Beale, B. Lavoie, M. McShane, S. Nirenburg, and T. Korelsky, "Question answering using ontological semantics," in *Proceedings of the 2Nd Workshop on Text Meaning and Interpretation*, ser. TextMean '04. Stroudsburg, PA, USA: Association for Computational Linguistics, pp. 41–48, 2004.

[2] J. Y. Chai and A. W. Biermann, "The use of word sense disambiguation in an information extraction system," in *Proceedings of the Sixteenth National Conference on Artificial Intelligence and the Eleventh Innovative Applications of Artificial Intelligence Conference Innovative Applications of Artificial Intelligence*, ser. AAAI '99/IAAI '99. Menlo Park, CA, USA: American Association for Artificial Intelligence, pp. 850–855, 1999.

[3] Y. S. Chan and H. T. Ng, "Domain adaptation with active learning for word sense disambiguation," in *Proceedings of the 45th Annual Meeting of the Association of Computational Linguistics*. Prague, Czech Republic: In Proceedings of Association for Computational Linguistics, pp. 49–56, June 2007.

[4] C.-C. Chang and C.-J. Lin, "Libsvm – a library for support vector machines," https://www.csie.ntu.edu.tw/~cjlin/libsvm/.

[5] C. Cortes and V. Vapnik, "Support-vector networks," *Machine Learning*, vol. 20, no. 3, pp. 273–297, 1995.

[6] N. Ide and J. Véronis, "Word sense disambiguation: The state of the art," *Computational Linguistics*, vol. 24, pp. 1–40, 1998.

[7] U. Kreßel, "Pairwise classification and support vector machines," *in Advances in Kernel Methods - Support Vector Learning*, 1999.

[8] T. Kudo, "Cabocha: Yet another japanese dependency structure analyzer," http://taku910.github.io/cabocha/.

[9] T. Kudo, "Mecab: Yet another part-of-speech and morphological analyzer," http://taku910.github.io/mecab/.

[10] D. D. Lewis and W. A. Gale, "A sequential algorithm for training text classifiers," in *Proceedings of the 17th Annual International ACM SIGIR Conference on Research and Development in Information Retrieval*, ser. SIGIR '94. New York, NY, USA: Springer-Verlag New York, Inc., pp. 3–12, 1994.

[11] R. Navigli, "Word sense disambiguation: A survey," *ACM Computing Surveys*, vol. 41, no. 2, pp. 10:1–10:69, Feb. 2009.

[12] M. Okumura, K. Shirai, K. Komiya, and H. Yokono, "Semeval-2010 task: Japanese wsd," in *Proceedings of the 5th International Workshop on Semantic Evaluation*, ser. SemEval '10. Stroudsburg, PA, USA: Association for Computational Linguistics, pp. 69–74, 2010.

[13] M. Pourvali and M. S. Abadeh, "Automated text summarization base on lexicales chain and graph using of wordnet and wikipedia knowledge base," *International Journal of Computer Science Issues*, vol. abs/1203.3586, 2012.

[14] Y. Takayama, M. Imamura, N. Kaji, M. Toyoda, and M. Kitsuregawa, "Active learning with pseudo negative examples for word sense disambiguation in web mining," *IPSJ TOD*, vol. 2, no. 2, pp. 1–9, jun 2009.

[15] V. N. Vapnik, *Statistical learning theory*, 1st ed. Wiley, Sep. 1998.

[16] D. Vickrey, L. Biewald, M. Teyssier, and D. Koller, "Word-sense disambiguation for machine translation," in *Proceedings of the Conference on Human Language Technology and Empirical Methods in Natural Language Processing*, ser. HLT '05. Stroudsburg, PA, USA: Association for Computational Linguistics, pp. 771–778, 2005.

[17] Z. Zhong and H. T. Ng, "Word sense disambiguation improves information retrieval," in *Proceedings of the 50th Annual Meeting of the Association for Computational Linguistics: Long Papers - Volume 1*, ser. ACL '12. Stroudsburg, PA, USA: Association for Computational Linguistics, pp. 273–282, 2012.

[18] J. Zhu, "Active learning for word sense disambiguation with methods for addressing the class imbalance problem," in *In Proceedings of Association for Computational Linguistics*, pp. 783–790, 2007.

A Semantic Web Multimedia Information Retrieval Engine

Miguel Bento Alves
ESTG, Instituto Politécnico de Viana do Castelo
4900-348 Viana do Castelo
Email: mba@estg.ipvc.pt

Carlos Viegas Damásio
NOVA LINCS, FCT-UNL
Universidade Nova de Lisboa
2829-516 Caparica, Portugal
Email: cd@fct.unl.pt

Nuno Correia
NOVA LINCS, FCT-UNL
Universidade Nova de Lisboa
2829-516 Caparica, Portugal
Email: nmc@fct.unl.pt

***Abstract*—We present a Semantic Web based approach that meets the requirements for multimedia information retrieval. For that, we developed a prototypical implementation using a Semantic Web framework, linking open data ontologies and image processing libraries. We show how the different mechanisms of the Semantic Web may help multimedia management, both for storage and in retrieval tasks.**

Keywords*–*Multimedia Retrieval; Semantic Multimedia; Ontologies; Semantic inference

I. INTRODUCTION

As a consequence of technology development in several fields, large image databases have been created. In this context, well-organized databases and efficient storing and retrieval algorithms are absolutely necessary. These databases must be able to represent multimedia resources and their descriptions, considering that they are complex objects, and make them accessible for automated processing [1]. To enable multimedia content to be discovered and exploited by services, agents and applications, it needs to be described semantically. Indeed, it is very easy and cheap to take pictures, store or publish them and share, but it is very difficult and expensive to organize pictures, annotate, and find or retrieve them. This "big mismatch" between these two groups of tasks summarizes some of the key motivations for multimedia retrieval and, particularly in our work, for semantic description of visual metadata and inference on it. Multimedia constitutes an interesting field of application for Semantic Web and Semantic Web reasoning, as the access and management of multimedia content and context strongly depends on the semantic descriptions of both [1]. Semantic multimedia is a field that has emerged as a multidisciplinary topic from the convergence of Semantic Web technologies, multimedia and signal analysis. In [2], the advantages of using Semantic Web languages and technologies for the creation, storage, manipulation, interchange and processing of image metadata are described in more detail.

Manual annotation is the most effective way of doing multimedia annotation, that consists in adding metadata to the image, such as keywords or textual descriptions, to support the retrieval process. However, this method ignores the rich contents that the images have which can not be described by small sets of tags [3]. Furthermore, the keywords are very dependent on the observer [4].

A visual content feature refers to part of a visual content that contains interesting details or a property of the image which we are interested in. For any object there are many features, interesting points of the object, that can be extracted to provide a "feature" description of the object. We can have global visual content features, which describe a visual content as a whole, or local features, which represent visual content details.

In this work, our purpose is to show that a Semantic Web approach meets the requirements for multimedia information retrieval. For that, we performed an implementation using the Jena framework [5], a free and open source Java framework for building Semantic Web applications. It provides a programmatic environment for RDF, RDFS, OWL, a query engine for SPARQL and it includes a rule-based inference engine. Jena is widely used in Semantic Web applications because it offers an "all-in-one" solution for Java. Jena includes a general purpose rule-based reasoner which is used to implement both the RDFS and OWL reasoners but it is also available for general use. Jena reasoner supports rule-based inference over RDF graphs and provides forward chaining, backward chaining and a hybrid execution model. To extract visual content features we make use of Lucene Image Retrieval (LIRE) [6] [7], a light weight open source Java library for content-based image retrieval. It provides common and state-of-the-art global image features.

This document is structured as follows. We discuss the benefits of representing multimedia data in ontologies in Section II. Furthermore, we present our domain ontology. In Section III we present how to retrieve multimedia data with Semantic Web technologies and we explored the functionalities of the used Semantic Web framework to maximize the retrieval task capabilities. In Section IV we illustrate how semantic rules can be used to add knowledge to our system, reuse the knowledge produced and adding expressivity to that knowledge. We finish by discussing this work and general conclusions in Section V.

II. STORING DATA WITH ONTOLOGIES

Ontologies [8], a formal representation of a set of concepts within a domain and the relationships between those concepts, are effective for representing domain concepts and relations in a form of semantic network. The motivation for the development of the MPEG-7 standard [9], an ontology for describing multimedia documents, summarizes well the use of ontologies to store multimedia data, namely, the need for a high-level representation that captures the true semantics of a multimedia object. Multimedia ontologies should provide metadata descriptors for structural and low-level aspects of multimedia documents. In [10] relevant ontologies are presented in the field of multimedia, providing a comparative study.

Reusing existing ontologies is always a good choice when it is appropriate to do so [11], because one of the requirements is to make sure that our system can communicate with other systems that have already committed to particular ontologies. Although it is a good practice to reuse existing ontologies, we need a domain ontology to capture the specifics of a given domain. In our work, we used the LIRE system to extract visual content features and we developed an ontology to represent the information extracted. In Figure 1, some excerpts of our LIRE ontology are presented, defining 19 global features and 5 local features. We performed mappings to the AceMedia ontology [12] and to Hunter's MPEG-7 Ontology [13], and we used Ontology for Media Resources (OMR) [14] to describe media resources. OMR is a W3C Media Annotations Working Group recommendation whose aim is to connect many media resource descriptions together, bridging the different descriptions of media resources, and provide a core set of properties that can be used to transparently express them. The mapping between our LIRE ontology and OMR allows the interoperability with other media metadata schemas, since the metadata of multimedia content can be represented in different formats. The mapping with AceMedia has the same purpose but is more focused on low-level features.

$lire{:}Feature \equiv vdo{:}Feature$

$lire{:}GlobalFeature \sqsubseteq lire{:}Feature$

$lire{:}LocalFeature \sqsubseteq lire{:}Feature$

$lire{:}EdgeHistogram \sqsubseteq lire{:}GlobalFeature$

$lire{:}EdgeHistogram \equiv mpeg7{:}EdgeHistogram$

$lire{:}ScalableColor \sqsubseteq lire{:}GlobalFeature$

$lire{:}ScalableColor \equiv mpeg7{:}ScalableColor$

$lire{:}FCTH \sqsubseteq lire{:}GlobalFeature$

$lire{:}SimpleExtractor \sqsubseteq lire{:}LocalFeature$

$lire{:}SurfExtractor \sqsubseteq lire{:}LocalFeature$

$lire{:}MPEG7features \equiv mpeg7{:}Texture \sqcup mpeg7{:}Color$

$\geq 1 lire{:}feature \sqsubseteq ma-ont{:}MediaResource$

$lire{:}globalFeature \sqsubseteq lire{:}feature$

$\top \sqsubseteq \forall lire{:}globalFeature.lire{:}Feature$

$lire{:}localFeature \sqsubseteq lire{:}feature$

$\top \sqsubseteq \forall lire{:}localFeature.lire{:}Feature$

$lire{:}edgeHistogram \sqsubseteq lire{:}globalFeature$

$\top \sqsubseteq \forall lire{:}edgeHistogram.lire{:}EdgeHistogram$

$lire{:}scalableColor \sqsubseteq lire{:}globalFeature$

$\top \sqsubseteq \forall lire{:}scalableColor.lire{:}ScalableColor$

$\geq 1 lire{:}featureProperty \sqsubseteq lire{:}Feature$

$lire{:}byteArrayRepresentation \sqsubseteq lire{:}featureProperty$

$\top \sqsubseteq \forall lire{:}byteArrayRepresentation.xsd{:}string$

$vdo{:}coefficients \sqsubseteq lire{:}featureVector$

$\top \sqsubseteq \forall lire{:}featureVector.xsd{:}string$

$lire{:}numberOfCoefficients \sqsubseteq lire{:}featureProperty$

$lire{:}numberOfBitplanesDiscarded \sqsubseteq lire{:}featureProperty$

$\geq 1 lire{:}numberOfBitplanesDiscarded \sqsubseteq lire{:}ScalableColor$

$\top \sqsubseteq \forall lire{:}numberOfBitplanesDiscarded.xsd{:}nonNegativeInteger$

$lire{:}numberOfBitplanesDiscarded \equiv vdo{:}numberOfBitPlanesDiscarded$

$lire{:}numberOfCoefficients \sqsubseteq lire{:}featureProperty$

$\geq 1 lire{:}numberOfCoefficients \sqsubseteq lire{:}ScalableColor$

$\top \sqsubseteq \forall lire{:}numberOfCoefficients.xsd{:}nonNegativeInteger$

$lire{:}numberOfCoefficients \equiv vdo{:}numberOfBitPlanesDiscarded$

Figure 1 - Excerpt of the domain ontology

The ontology can be downloaded from here [15]. Figure 2 exemplifies the descriptions of the visual features of an image. Notice that since we mapped our domain ontology to the AceMedia ontology, the same data can be obtained using the visual descriptions defined in AceMedia.

```
:im247581.jpg rdf:type ma-ont:Image ;
   lire:colorLayout [
      lire:featureVector "[34.0,20.0,28.0,...,13.0]";
      lire:byteArrayRepresentation "[21,6,34,...,13]"
      lire:numberOfCCoeff 6;
      lire:cbCoeff "[24,15,18,17,15,15,16,16,...,16]"
      lire:numberOfYCoeff 21;
      lire:yCoeff "[34,20,28,22,15,23,12,18,...,15]";
      lire:crCoeff "[40,16,11,14,17,13,...,15]" ];
   lire:scalableColor [
      lire:featureVector "[0.0,-9.0,50.0,...,-3.0]";
      lire:byteArrayRepresentation "[0,0,0,0,...,-3]"
      lire:numberOfCoefficients 64;
      lire:haarTransformedHistogram "[-129,57,...,1]"
      lire:numberOfBitplanesDiscarded 0 ];
```

Figure 2 - The descriptions of the visual features of an image

Some mappings require the use of the Jena rule engine, since they cannot be represented with OWL axioms. In Figure 3, we give an example where the property *coefficients* correspond to the property *featureVector* when this last property is defining a property of a *ScalableColor*. Notice that the inference done by the rules listed in Figure 3 cannot be modelled in OWL, namely by the OWL 2 role inclusion chain axioms, because the target is a literal. In Section IV it is explained why rules are important in the Semantic Web stack.

```
(?a lire:scalableColor ?b), (?b lire:featureVector ?c
   -> (?b vdo:coefficients ?c).
```

Figure 3 - Rule example

III. RETRIEVING MULTIMEDIA DATA WITH SPARQL USING JENA

Sparql Protocol And Rdf Query Language(SPARQL) [16] is the language most used in Semantic Web frameworks to query RDF. SPARQL can be employed to express queries across diverse data sources, when the data is stored as RDF. The SPARQL query language is based on matching graph patterns and the results of the queries can be result sets or RDF graphs.

```
PREFIX ma-ont: <https://www.w3.org/ns/ma-ont.rdf#>
SELECT ?x ?z WHERE {
  ?x rdf:type ma-ont:Image .
  ?x lire:scalableColor ?x_sc .
  ?x_sc lire:byteArrayRepresentation ?bx .
  ex:im247581.jpg lire:scalableColor ?y_sc .
  ?y_sc lire:byteArrayRepresentation ?by .
  BIND (lire:SFDistance('ScalableColor', ?bx, ?by)
    as ?z) .
} ORDER BY ?z
```

Figure 4 - SPARQL query example with built-in functions

The Jena framework allows the definition of SPARQL functions to be used in the query engine. A SPARQL value function is an extension point of the SPARQL query language that uses an URI to name a function in the query processor. In this way, we can develop SPARQL functions to perform operations with multimedia data. In Figure 4, we provide a SPARQL query that retrieves the distance of the *ScalableColor* feature of all images to a given image. In all code examples, both the well-know prefixes and the prefix of our ontology, *lire*, are omitted. In this example, *SFDistance* is a custom SPARQL function that calculates the distance between two images, considering the *ScalableColor* feature, represented by its byte array. This custom function developed uses the algorithm of LIRE to calculate distances between images. However, it is very easy to implement other algorithms to calculate the difference between two images and deploy them in the system as custom SPARQL functions.

Jena also provides a Java API, which can be used to create and manipulate RDF graphs. Jena has object classes to represent graphs, resources, properties and literals. In this way, we can retrieve multimedia data in Java programs without SPARQL.

IV. SEMANTIC RULES FOR MULTIMEDIA INFERENCING

It is recognised that OWL has some limitations [17]. To overcome the OWL limitations, semantic rules allow to add expressivity and expertise to our model. SWRL [18] is a proposal for representing rules/axioms for the Semantic Web, implemented by several Semantic Web frameworks. Other Semantic Web frameworks have their own rule formats, e.g., Jena framework with Jena rules [19]. Since SWRL and Jena rules are an extension of the OWL ontology language, they are restricted to unary and binary DL-predicates. In Figure 5, we give an example of how semantic rules can easily encode expert knowledge, where an image is concluded to be a member of a particular concept if some of its features are close to another image that is already classified as representing that concept.

```
(?image rdf:type ?concept) <-
  (?image lire:colorLayout ?cl1),
  (?cl1 lire:byteArrayRepresentation ?b_cl1),
  (?image lire:edgeHistogram ?eh1),
  (?eh1 lire:byteArrayRepresentation ?b_eh1),
  (?image_concept rdf:type ?concept),
  (?concept exa:minDistances ?MinD),
  (?MinD exa:minDistance ?MinD_CL),
  (?MinD_CL exa:featureClass lire:ColorLayout),
  (?MinD_CL exa:value ?min_d_cl),
  (?MinD exa:minDistance ?MinD_EH),
  (?MinD_EH exa:featureClass lire:EdgeHistogram),
  (?MinD_EH exa:value ?min_d_eh),
  (?image_concept lire:colorLayout ?cl2),
  (?cl2 lire:byteArrayRepresentation ?b_cl2),
  (?image_concept lire:edgeHistogram ?eh2),
  (?eh2 lire:byteArrayRepresentation ?b_eh2),
  ColorLayoutDistance(?b_cl1, ?b_cl2, ?Dist_cl),
  EdgeHistogramDistance(?b_eh1, ?b_eh2, ?Dist_eh),
  le(?Dist_cl, ?min_d_cl), le(?Dist_eh, ?min_d_eh).
```

Figure 5 - Semantic rule example

In the example of Figure 5, *ColorLayoutDistance* and *EdgeHistogramDistance* are custom built-in functions, provided via the Jena framework. Both use the algorithm of LIRE to calculate distances between images, as was done previously in SPARQL functions. Therefore, different algorithms can be developed and linked to the system library. In Figure 6, we give a similar example but using the work developed in [20], a system that allows the definition of SPARQL queries on Jena rules, where an image is considered an image from a given concept if there are at least 100 photos to which the features are close enough.

```
(?image rdf:type ?concept) <-
  (?image lire:colorLayout ?cl1),
  (?cl1 lire:byteArrayRepresentation ?b_cl1),
  (?image lire:edgeHistogram ?eh1),
  (?eh1 lire:byteArrayRepresentation ?b_eh1),
  (\\\SPARQL
    SELECT (COUNT(*) AS ?nCnt) WHERE {
      ?image_concept rdf:type ?concept .
      ?concept exa:minDistances ?MinD .
      ?MinD exa:minDistance ?MinD_CL .
      ?MinD_CL exa:featureClass lire:ColorLayout .
      ?MinD_CL exa:value ?min_d_cl .
      ?MinD exa:minDistance ?MinD_EH .
      ?MinD_EH exa:featureClass lire:EdgeHistogram .
      ?MinD_EH exa:value ?min_d_eh .
      ?image_concept lire:colorLayout ?cl2 .
      ?cl2 lire:byteArrayRepresentation ?b_cl2 .
      ?image_concept lire:edgeHistogram ?eh2 .
      ?eh2 lire:byteArrayRepresentation ?b_eh2 .
      BIND (lire:SFDistance('ColorLayout',
        ?b_cl1, ?b_cl2) as ?Dist_cl) .
      BIND (lire:SFDistance('EdgeHistogram',
        ?b_eh1, ?b_eh2) as ?Dist_eh) .
      FILTER (?Dist_cl <= ?min_d_cl) .
      FILTER (?Dist_eh <= ?min_d_eh) . }
  \\\SPARQL),
  ge(?nCnt, 100).
```

Figure 6 - Semantic rule with a SPARQL query

```
(?image rdf:type ?concept) <-
  (?image rdf:type ma-ont:image),
  (?beach_image rdf:type dbp_onto:Beach),
  (?image_concept rdf:type ?concept),
  (?concept exa:minDistances ?MinD),
  (?MinD exa:minDistance ?MinD_CL),
  (?MinD_CL exa:featureClass lire:ColorLayout),
  (?MinD_CL exa:value ?min_d_cl),
  (?MinD exa:minDistance ?MinD_EH),
  (?MinD_EH exa:featureClass lire:EdgeHistogram),
  (?MinD_EH exa:value ?min_d_eh),
  ColorLayoutDistance2(?image, ?beach_image,
    ?Dist_cl),
  EdgeHistogramDistance2(?image, ?beach_image,
    ?Dist_eh),
  le(?Dist_cl, ?min_d_cl),
  le(?Dist_eh, ?min_d_eh).
```

Figure 7 - Semantic rule

In Jena custom built-ins, we can use the Java API which allows to create and manipulate RDF graphs. In this way, high-level functions can be used to retrieve the data necessary to the processing inside the function. It is like a "black box", where the details are hidden. In Figure 7, we give an example based on the previous examples but using built-in functions that receive an image as parameter instead of the lower-level data.

Finally, we present in Figure 8 a rule that infers a set of consequences starting by a set of premises and using built-in functions. In this example, the knowledge base keeps the relation of two images with respect to a given feature (*ColorLayoutDistance*).

```
(?img1 rdf:type ma-ont:Image),
(?img2 rdf:type ma-ont:Image),
ColorLayoutDistance(?img1, ?img2, ?Dist),
makeTemp(?bn) ->
   (?img1 lire:hasRelatedMediaResource ?bn),
   (?bn lire:feature lire:ColorLayout),
   (?bn lire:relatedMediaResource ?img2),
   (?bn lire:distance ?Dist).
```

Figure 8 - Semantic rule

V. CONCLUSIONS AND DISCUSSION

The effectiveness of the Semantic Web technologies in the multimedia field have already been widely reported. In this work, we contribute to support the advantages of using Semantic Web languages and technologies in the multimedia field, through development of a multimedia store and retrieval system in a Semantic Web framework, namely, Jena. We gave some focus to the low-level features and we also used the LIRE system to image processing. We showed how ontologies can meet the store requirements of multimedia objects, with different mechanisms of inference that can be associated with them. It was also shown how a good design of a multimedia ontology can be useful to integrate semantic data of multimedia objects with other systems. We have shown how a powerful language as SPARQL can be useful in data retrieval. To increase the power of data retrieval, we make use of the mechanisms of the Jena framework that allow the development of multimedia custom SPARQL functions. Notice that all knowledge obtained by using the system developed in this work is open, well-known and can be shared. For example, the use of machine learning techniques to annotate multimedia content can provide a relatively powerful method for discovering complex and hidden relationships or mappings. However, it can be difficult to develop and maintain because its effectiveness depends on the design and configuration of multiple variables and options. The relationships discovered between low-level features and semantic descriptions remain hidden and are not able to be examined or manipulated [21]. The knowledge is "closed" and hidden in the systems and these systems are used as "black boxes". We have also shown how semantic rules can increase the expertise of our system. Furthermore, it gives a better expressivity to the developer and the knowledge produced can be reused in other parts of the system or even by other systems. One of the most important purposes of multimedia systems is mapping the data produced by the visual descriptor extraction systems to higher-level semantic terms, such as objects and events. The system developed in our work is tailored to allow multimedia developers to find out these mappings. As a future work, we foresee the development of semantic rules that can represent concepts with low-level features and with a good precision and recall.

REFERENCES

[1] D. J. Duke, L. Hardman, A. G. Hauptmann, D. Paulus, and S. Staab, Eds., Semantic Multimedia, Third International Conference on Semantic and Digital Media Technologies, SAMT 2008, Koblenz, Germany, December 3-5, 2008. Proceedings, ser. Lecture Notes in Computer Science, vol. 5392. Springer, 2008.

[2] R. Troncy, J. van Ossenbruggen, J. Z. Pan, and G. Stamou, "Image annotation on the semantic web," World Wide Web Consortium, Incubator Group Report XGR-image-annotation-20070814, August 2007.

[3] R. Datta, D. Joshi, L. Li, and J. Wang, "Image retrieval: Ideas, influences, and trends of new age," 2008.

[4] C. Ventura, "Image-based query by example using mpeg-7 visual descriptors," Master's thesis, 2010. [Online]. Available: http://upcommons.upc.edu/pfc/handle/2099.1/9453

[5] B. Mcbride, "Jena: A semantic web toolkit," IEEE Internet Computing, vol. 6, no. 6, 2002, pp. 55–59.

[6] M. Lux and S. A. Chatzichristofis, "Lire: Lucene image retrieval: An extensible java cbir library," in Proceedings of the 16th ACM International Conference on Multimedia, ser. MM '08. New York, NY, USA: ACM, 2008, pp. 1085–1088.

[7] M. Lux and O. Marques, "Visual information retrieval using java and lire," Synthesis Lectures on Information Concepts, Retrieval, and Services, vol. 5, no. 1, jan 2013, pp. 1–112 pp.

[8] T. Hofweber, "Logic and ontology," in The Stanford Encyclopedia of Philosophy, spring 2013 ed., E. N. Zalta, Ed., 2013.

[9] P. Salembier and T. Sikora, Introduction to MPEG-7: Multimedia Content Description Interface. John Wiley & Sons, Inc., 2002.

[10] M. C. Suárez-Figueroa, G. A. Atemezing, and O. Corcho, "The landscape of multimedia ontologies in the last decade," Multimedia Tools Appl., vol. 62, no. 2, Jan. 2013, pp. 377–399.

[11] L. Yu, A Developer's Guide to the Semantic Web. Springer, 2011.

[12] S. Bloehdorn, K. Petridis, C. Saathoff, N. Simou, Y. Avrithis, S. H, Y. Kompatsiaris, and M. G. Strintzis, "Semantic annotation of images and videos for multimedia analysis," In Proc. of the 2nd European Semantic Web Conference, ESWC 2005, 2005, pp. 592–607.

[13] J. Hunter, "Adding Multimedia to the Semantic Web - Building an MPEG-7 Ontology," in Proceedings of the 1st International Semantic Web Working Symposium, Stanford, USA, August 2001.

[14] P.-A. Champin, T. Bürger, T. Michel, J. Strassner, W. Lee, W. Bailer, J. Söderberg, F. Stegmaier, J.-P. EVAIN, V. Malaisé, and F. Sasaki, "Ontology for media resources 1.0," W3C, W3C Recommendation, Feb. 2012, http://www.w3.org/TR/2012/REC-mediaont-10-20120209/.

[15] https://github.com/mbentoalves/LIRE_Ontology/blob/master/lire.ttl

[16] E. Prud'hommeaux and A. Seaborne, "SPARQL Query Language for RDF," W3C, Tech. Rep., 2006. [Online]. Available: http://www.w3.org/TR/rdf-sparql-query/

[17] B. Parsia, E. Sirin, B. C. Grau, E. Ruckhaus, and D. Hewlett. Cautiously approaching swrl. Preprint submitted to Elsevier Science. [Online]. Available: http://www.mindswap.org/papers/CautiousSWRL.pdf (2005)

[18] I. Horrocks, P. F. Patel-Schneider, H. Boley, S. Tabet, B. Grosof, and M. Dean, "SWRL: A semantic web rule language combining OWL and RuleML," World Wide Web Consortium, W3C Member Submission, 2004. [Online]. Available: http://www.w3.org/Submission/SWRL

[19] Jena Documentation. Reasoners and rule engines: Jena inference support. [Online]. Available: http://jena.apache.org/documentation/inference/

[20] M. B. Alves, C. V. Damásio, and N. Correia, "SPARQL commands in jena rules," in Knowledge Engineering and Semantic Web - 6th International Conference, KESW 2015, Moscow, Russia, September 30 - October 2, 2015

[21] L. Hollink, S. Little, and J. Hunter, "Evaluating the application of semantic inferencing rules to image annotation," in Proceedings of the 3rd international conference on Knowledge capture, ser. K-CAP '05. New York, NY, USA: ACM, 2005, pp. 91–98.

Inference and Serialization of Latent Graph Schemata Using ShEx

Daniel Fernández-Álvarez*, Jose Emilio Labra-Gayo† and Herminio García-González‡
Department of Computer Science
University of Oviedo
Oviedo, Spain
Email: *danifdezalvarez@gmail.com, †labra@uniovi.es, ‡herminiogg@gmail.com

***Abstract*—Shape Expressions have recently been proposed as a high-level language to intuitively describe and validate the topology of RDF graphs. Current implementations of Shape Expressions are focused on checking which nodes of certain graph fit in which defined schemata, in order to get automatic typings or to improve RDF data quality in terms of completion and consistency. We intend to reverse this process, i.e., we propose to study the neighborhood of graph nodes that have already been typed in order to induce templates in which most of the individuals fit. This will allow to discover latent schemata of existing graphs, which can be used as a guideline for introducing coherent information in existing structures or for quality verification purposes. We consider that collaborative or general-purpose graphs are a specially interesting domain to apply this idea.**

Keywords–Inference, Graph schemata, Shape Expressions, RDF

I. INTRODUCTION

When tackling the task of adding knowledge to an existing RDF (Resource Description Framework) graph it is necessary to know the current topology of the data in order to be consistent with the ontologies already used. The success of this work is directly linked to the degree of coherence, completion and documentation of the targeted graph. Ontologies define the meaning and correct use for each class or property in terms of domain and range, but they are not able to declare how they should be combined in a concrete use in which a node is implementing several roles at a time or offering partial information. In some other contexts, such as XML world, several syntaxes, including RelaxNG[1] and XML Schema[2], cover those needs. Nowadays, there is not a standard syntax equivalent in RDF. However, there are some approaches under development, such as ShEx (Shape Expressions)[3].

Due to that lack of syntax to define how the neighborhood of specific nodes should look like, it is usual to use some SPARQL queries against certain key entities in order to get an approximate idea of local graph shapes and used ontologies. If we are manipulating small structures, maybe oriented to a very specific field of knowledge and possibly created by automatic processes, we may need few example queries. On the other hand, in cases of general-purpose collaborative graphs, finding correct and universal interfaces for certain type of data may be tricky and hard.

We can illustrate this idea using real examples extracted form DBpedia [4]. Precisely, we are going to check how the fact "Barack Obama and John F. Kennedy have studied at Harvard University" is represented. At the moment this paper is being written, Obama's URI in the DBpdia is linked to Harvard's one with the triple of Figure 1. John F. Kennedy is also linked with this node, but using a different property. In addition, the very same reality is expressed with the triples shown in Figure 2.

```
dbr:Harvard_people    dbp:name    dbr:B_Obama
```

Figure 1: Links of B. Obama with Harvard

```
dbr:Harvard_people    dbp:leadfigures    dbr:JFK
dbr:JFK    dbo:almaMater    dbr:Harvard
dbr:JFK    dbp:almaMater    "Harvard"@en
dbr:JFK    dct:subject    dbc:Harvard_alumni
dbr:JFK    rdf:type    yago:HarvardAlumni
```

Figure 2: Links of JFK with Harvard

The information is actually contained in the graph. However, since the same notion has been expressed using too many different ways, it looks hard to design a single SPARQL query for tracking all those individuals that have studied at Harvard.

Our hypothesis is that it is possible to analyze the neighborhood of certain nodes that fit in a condition or few simple conditions, such as a link "dbo:profession dbr:Politician", in order to detect a schema shared by all these nodes. With this, we could obtain latent topologies with certain degree of trustworthiness, that would be helpful for:

- Documentation: guideline to introduce new content.
- Verification of quality: the process of inferring an schema may produce a clear result with a high level of trustworthiness, that would be synonym of a highly coherent graph, or vice versa. Also, once a schema has been human-reviewed and accepted, it can be used to detect errors or inconsistencies across already typed entities.
- Discovering hidden entities: we may find nodes that perfectly fit in a defined shape but are not appropriately typed, which can make them "hidden" to certain SPARQL queries.

We think that our proposal can be applied to any kind of

```
<PoliticianShape> {
    foaf:name   xsd:string ,
    dbr:almaMater   @<UniversityShape>?,
    owl:sameAs   @<PoliticianShape>*
}
```

Figure 3: Politician Shape

graph, but would have special interest in collaborative, general-purpose graphs such as DBpedia or Wikidata [5]. These initiatives are thought to be a massive store of information, growing in unexpected directions with contributions from the community. Because of that, it may be hard to design an expected schema for every possible type of entity. In such structures, the schemata is not planned; there are latent and hidden forms that just emerge with community tendencies and self-moderation. Guiding users' efforts with induced graph topology based on their own actions can be a powerful tool to improve data quality of collaborative graphs.

In section II we will dig into ShEx syntax and possibilities. We will use section III to discuss some approaches for the task of schemata induction. In section IV we will explain the special interest of collaborative graphs. Finally, in section V we present the conclusions of our work.

II. SHEX TO EXPRESS GRAPH TOPOLOGY

There are several proposals under development to describe constraints for RDF graphs topology. We are considering ShEx [3] and we may also consider SHACL (Shapes Constraint Language)[6]. Although they cover similar issues, we are planning to work with ShEx instead of SHACL because it presents a more readable, human-friendly syntax, it offers support for recursive or cyclic data models and it is more grammar-oriented. On the other hand, SHACL follows a more constraint-oriented approach. Nevertheless, core SHACL could also be a valid candidate for this task once its definition is more stable. A ShEx schema is composed of several expressions, called shapes, that specify which are the expected relations that a node of certain type (class) should include. ShEx has already been employed for documentation purposes [7], and some implementations for quality verification against defined shapes have been provided [8], [9].

If we come back to the example of USA presidents and we assume that the most usual way to link a politician with his university is the use of "dbo:almaMater", the resulting shape would look like the one in Figure 3. In order to provide some extra examples of ShEx expressibility, we have made some other assumptions: politician nodes use to have a name specified through "foaf:name" and they are linked to an unbound number of equivalent DBpedia entries of type politician through "owl:sameAs".

III. TECHNICAL DISCUSSION

XML shares some distinguishing features with RDF. Both of them can be employed to define data structures (tree-like in case of XML and graph-like in the case of RDF) with an unbounded number of possible node types. The XML community has already faced the described issues of schema specification, inference and verification. Syntaxes such as RelaxNg [1] and XML Schema [2] are handy to define the expected form and constraints of an XML document. At the same time, there are several tools that effectively check if a certain document fits in a given schema. ShEx syntax and their implementations have been thought to cover those needs for RDF and so, they could be applied in the same scenarios.

The problem of inferring a latent schema for an XML document and expressing it in some of the mentioned syntaxes has been studied in the past decade [10]. RDF world is yet a step back in that sense, since both ShEx and SHACL are recent proposals. However, the problem of exploring RDF graphs in order to induce latent or hidden structures is not new. Several works in the last years have provided techniques and frameworks that are able to find commonly used ontology elements across big RDF datasets, to discover logical axioms for type inference or even to induce common shapes of a class or type of element.

In [11], a framework for ontology learning is presented. This approach uses mining graph algorithms and machine learning techniques to extract, among other notions, which are the core or most usual properties associated with a certain class. Their main goal is to integrate ontologies of several datasets in order to find shared core elements.

In [12], an approach to extract graph schemata from large RDF datasets is presented. Association rule mining is used to induce non trivial axioms of logical descriptions relative to TBox (terminological box) knowledge. Those axioms are expressed with the EL profile of the Web Ontology Language OWL 2, which is based on the description logic $\mathcal{EL}^{++}$ [13]. Through this, the authors are able to extract graph schemata at ontology-level in a fully automatic manner.

In [14] a framework to discover common properties in clusters of individuals of an RDF graph is described. Each cluster, in an ideal situation, is identified with a class. The clusters are explored in order to detect properties widely used, which allows to elaborate descriptions of the clusters themselves and to detect domain and range restrictions when linking two instances of different classes in a general schema. This approach shares with ours the fact that is more class-centered (aka shape-centered) instead of ontology-centered. However, the results obtained are expressed in an ad-hoc syntax, less expressive compared with ShEx.

At this stage, we think we need further investigation in order to decide which are the techniques that may work better to achieve our goals. Several challenges will be faced, some of which linked to the targeted source, including graph size, adaptation to data model or noise management. However, we consider that the mentioned work proves that it is feasible to induce latent structures in RDF datasets, even when dealing with huge graphs such as DBpedia. The techniques that they employ, including association rule mining or instance clustering, may be appropriate approaches to cover most of our requirements for schema inference.

IV. SPECIAL CASE OF COLLABORATIVE GRAPHS

General purpose and collaborative graphs are study cases where this proposal could be specially well exploited. Since they grow with unpredictable community contributions, the latent schemata may also vary in time depending on the users' agreement on the use of certain properties. Trying to limit the possible links between nodes by forcing them to fit in safe inferred shapes may be a wrong idea since it cuts the freedom philosophy that underlies this kind of initiatives. However, ShEx can be useful as a mechanism to guide this evolution.

In addition, the changeable and entropic nature of these graphs generates scenarios that support hypothesis which may make less sense in more constrained contexts. From a purist point of view, it may be desirable to obtain non-overlapped shapes of each existing class. For instance, a priori, it looks obvious that the shape of graduate should tell how to properly establish a relation between a person and his alma mater. Meanwhile, the shape of politician may indicate how to link someone to a political party. With this, if a user wants to add information about an entity that implements both roles at a time, such as B. Obama, he should look for two different shapes in order to discover the appropriate way to express these two pieces of information. Because of that, it may be interesting to discover "which information is associated in this context to entities of certain type" instead of "which information must be necessarily associated to a certain type". It could happen that most of the politicians have higher education. If a common property used to link politicians and universities is discovered and appears in the latent schema of the shape politician, the user who wants to add studies to certain politician would not need to query different shapes.

It even may be feasible to elaborate schema inference on users' demand to obtain a view of the state of a shape in nearly real-time. This could be done analyzing a representative set of entities of certain type. A periodical checking of the inferred schema, or an automatic update triggered by a significant number of modifications/additions would also reflect the nature of these graphs.

V. Conclusions

We propose to apply automatic schema inference over existing RDF graphs in order to discover latent structures. Our aim is to create automatic graph documentation and to provide the basis for a tool able to check data completion and coherence using ShEx syntax.

We consider collaborative general-purpose graphs, such as DBpedia or Wikidata, an specially interesting scenario to apply this idea, since it is hardly possible to design graph shapes a priori. The schemata just emerge and evolve with the community's efforts.

References

[1] E. van der Vlist, Relax NG: A Simpler Schema Language for XML. Beijing: O'Reilly, 2004.

[2] S. Gao, C. M. Sperberg-McQueen, H. S. Thompson, N. Mendelsohn, D. Beech, and M. Maloney, "W3c xml schema definition language (xsd) 1.1 part 1: Structures," W3C Candidate Recommendation, vol. 30, no. 7.2, 2009.

[3] E. Prud'hommeaux, J. E. Labra Gayo, and H. Solbrig, "Shape expressions: an rdf validation and transformation language," in Proceedings of the 10th International Conference on Semantic Systems. ACM, 2014, pp. 32–40.

[4] J. Lehmann, R. Isele, M. Jakob, A. Jentzsch, D. Kontokostas, P. N. Mendes, S. Hellmann, M. Morsey, P. van Kleef, S. Auer, and Others, "DBpedia–a large-scale, multilingual knowledge base extracted from Wikipedia," Semantic Web, vol. 6, no. 2, 2015, pp. 167–195.

[5] D. Vrandečić and M. Krötzsch, "Wikidata: a free collaborative knowledgebase," Communications of the ACM, vol. 57, no. 10, 2014, pp. 78–85.

[6] A. Ryman, "Z specification for the w3c editor's draft core shacl semantics," arXiv preprint arXiv:1511.00384, 2015.

[7] J. E. L. Gayo, E. Prud'hommeaux, H. R. Solbrig, and J. M. Á. Rodríguez, "Validating and describing linked data portals using rdf shape expressions." in LDQ@ SEMANTICS. Citeseer, 2014.

[8] https://www.w3.org/2013/ShEx/FancyShExDemo, accessed: 2016-01-10.

[9] http://rdfshape.weso.es, accessed: 2016-01-10.

[10] G. J. Bex, F. Neven, and S. Vansummeren, "Inferring xml schema definitions from xml data," in Proceedings of the 33rd international conference on Very large data bases. VLDB Endowment, 2007, pp. 998–1009.

[11] L. Zhao and R. Ichise, "Instance-based ontological knowledge acquisition," in The Semantic Web: Semantics and Big Data. Springer, 2013, pp. 155–169.

[12] J. Völker and M. Niepert, "Statistical schema induction," in Extended Semantic Web Conference. Springer, 2011, pp. 124–138.

[13] F. Baader, S. Brandt, and C. Lutz, "Pushing the el envelope," in IJCAI, vol. 5, 2005, pp. 364–369.

[14] K. Christodoulou, N. W. Paton, and A. A. Fernandes, "Structure inference for linked data sources using clustering," in Transactions on Large-Scale Data-and Knowledge-Centered Systems XIX. Springer, 2015, pp. 1–25.

Cyber-Physical System for Gait Analysis and Fall Risk Evaluation by Embedded Cortico-muscular Coupling Computing

V. F. Annese, G. Mezzina, D. De Venuto,
Politecnico di Bari, Dept. of Electrical and Information Engineering (DEI)
Via Orabona 4, 70125 Bari – Italy
{valeriofrancesco.annese, daniela.devenuto}@poliba.it; g.mezzina23@gmail.com

Abstract— **The paper describes the architecture of a non-invasive, wireless embedded system for gait analysis and preventing involuntary movements including falls. The system operates with synchronized and digitized data samples from 8 EMG (limbs) and 8 EEG (motor-cortex) channels. An embedded Altera Cyclone V FPGA operates the real-time signal pre-processing and the computation (resource utilization: 85.95% ALMs, 43283 ALUTs, 73.0% registers, 9.9% block memory; processing latency < 1ms). The system has been tested on patients affected by Parkinson disease (PD) under physician guide and compared with healthy subjects' results. Both PD and healthy subjects have been involved in the standard diagnostic protocol (normal gait and pull test). The developed cyber-physical system detects differences between the PD and the healthy subjects in terms of walking pattern, i.e., agonist-antagonist co-contractions (Typ time: PD's 148ms vs Healthy 88ms; Max: PD's 388ms vs Healthy 314ms). The PD's cerebral Movement Related Potentials (i.e., Bereitschaft) analysis during the pull-test showed an increasing from 59dBμ to 66dBμ after 3 settling steps while measurements on healthy subject return, respectively, 57dBμ, 62dBμ in 1 settling step. The system is able to prevent fall enabling the actuator in 168ms, i.e., better than the normal human time reaction (300ms).**

Keywords-Fall prevention; EEG; EMG; MRPs; FPGA.

I. INTRODUCTION

Due to neurological diseases, muscular deformities, ageing and further numerous factors, the normal gait frequently tends to degenerate into gait disorders. They constitute a contributive intrinsic falling cause, heavily increasing the risk of falling. Nowadays, 28–35% of people aged 65 years and above fall and, as consequence, each year more than 424000 fall events are fatal [1][2]. The economic impact of this phenomenon is impressive: 43.8 billion dollars are estimated to be used in fall-related medical care expenditures by 2020 [3]. Despite the extensive research in this field, developed tools for fall risk have not been successful in predicting and preventing falls [3]. Indeed, although fall detection technology is now mature (detectors for domestic use can be implemented using artificial vision techniques, tri-axial gyroscopes and accelerometers, Microsoft Kinect's infrared sensors, floor vibrations and sounds and numerous others) [4], fall prevention solutions are still far to be implemented. Fall prevention systems can be mainly divided into four categories: static fall-risk assessment, pre-fall intervention, fall-injury prevention and fall prevention [5][6]. The static fall-risk assessment category includes all the protocolled clinical tools which aim to identify people with high fall-risk due to neuro-muscular diseases (i.e., Barthel Index [7], the TGBA index [8], STRATIFY [9], TUG [10]). The static fall-risk assessment tools are indispensable for the beginning of a drug/rehabilitation plan but do not perform any intervention for preventing falls. The pre-fall intervention category includes all the methods oriented to the improvement of balance, stability and muscular strength of the subject. In recent years, in order to create more appealing exercises, assistive technology has been successfully implemented to drive the patients into a kind of game-exercise (i.e., Microsoft Kinect, Nintendo Wii, VR tools [11][12]). They can be part of a wider preventive plan but they cannot constitute a standalone solution since they do not limit the consequent damage of a fall. The fall-injury prevention category groups all the technologies implementing a shock absorber when a fall event is detected. Those systems are made up by the fall detection system and by the actuator, which timely manage the shock absorber. The shock absorption is conducted by an airbag that is promptly inflated. Toshiyo et al. [13] present a system protection against impact with the ground using accelerometers and gyroscopes for the fall detection and a jacket-worn airbag to be timely inflated before the impact. These systems, although reduce effectively the damage due to the fall, fail to cover all the scenarios and do not limit the brain damage associated with it (i.e., fair of falling). The fall prevention category aims to definitively avoid the fall event [14-17]. In [14], Zeilig et al., describe a fall prevention system named "ReWalk" consisting of a multi-sensing platform (blood pressure, ECG, etc.) for fall detection combined to an exoskeleton to assist the movement of the subject. Vuillerme et al. [15] propose to use a combination of pressure sensors and electro-tactile biofeedback to prevent the fall. Additionally, Munro et al. [16] describe a fall prevention tool based on an intelligent wearable knee flexion controller. These systems are the most suitable for fall prevention since if a fall event is detected, a feedback aiming to correct the movement is delivered to the subject and the fall is avoided. In this frame, we propose a novel digital back-end architecture for fall prediction in the everyday life. The architecture, implemented on a field programmable gate array (FPGA), combines both electroencephalography (EEG) and electromyography to take decision for processing and eventual corrective actions on the muscles. To the best of our knowledge, our architecture is the first fully implemented cyber-physical system, which allows fall prevention by real-time processing of coupled EMG and EEG.

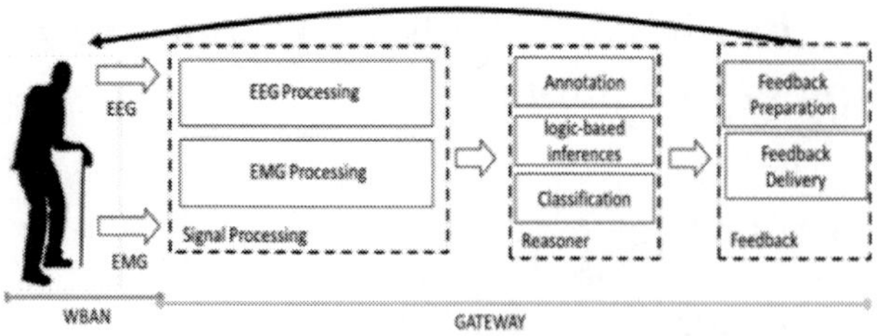

Figure 1. Architecture of the proposed system.

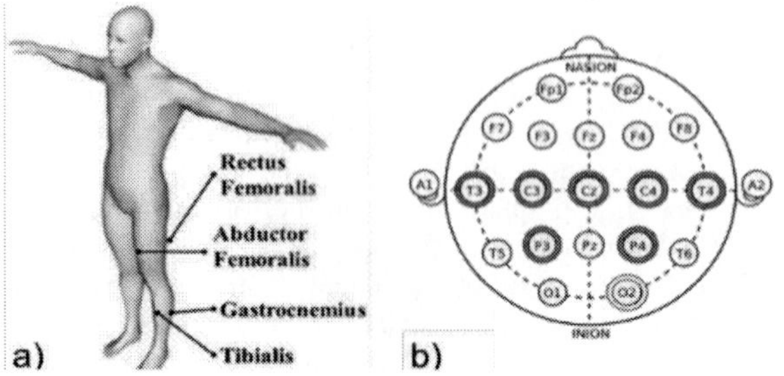

Figure 2. EMG (a) and EEG (b) electrodes setting

The paper is structured as follows. Section II introduces basic medical knowledge for the fall prediction. Section III discusses the cyber-physical system architecture. Section IV presents experimental data from a Parkinson's diseased (PD) patient and a healthy subject.

II. Medical Background

Literature studies demonstrate the possibility to predict a fall by a combined analysis of muscular movement (EMG) and its brain pre-processing (EEG) by monitoring EEG Movement Related Potentials (MRP) anticipating muscle activations [1-4, 17-18]. Currently none of the above remarked solutions enables such analysis: indeed only partial solutions have been proposed in literature. In fact, some systems measure individually EEG or EMG; others measure both of them, but only on a few EEG/EMG electrodes without relative synchronization, using an external clock and delivering filtered data to be post-processed and not handled in real time [19]. We mainly focus on Bereitschaftspotential (BP), μ and β rhythms that can be detected in the motor-cortex area even one second before the muscle activation in the band of 2–5Hz, 7–12Hz, and 13–30Hz respectively. In movement disorders, mobility impairment is indicated by an altered modulation of the MRPs as well as a mismatch between the MRPs and the movement. EMG data are processed in parallel, aiming to evaluate the co-contraction time among agonist-antagonist muscles. The co-contraction time is the period during which an agonist and antagonist muscles (i.e., Gastrocnemius and Tibialis) are contracted at the same time. During normal gait where agonist and antagonist muscles are alternately activated, the co-contraction time is low (< 300ms) and depends on the particular subject. High EMG co-contraction time during gait (larger than 500/600ms depending on the subject) is a significant index of unbalance and instability. According to [20], a reaction time of 300ms or lower returns a probability $p < 0.01$ of falling. Therefore, if the system reacts within this time limit and delivers a corrective action, the fall can be avoided.

III. The Cyber-Physical System

The high-level architecture of the cyber-physical system is outlined in Fig. 1. The wireless body area network (WBAN) allows synchronized collection of EEG and EMG. Eight EEG (according to the international 10-20 system T3, T4, C3, C4, CZ, P3, P4, O2, – 500Hz and 24bit resolution) and as many EMG channels (Gastrocnemius, Tibialis, Rectus and Biceps Femoralis of both the legs – 500Hz sampling rate and 16bit resolution [21]) are collected by a wireless and wearable recording systems, and sent to a gateway as shown in Fig. 2. The signal processing is performed on an FPGA. Signal processing outcomes are subsequently passed to a reasoner, which detect critical situation by analyzing EEG, EMG, inertial sensor data, environment and clinical condition information. When a potential fall is detected, a feedback is generated and delivered to the subject. The global vision of the project includes the electrical stimulation of the antagonist limb muscles in order to favor the postural correction, drastically reducing the probability of fall. The electrostimulation sub-system is part of our future works.

A. *High-Level Algorithm Description*

EMG and EEG follow two different processing branches. A trigger signal is extracted from EMG raw data using a dynamic-threshold approach. The trigger signal is computed as follows. First, the EMG signal is rectified, squared and stored in an M samples shift-register (in our algorithm $M = 512$, that is 1s data). The mean value of all register samples (global average) is therefore directly the EMG power in the M samples window and it is used as threshold. A second mean value (local average) is computed on the last N samples (i.e., corresponding to just a part of the complete M samples shift register, being $N<M$, in our design $N = 128$) and compared with the threshold. As a new EMG sample arrives, both global and local average are refreshed, making the thresholding scheme dynamic. The EMG trigger rises and stays high only if the local power is larger than the dynamic global average threshold. This approach heavily compresses the EMG signals, providing and unambiguous muscle activation signal (only 1bit trigger signal per muscle). For the EEG part running in parallel with respect to the EMG one, the time-frequency analysis is run on seven motor-cortex channels only (T3, T4, C3, C4, CZ, P3, P4), while the occipital one (O2) is used for noise reduction. As soon as new EEG samples arrive, data are stored in a 256 samples register. When a coupled EMG rising edge is detected, a 256 points 24bit resolution Fast Fourier Transform (FFT) is computed on the previous 256 EEG samples stored into the register. The cortical involvement is opposite with respect to the movement performed: if a right limb movement is detected (right

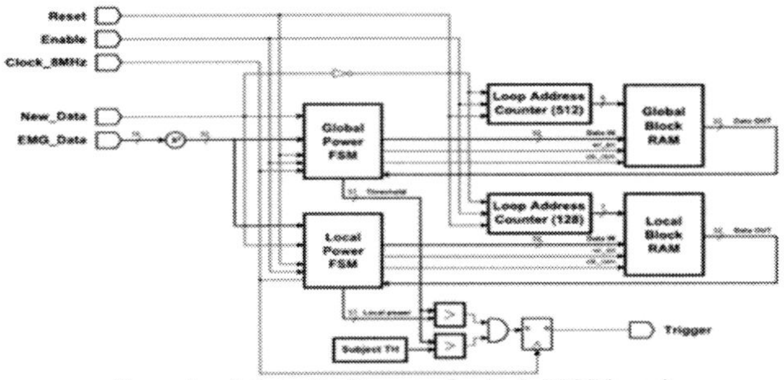

Figure 3. Schematic diagram of a single EMG branch

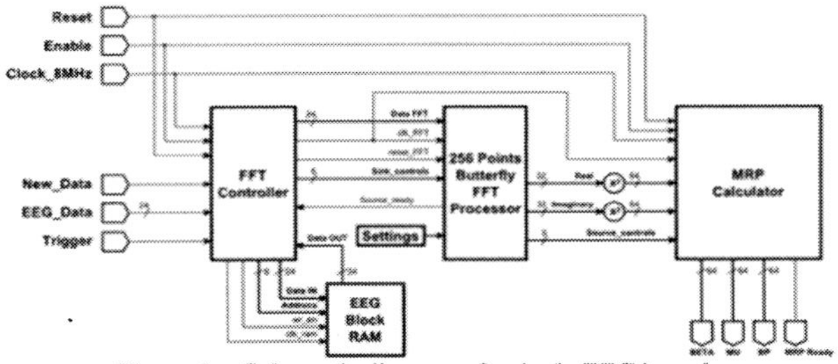

Figure 4. Schematic diagram of a single EEG branch

Gastrocnemius), the analysis is performed on left motor-cortex channels (Cz, C3, T3, P3) and vice versa (left Gastrocnemius triggers Cz, C4, T4, P4, note that since Cz is a central channel is triggered by both). The FFT output data are processed to compute the square magnitude and the appropriate frequency components summed in order to calculate the spectral powers in the MRPs bands. When the EMG trigger arrives, the EEG power levels in the MRPs band are referred to approximately 500ms before the movement occurs. The obtained power levels for each EEG channel are then compared to fixed thresholds (which need to be trimmed on the subject) in order to evaluate the voluntariness of the EMG contraction. Thresholds are customized on the individual after a period of learning (the subjects were asked to rest for 1 minute).

B. FPGA Architecture: Processor System-level Design

In the aim of a future ASIC implementation, the architecture has been validated on a FPGA (Altera Cyclone V). A more detailed description of the FPGA implementation has been presented in [21][22]. The input-output interface of our design is characterized by:16 bio-signals inputs (eight 16bit EMG and eight 24bit EEG); 25 outputs (BP, μ and β 1bit flags for the seven EEG motor-cortex channels and 4 co-contraction 1bit signals). The System clock is set to 8.19209MHz (signal 8 MHz CLK), obtained with an on-chip Phase-Locked Loop (PLL, block named PLL) from the embedded 50MHz oscillator (50 MHz CLK). The global signals of the whole implementation are: Reset, an asynchronous reset (derived from the Reset KEY input) ; Enable SW, an enable signal which freezes the processing; 500Hz CLK, an input data clock signal from the EMG and EEG channels (500Hz frequency); 8 MHz CLK, a 8.19209MHz system clock obtained by the on-chip PLL. In the complete system, 8 EMG and 7 EEG processing branches are replicated in parallel on the FPGA. In the following sub-section, we summarize the processing data path for a generic combined [21][22].

EMG Processing Branch (see Fig. 3). Incoming squared EMG samples passed to two FSMs, Global Power FSM and Local Power FSM, to calculate in parallel, respectively, the dynamic threshold (global power) and the local power. Based on two block RAM (Global Threshold and Local Threshold Block RAM of M = 512 and N = 128, 32bit words), when a new EMG sample arrives (500Hz CLK = '1') the last inserted sample is pointed and "pop" (512th and 128th for, respectively, Global Power and Local Power Block RAM). Then, the read sample is subtracted and the new sample is added to refresh the overall power Sum within the window. An asynchronous 64bit comparator (>) compares the powers calculated in parallel by the two blocks (THR and Local THR). Local THR is also compared to a fixed threshold (evaluated on the subject resting) that prevents unpredictable behavior due to noise when the subject stops walking. The output of the comparator is the 1bit EMG trigger (signal Trigger), used both in the EEG computation to enable the time-frequency analysis and in the co-contraction calculation. The co-contraction signal is obtained by computing an AND logic operation on agonist-antagonist coupled muscles. The adopted approach allows the efficient calculation of the powers in the desired windows, without necessarily having to re-compute, at each 8MHz clock rising edge, the overall sum of the RAMs.

EEG Processing Branch (see Fig. 4). The EEG branch comprises a 256 points 24bit resolution FFT processor based on a butterfly structure [24, 25]. The 256 EEG samples to be transformed are dynamically stored in a 256 24bit words RAM(EEG Block RAM) addressed by a loop address counter in the FFT Controller. When EMG Trigger rises to '1', the 256 samples stored into the RAM are passed the FFT block by properly temporizing the Sink_controls signals through a series of dedicated states. After data is sent and validated (Source_controls), the FSM waits for another Trigger rising edge to repeat the sequencing. The FFT output data is interpreted by the MRP Calculator where they are squared and opportunely summed (both real and imaginary parts) using a 64bit adder in order to extract the BP, μ and β powers, in natural units (BP, MU, BETA signals). Finally, when MRP Ready is asserted, BP, μ and β are compared to fixed thresholds related to the subject, preloaded on the FPGA.

C. The Reasoner

The decision algorithm is based on the annotation of EMG/EEG wireless wearable electrodes signals and on the application of logic-based inferences in order to classify fall patterns and calculate a response for feedback delivery.

EMG co-contractions, EEG MRPs and data acquired from an inertial sensor are used to distinguish when a fall is starting and to trigger the further processing steps. The environmental conditions and the medical history of the patient are taken into account. The reasoner has been already developed in previous works: a more detailed description of the semantic matchmaking algorithm is reported in [19].

IV. RESULTS

Experimental results on healthy subjects have been already presented in [21-23, 25, 31-33]. In the present paper, we propose a dataset including EEG/EMG recordings of a subject affected by Parkinson disease (PD) and a healthy one, both performing natural gait (120s) and 'pull tests' [26]. Those tests are performed in a controlled environment (local hospital), under the supervision of specialized staff. The use of the proposed system in these analyses provides a systematic and objective quantification of diagnostic indexes. Overall, the worst case power consumption (when unrealistically all blocks are simultaneously operating) can be estimated as 150mW, which is a feasible upper bound for portable applications [21, 24, 28, 29]. The system is able to deliver the corrective action in 168ms well within the 300ms time limit (data collection: 14ms; data processing: 42ms; reasoning: 12ms; feedback: 100ms) [19].

A. *Cyber-Physiscal System Performance*

The FPGA system implementation with 16 bio-signals inputs and 25 outputs requires 81.7% ALMs (arithmetic logic module), 44808 ALUTs, 73.4% registers, 10.3% block memory of the available resources. FPGA results present a mean relative error of 0.01% if compared with Matlab outcomes on the same dataset. The most power hungry part of the system is the FFT. In a 180nm CMOS ASIC, a 16bit butterfly 256 points FFT at 4MHz would consume about 13mW during continuous operation including block RAM, which at 4MHz would consume approximately 1mW [27].

B. *Experimental Results: Gait Analysis*

For the gait analysis, the subjects are asked to perform a natural and fluid walk. The results are summarized in table I, which reports, from the top of the table, the failure rate of the EMG trigger generation, maximum, typical and number/second co-contractions, limb muscles activation/deactivation and their ratio (duty cycle) during a single step. Table I distinctly shows the parameters for PD and healthy subjects. The results quantify the differences between the PD and the healthy subjects in terms of walking patterns.

i. The EMG trigger failure rate to detect EMG contraction is only 0.07% (worst-case).

ii. The Haste rate (HR), defined as number of co-contractions (ccs) per second, is 1.17 ccs/s for the PD subject against 0.44 ccs/s for a healthy subject: co-contractions are more frequent in PD than the healthy.

iii. Typical co-contraction times show an increase of 58ms (average value on all the four muscles couples) between PD subject and healthy one with greater incidence on the right leg (Δt=+120ms on R.Gast-R. Tib and Δt=+90ms on R. Bic – R. Rect): the co-contraction times are, on average, higher in PD than the healthy during gait.

iv. The maximum co-contraction time for the PD subject is higher for all the muscles if compared with the healthy subject (e.g. PD Max= 756ms and Healthy Max=548ms on L. Rect-L. Bic). The maximum co-contraction time is higher in PD than the healthy during gait.

v. On single muscle, PD subject shows contraction times that cover, on average, the 48.56% of the step time length. The healthy subject returns a value of 33.62%. The PD outlines muscular hyperactivity during gait. During normal gait, no significant differences on MRPs were found.

Indeed, both subjects present a BP that ranges from 58-65 dBμ, μ-rhythm ranges from 51-55 dBμ and β-rhythm sweeps between 41-44 dBμ. However, considering the BP, evident differences have been highlighted in both subjects between the state of resting and the time slot preceding the step. Considering the healthy subject, in the resting state the BP mean value was 49±4.6 dBμ while before a step the BP mean value reached 60.8±6.4 dBμ (see Fig. 5). The difference of the walking patterns is also evident from the diagram presented in Fig. 6, on which is reported a BP vs. co-contraction times plot for PD (in blue) and healthy (in red) subjects is shown. For clarity, the shown co-contraction times are computed on the left gastrocnemius/tibialis pair while the shown BP are referred to the right-motor

TABLE I. GAIT ANALYSIS OF A PD AND A HEALTHY SUBJECT ACHIEVED BY THE PROPOSED CYBER-PHYSISCAL SYSTEM

PARKINSON'S DISEASED SUBJECT								
	L REC	L BIC	R TIB	R GAS	L TIB	L GAS	R REC	R BIC
Detection fails (%)	0.03	0.07	0.07	0.02	0.06	0.01	0.02	0.07
Co- contractions								
Max (ms)	756		630		446		640	
Typ (ms)	265.3±120.4		260.4±136		127.5±94		336.0±84	
Haste rate (num/s)	1,53 (184/120)		1,1 (132/120)		1.07 (129/120)		0,99 (119/120)	
Contractions								
Active (ms)	381±1 38	434±1 97	553±2 59	381±8 6	285±1 51	462±8 0	352±1 41	426±7 7
Deactive (ms)	232±1 24	329±1 57	260±1 29	696±1 39	997±3 66	637±1 53	208±1 23	673±1 10
Duty cycle (%)	62.2	56.9	68.0	35.4	22.3	42.1	62.8	38,8

HEALTHY SUBJECT								
	L REC	L BIC	R TIB	R GAS	L TIB	L GAS	R REC	R BIC
Detection fails (%)	0.02	0.03	0.06	0.02	0.04	0.01	0.02	0.03
Co- contractions								
Max (ms)	548		364		270		542	
Typ (ms)	268±138		140±103		100±55		246±140	
Haste rate (Num/s)	0.68 (82/120)		0.25 (30/120)		0.25 (30/120)		0.59 (71/120)	
Contractions								
Active (ms)	353 ±129	509 ±197	575 ±208	383 ±170	566 ±255	445 ±110	330 ±142	497 ±182
Deactive (ms)	1179 ±650	788 ±361	633 ±282	868 ±392	949 ±266	1010 ±228	1127 ±470	814 ±369
Duty cycle (%)	23.0	39.2	47.6	30.6	37.4	30.6	22.7	37.9

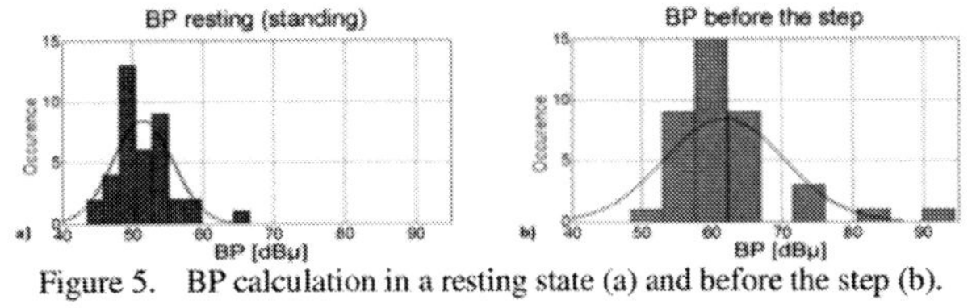

Figure 5. BP calculation in a resting state (a) and before the step (b).

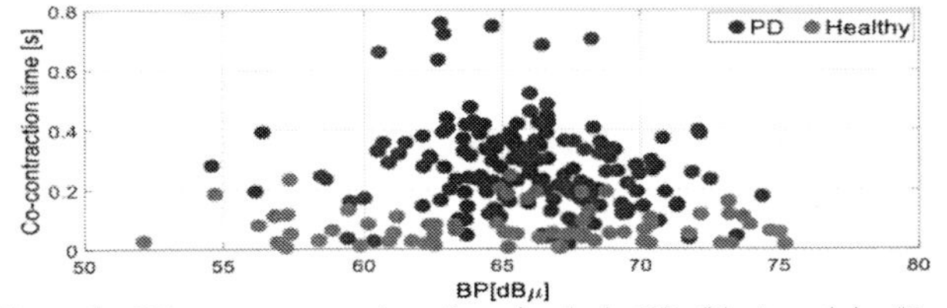

Figure 6. BP vs co-contraction time for both PD (blue) and healthy subjects (red).

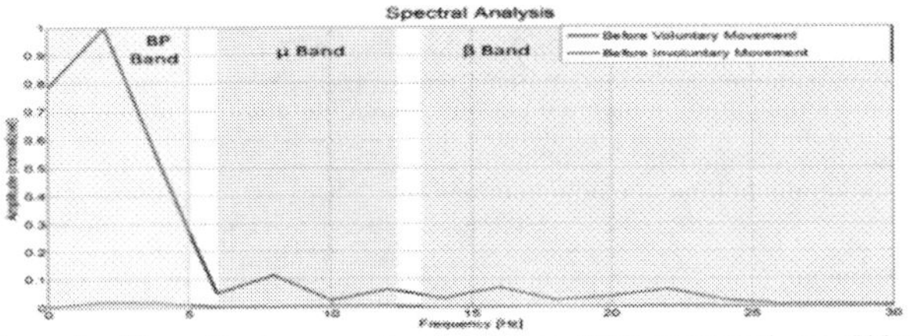

Figure 7. Normalized comparison between FFT computed on 500ms before a voluntary (blue) and involuntary (red) movement on Cz.

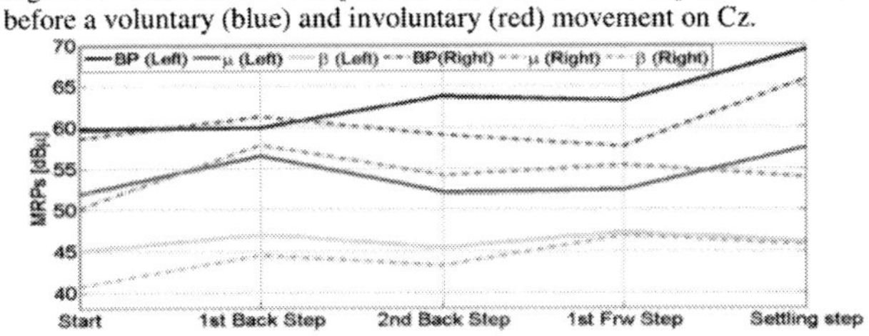

Figure 8. Demonstrative evidence of MRP power levels increment in the PD patient in order to recovery his stability.

TABLE II. MRPS AND CO-CONTRACTION VALUES DURING PULL TEST

	START PULL TEST		1ST UNBALANCED STEP		2ND UNBALANCED STEP		1ST RECOVERY STEP		2ND RECOVERY STEP	
MRPs ON PARKINSON'S SUBJECT										
	R	L	R	L	R	L	R	L	R	L
BP(dBμ)	62.8	59.9	65	62.4	66	66.3	69.3	66	66	68.2
μ (dBμ)	49.6	54	54.5	54.7	55.4	55.7	55.8	57.9	57.6	59.5
β (dBμ)	46.06	45.6	46.33	44.26	48.16	43.7	44.58	47.9	46.27	47
MRPs ON HEALTHY SUBJECT										
	R	L	R	L	R	L	R	L	R	L
BP(dBμ)	58.40	56.40	-	-	-	-	69.20	64.20	-	-
μ (dBμ)	47.30	52.20	-	-	-	-	53.07	58.40	-	-
β (dBμ)	42.70	38.08	-	-	-	-	44.23	44.12	-	-
CO-CONTRACTIONS ON PARKINSON'S DISEASED SUBJECT DURING PULL TEST										
Max (ms)	L. RECT – L. BICEP		R. TIB – R. GAST			L. TIB – L. GAST		R. RECT – R. BICEP		
	751		462			598.6		1060.6		
CO-CONTRACTIONS ON HEALTHY SUBJECT DURING PULL TEST										
Max (ms)	L. RECT – L. BICEP		R. TIB – R. GAST			L. TIB – L. GAST		R. RECT – R. BICEP		
	549		370			284		568		

channels average. The analysis demonstrates that, while for the MRPs similar results are obtained for both subjects, the co-contractions for the PD subject are more frequent and reach values much higher in comparison with the healthy subject. In Fig. 7, a comparison between the EEG spectra computed before a voluntary movement (in blue) and before an involuntary movement (in red) are compared. The spectra are normalized. Considering the bands of interest (BP, μ and β), the power computed in the BP band during a voluntary movement is more than 100 times higher than the one calculated during an involuntary one. Similarly, the μ and β powers are about 10 times higher during a voluntary movement.

C. *Experimental Results: Pull Test*

The postural stability is tested in specialized centers by the "pull test" protocol [26]. During this test, the neurologist gives a moderately forceful backwards tug on the standing individual and observes how the person recovers his stability. The normal response is one or more quick backwards steps to prevent a fall. Usually during this test, the physician associates a numeric index basing on the subject response. Using the proposed cyber-physical system, we were able to quantify the instability of the subject and his intentionality in the stability recovery by MRPs. Pull test results for both PD and healthy subjects are summarized in Table II, which includes MRPs for both right (R) and left (L) EEG channels and the maximum co-contraction value reached. The EMG triggers analysis highlights that, when the sudden unbalancing is externally induced from the operator, PD subject reacted with four step. Two of these are backward, while two forward, until complete settling. The healthy subject reacted to the unbalancing with a single settling step. PD subject co-contractions in pull test increase, on average, of 98.75ms in comparison with gait's values. The healthy subject co-contraction values show no relevant change with an increase of 11.75ms. The PD subject co-contraction maximum value was 1.06s and was recorded on right biceps-rectus Femoralis. The MRPs have an interesting behavior when the sudden unbalancing happens. For the PD subject, MRPs increase their initial value (that sweep between 59.9-62.8dBμ) of 6.5dBμ on right EEG channels and 6dBμ on left ones. The increase is distributed over the steps showing the recovery of voluntariness during the movements. The healthy subject showed an initial range of 56.4-58.4dBμ and reached 64.2 dBμ (increase of 7.8 dBμ) and 69.2dBμ (increase of 7.8 dBμ) on left and right EEG channels respectively. The MRPs evolution during a single entire pull test for the PD subject is presented in Fig. 8. When the unbalance is externally induced, the recorded MRPs values are comparable to the resting values. However, in the subsequent recovery steps the MRPs increase both on right (ΔBP = +11.9% ; $\Delta\mu$ =5.5% ; $\Delta\beta$ = + 11.1%) and left (ΔBP = +14.3% ; $\Delta\mu$ = +8.8% ; $\Delta\beta$ = +2.2%) EEG channels.

V. CONCLUSION

In this work, a cyber-physical system for gait analysis and fall risk evaluation has been presented. EEG/EMG wireless nodes for real-time synchronous data collection make up the system. The system is able to evaluate different indexes, in order to establish the coupling between brain activity and movement, leading to the assessment of the intentionality level of a muscle contraction. An FPGA

(Altera Cyclone V) implementation, including test and validation of the system has been presented. The FPGA results show low residual numerical error (0.012%) if compared to Matlab ones and the maximum power consumption is of about 150mW. A further stage of semantic matchmaking collects, interprets and contextualizes the processed data. In this article, the system has been tested on a subject affected by the Parkinson's syndrome and on a healthy subject performing a natural gait and pull tests [28]. The system is able to detect critical conditions in 168ms (data collection: 14ms; data processing: 42ms; reasoning: 12ms; feedback: 100ms), within the 300ms, i.e., the standard time limit to avoid the fall [23].

REFERENCES

[1] World Health Organization. "Neurological Disorders. Public health challenges", Report., 2006

[2] M.E. Tinetti "Preventing falls in elderly persons", New England journal of medicine", 348.1:42–49, 2003.

[3] D. Oliver. "Falls risk-prediction tools for hospital inpatients. Time to put them to bed", Age Ageing, 37:248–50, 2008.

[4] Y. S. Delahoz et al. "Survey on fall detection and fall prevention using wearable and external sensors", Sensors: 19806–19842, 2014.

[5] M. De Tommaso, E. Vecchio, K. Ricci, A. Montemurno, D. De Venuto, V. F. Annese. "Combined EEG/EMG evaluation during a novel dual task paradigm for gait analysis." Proceedings - 2015 6th IEEE International Workshop on Advances in Sensors and Interfaces, IWASI 2015, art. no. 7184949, pp. 181-186. DOI: 10.1109/IWASI.2015.7184949. 2015.

[6] D. De Venuto and A.S. Vincentelli. "Dr. Frankenstein's dream made possible: Implanted electronic devices" Proceedings -Design, Automation and Test in Europe, DATE, art. no. 6513757, pp. 1531-1536. 2013.

[7] C. Collin et al. "The Barthel ADL Index: a reliability study." International disability studies. 2009.

[8] S. L. Vaught "Gait, balance, and fall prevention." The Ochsner Journal 3.2: 94-97. 2011.

[9] D. Oliver et al. "A systematic review and meta-analysis of studies using the STRATIFY tool for prediction of falls in hospital patients: how well does it work?." Age and ageing 37.6: 621-627. 2008.

[10] E. Nordin et al. "Prognostic validity of the Timed Up-and-Go test, a modified Get-Up-and-Go test, staff's global judgement and fall history in evaluating fall risk in residential care facilities." Age and ageing 37.4: 442-448. 2008.

[11] J. Hamm et al.. "Fall prevention intervention technologies: A conceptual framework and survey of the state of the art". Journal of Biomedical Informatics. 2016.

[12] M. Tinetti et al. "Fall risk index for elderly patients based on number of chronic disabilities." The American jour. of medicine 80.3,1986, 429-434.

[13] T. Toshiyo et al. "A wearable airbag to prevent fall injuries." Information Technology in Biomedicine, IEEE Transactions on 13.6: 910-914. 2009.

[14] Z. Gabi et al. "Safety and tolerance of the ReWalk™ exoskeleton suit for ambulation by people with complete spinal cord injury: A pilot study." The journal of spinal cord medicine 35.2: 96-101. 2012

[15] N. Vuillerme et al. "Pressure sensor-based tongue-placed electrotactile biofeedback for balance improvement-Biomedical application to prevent pressure sores formation and falls." Engineering in Medicine and Biology Society, 2007. EMBS 2007. 29th Annual International Conference of the IEEE. IEEE, 2007.

[16] B. J. Munro et al. "The intelligent knee sleeve: A wearable biofeedback device." Sens. Actuators B: Chemical 131:541. 2008.

[17] D. De Venuto, D. T. Castro, Y. Ponomarev, E. Stikvoort. "Low power 12-bit sar adc for autonomous wireless sensors network interface". 3rd International Workshop on Advances in Sensors and Interfaces, IWASI 2009, art. no. 5184780, pp. 115-120.DOI: 10.1109/IWASI.2009.5184780. 2009.

[18] V. F. Annese and D. De Venuto. "FPGA based architecture for fall-risk assessment during gait monitoring by synchronous EEG/EMG." Proceedings - 2015 6th IEEE International Workshop on Advances in Sensors and Interfaces, IWASI 2015, art. no. 7184953, pp. 116-121. DOI: 10.1109/IWASI.2015.7184953. 2015.

[19] D. De Venuto, V. F. Annese, M. Ruta, E. Di Sciascio, A. L. Sangiovanni Vincentelli. "Designing a Cyber-Physical System for Fall Prevention by Cortico-Muscular Coupling Detection.". IEEE Design and Test, 33 (3), art. no. 7273831, pp. 66-76. DOI: 10.1109/MDAT.2015.2480707. 2016.

[20] Y. Lajoie et al. "Predicting falls within the elderly community: Comparison of postural sway, reaction time, the Berg balance scale and the Activities-specific Balance Confidence (ABC) scale for comparing fallers and non-fallers", Arch. gerontology-geriatrics, 38.1:11-26, 2014.

[21] V. F. Annese, M. Crepaldi, D. Demarchi, D. De Venuto. "A digital processor architecture for combined EEG/EMG falling risk prediction". Proceedings of the 2016 Design, Automation and Test in Europe Conference and Exhibition, DATE 2016, art. no. 7459401, pp. 714-719. 2016.

[22] V. F. Annese and D. De Venuto. "The truth machine of involuntary movement: FPGA based cortico-muscular analysis for fall prevention" 2015 IEEE International Symposium on Signal Processing and Information Technology, ISSPIT 2015, art. no. 7394398, pp. 553-558. DOI: 10.1109/ISSPIT.2015.7394398. 2015.

[23] D. De Venuto, M. J. Ohletz, B. Ricco. "Automatic repositioning technique for digital cell based window comparators and implementation within mixed-signal DfT schemes". Proceedings - International Symposium on Quality Electronic Design, ISQED, 2003-January, art. no. 1194771, pp. 431-437. DOI: 10.1109/ISQED.2003.1194771. 2003.

[24] D. De Venuto, M.J. Ohletz, B. Riccò. "Digital window comparator DfT scheme for mixed-signal ICs" Journal of Electronic Testing: Theory and Applications (JETTA), 18 (2), pp. 121-128. DOI: 10.1023/A:1014937424827. 2002.

[25] V. F. Annese and D. De Venuto. "Fall-risk assessment by combined movement related potentials and co-contraction index monitoring". IEEE Biomedical Circuits and Systems Conference: Engineering for Healthy Minds and Able Bodies, BioCAS 2015 - Proceedings, art. no. 7348366. DOI: 10.1109/BioCAS.2015.7348366. 2015.

[26] R. P.Munhoz et al. "Evaluation of the pull test technique in assessing postural instability in Parkinson's disease." Neurology 62.1, 2004.

[27] Y. Han Bo, et al. "A low power ASIP for precision configurable FFT processing", Conf. Signal & Inform. Processing Association. 2012.

[28] D. De Venuto, S. Carrara, B. Riccò. "Design of an integrated low-noise read-out system for DNA capacitive sensors." Microelectronics Journal, 40 (9), pp. 1358-1365. DOI: 10.1016/j.mejo.2008.07.071. 2009.

[29] D. De Venuto, M. J. Ohletz, B. Riccò. "Testing of analogue circuits via (standard) digital gates". Proceedings - International Symposium on Quality Electronic Design, ISQED, 2002-January, art. no. 996709, pp. 112-119. DOI: 10.1109/ISQED.2002.9967097. 2002.

[30] D. De Venuto, M. J. Ohletz. "On-chip test for mixed-signal ASICs using two-mode comparators with bias-programmable reference voltages" (2001) Journal of Electronic Testing: Theory and Applications (JETTA), 17 (3-4), pp. 243-253. DOI: 10.1023/A:1013377811693. 2001.

[31] V. F. Annese and D. De Venuto. "Gait analysis for fall prediction using EMG triggered movement related potentials." Proceedings - 2015 10th IEEE International Conference on Design and Technology of Integrated Systems in Nanoscale Era, DTIS 2015, art. no. 7127386. DOI: 10.1109/DTIS.2015.7127386. 2015

[32] V. F. Annese, C. Martin, D. R. S. Cumming, D. De Venuto. "Wireless capsule technology: Remotely powered improved high-sensitive barometric endoradiosonde". Proceedings of 2016 IEEE International Symposium on Circuits and Systems (ISCAS) (pp. 1370-1373). DOI: 10.1109/ISCAS.2016.7527504. 2016, May. 2016.

[33] D. De Venuto, V. F. Annese, A. L. Sangiovanni-Vincentelli. "The ultimate IoT application: A cyber-physical system for ambient assisted living". Proceedings of *2016 IEEE International Symposium* on Circuits and Systems (ISCAS) (pp. 2042-2045). DOI: 10.1109/ISCAS.2016.7538979. 2016.

Semantic-Based Context Mining and Sharing in Smart Object Networks

Eliana Bove

DEI - Politecnico di Bari
Via E. Orabona 4
Bari, Italy I-70125
Email: eliana.bove@poliba.it

Abstract—**The Semantic Web of Things is the evolution of Internet of Things paradigms introducing novel Knowledge Base models, in order to associate semantic representation to real-world objects and events. The paper proposes a semantic-based approach for high-level information representation, knowledge discovery, allotment and sharing in distributed scenarios populated by smart objects. By leveraging the integration of standard supervised machine learning techniques with non-standard semantic-based reasoning services, smart objects annotate in a fully automatic way the context they are in and expose their acquired knowledge to the outside world as in a blog, exploiting a layered architecture built on a publish/subscribe Message Oriented Middleware. The feasibility of the envisioned framework is supported by a case study and an early experimental campaign.**

Keywords–Logic-based matchmaking; Pervasive Computing; Machine Learning; Ubiquitous Knowledge Base; Mobile Resource Discovery.

I. INTRODUCTION

Increasingly available *Internet of Things* (IoT) technologies are enabling the pervasive computing paradigm, where information is really scattered in a given environment in the form of atoms which deeply permeate the context [1]. Heterogeneous data streams must be continuously retrieved and locally processed by mobile ad-hoc networks of *smart objects* dipped in the environment in order to detect events of interest in observed areas. A smart object [2] is an intelligent software agent acting on a mobile device, equipped with embedded sensors, actuators, communication ports as well as limited computation and storage facilities. Each smart object describes itself and the context where it operates toward a variety of external devices and IoT applications. The interoperability and the relevance of the IoT could be further enhanced by associating semantically rich (compact) descriptions to real-world objects and to data they retrieve, so featuring novel classes of smart applications. This is the so-called *Semantic Web of Things* evolution of classic Internet of Things paradigms. This paper proposes a novel semantic-based framework for knowledge high-level representation, discovery and sharing within smart object networks in the Semantic Web of Things. By leveraging the integration of standard supervised Machine Learning (ML) techniques with non-standard semantic-based inference services [3] on annotations in Semantic Web languages, smart objects become able to annotate in a fully automatic way the context they are in, continuously enriching their basic descriptive core according to events they detect and exposing them to the outside world as in a blog. Identification and sensing information are expressed in OWL 2 (Web Ontology Language) annotations [4] via a semantic-based evolution of standard *k Nearest Neighbors* (k-NN) ML algorithm. For knowledge sharing in smart object networks, the proposed framework interconnects distributed components by exploiting the publish/subscribe (pub/sub) Message-Oriented Middleware (MOM) architectural model. In detail, the topmost layer provides resource/service discovery based on standard and non-standard inference services for semantic matchmaking. It enables a fine-grained categorization and ranking of resources matching a request. An optimized Description Logic (DL) reasoner for mobile and embedded devices [5] is integrated for this purpose. The middle layer is a distributed collaborative protocol to collect ontology fragments (*chunks*) disseminated among the devices in an environment, in order to rebuild a minimal ontology core needed for supporting inference procedures on a particular set of semantic annotations. As ontologies can be large and Semantic Web languages use the verbose XML syntax, both compression and ontology partitioning are needed. The proposal adopts a novel scheme for rebuilding partitioned ontologies. It seeks a practical trade-off between the size of individual ontology chunks managed by devices –also exploiting compressed encoding– and the number of message exchanges required for on-the-fly reassembly. This layer implements a *ubiquitous KB* (u-KB) [6] model, where a node of the distributed system endowed with a reasoner fetches on the fly all and only the KB parts required for the current inference problem. Finally, the lowest layer is a message-oriented middleware based on the publish-subscribe model. It provides reliable communication among loosely-coupled components to support functionalities of the higher-level layers. The proposed approach results as a general-purpose, cross-domain semantic-based context mining, knowledge discovery and sharing facilitator among pervasive smart devices. In order to evaluate the usefulness of the proposed theoretical approach in a real scenario, the framework has been implemented in a prototypical smart farmer robot team. The proposal makes every entity involved in the scenario able to summarize the information gathered via its sensing interfaces into a semantically annotated description of the environment and relevant objects in it. Furthermore, robots can interact and communicate with each other by leveraging the proposed knowledge sharing approach which integrates a scalable off-the-shelf middleware as pub/sub communication layer, namely Bee Data Distribution System (Bee-DDS) [7]. A prototype was implemented and tested in experimental evaluations, to ensure correctness of the approach and perform a preliminary performance evaluation. The remainder of the paper is organized as follows. Section II provides a survey of related work. Section III discusses the proposed framework in detail. An illustrative case study is described in Section IV to allow a better understanding of the proposal. Finally, experimental results are in Section V and Section VI closes the paper.

II. Related Work

A smart object is a software agent able to process and analyze sensory raw data and further combine data classifications to identify patterns, situations and events. It can collect data sources either by exploiting on-board sensors or querying short-range wireless communication protocols. The interpretation of raw, low-level gathered data and the behavior adaptation characterize different works existing in literature. Threshold detectors or standard ML techniques are exploited by current event classification approaches [8]. This paper is based on the integration between low-level data analysis and the high-level context interpretation to trigger actions, assume decisions or make interventions on the environment. Although noisy, uncertain and incomplete sensor data are well handled by probabilistic learning models, several limitations such as scalability, ad-hoc static models and data scarcity characterize these models. An event detection fuzzy logic approach based on a rule-base was presented in [9] in order to overtake the low level of model accuracy leveraging crisp threshold values. However, in addition to high accuracy, another important requirement of a smart object is the computational efficiency for working on pervasive computing platforms. Ontology based reasoning approaches for home and office activity recognition were presented in [10] and [11], respectively. They support only full matches and this is a limit in pervasive scenarios featured by several heterogeneous information sources. This paper merges the strengths of Machine Learning and high-level semantic interpretation in order to depict and detect more complex context state. Useful classification surveys about different particularities of ML techniques are in [12]. Particularly, good accuracy, insensitivity to outliers, high performance with both nominal and numerical features and incremental learner characteristics make the k-NN algorithm very useful for smart objects. In recent years, the Semantic Web research community dealt with the task of describing sensor features and recover data through ontologies. The most relevant and widely used vocabularies are *OntoSensor* [13] and *SSN-XG* [14]. Both are general enough to cover different application domains, unfortunately they are too large and complex to be processed by a single node in pervasive computing contexts where semantic-based knowledge sharing among different smart objects is required for auto-coordination and collaboration. Therefore, strategies for modularizing terminologies are necessary. Solutions in literature are strongly influenced by the specific applications. In general, the issue faced on this paper is somewhat different from the above classical ontology modularization, as it requires a dynamic, problem-oriented approach compatible with resource-constrained devices. [15] presents a relevant work enabling ontology decomposition and run-time rebuilding based on service instance descriptions, albeit giving slightly less flexibility in run-time ontology distribution. Furthermore, by construction the framework supports only semantic matchmaking based on Subsumption, preventing inference services which evaluate non-full matches. In order to derive implicit information starting from explicit event and context detection, supporting approximate matches and service ranking metrics is very important. That is why ubiquitous logic-based matchmakers implementing non-standard inference services [5] appear as enabling technologies in mobile and pervasive contexts. The knowledge-based information sharing needed for smart object cooperation is achieved by exploiting middleware software infrastructure. Different semantically enriched middleware platforms exist in literature [16][17], however, they take into account only full matches, which are quite rare in complex pervasive domains. The current proposal aims to a more principled and general solution supporting distributed knowledge representation, management, sharing and discovery in pervasive context where mobile computing devices provide minimal computational capabilities and where the exploitation of logic-based and approximate discovery strategies manage non-full matching results, typical in these scenarios.

III. Proposed Approach

The proposed framework introduces a semantic-based approach for knowledge high-level representation, discovery and sharing in distributed smart object networks. The approach aims to: (i) characterize the descriptive core of each smart object in a fully automatic way starting from sensed context data; (ii) share the learned semantic-based knowledge within the network and (iii) achieve objects cooperation for triggering actions, taking decisions or making interventions on the environment.

The starting point is represented by raw data collected by object sensors. Each object processes data and produces an annotation in a semantically rich formalism grounded on the Attributive Language with unqualified Number restrictions ($\mathcal{ALN}$) Description Logics [18], which is a subset of OWL 2 language. In order to guarantee the delivery of this information within the network, the proposed approach includes a layered architecture where a semantic-based knowledge discovery supports resource allotment in scenarios populated by a large number of resource-constrained nodes. The envisioned framework exploits a pub/sub MOM for inter-node communication. In what follows, proposed framework details are provided.

A. Data Mining and Semantic Annotation

Each intelligent entities continuously executes three steps, as shown in Fig. 1.

1. Clustering: adopts an unsupervised clustering approach to

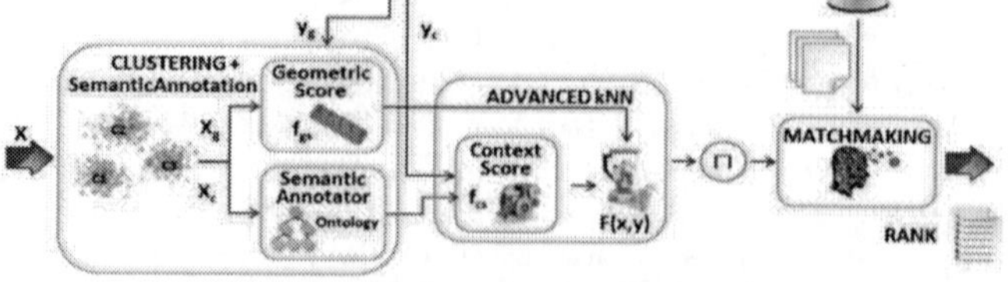

Figure 1. Sketch of the log information flow

pre-process input data. The previous knowledge of the object is represented by a training data set grouped into clusters. Each cluster is characterized by two components: geometry and context. *Geometry* describes data through statistical parameters. *Context* annotates data w.r.t. an OWL 2 reference ontology, which is different for each application domain. An unknown input instance is linked with the description of the nearest cluster [19].

2. Advanced k Nearest Neighbors: exploits an enhanced version of the *k-NN* algorithm to give high-level data representation. A semantic-based similarity measure f_{cs} (context distance) and a partial scores f_{gs} deriving from geometry (i.e., quantitative statistical attributes) are combined by a utility function F. A peculiar aspect of the approach proposed here consists in the integration of classic k-NN supervised machine learning with semantic-based matchmaking. In what follows, x and y are input arguments of F: the first is the instance to be examined and the latter represents each element of the training set. Both are described by two components: the geometric (x_g, y_g) and the contextual (x_c, y_c) ones.
The *geometric score* $f_{gs}(x_g, y_g)$ numerically expresses the similarity between y_g and x_g, as proposed in [20]. This numerical assessment is referred to the statistical distribution parameters featuring the data point and the training examples. Since x_g is the value to be matched, only the k dimensions describing x must be taken into account. Therefore, a basis vector $B(x_g) = \langle b_1, b_2, \ldots, b_k \rangle$ is defined, where $b_i \in [0,1]$ and $b_i = 0 \Leftrightarrow x_{g_i} = \emptyset$. The matching value on a single dimension is computed as:

$$dmatch(x_{g_i}, y_{g_{ji}}) = \begin{cases} \frac{|x_{g_i} \sqcap y_{g_{ji}}|}{|x_{g_i}|} & if\ B(x_{g_i}) = 1 \wedge \\ & B(y_{g_{ji}}) = 1 \\ 0 & else \end{cases} \quad (1)$$

According to (1), the value $dmatch(x_{g_i}, y_{g_{ji}})$ is computed by determining the overlap between x_{g_i} and $y_{g_{ji}}$ (the i-th dimension of the j-th training example) divided by the length of x_{g_i}. The overall matching score is defined as:

$$f_{gs}(x_g, y_g) = 1 - \frac{\sum_{i=1}^{k} dmatch(x_{g_i}, y_{g_{ji}})}{k} \quad (2)$$

Division by k produces normalization w.r.t. the highest cardinality of x_g.
The *contextual metric* $f_{cs}(x_c, y_c)$ is calculated on features annotated in *OWL 2* language [4] according to the reference terminology and exploits non-standard inference services presented in [3]. Concept Abduction and Concept Contraction non-standard inferences are used in order to consider non-full matches. Given an ontology $\mathcal{T}$ and two concept expressions A and B (acting as resource and request descriptions, respectively), if the conjunction $A \sqcap B$ is unsatisfiable w.r.t. the ontology $\mathcal{T}$, i.e., A, B are not compatible with each other, Concept Contraction determines what features G (for *Give up*) can be retracted from B to obtain a subset K (for *Keep*) such that $K \sqcap A$ is satisfiable in $\mathcal{T}$, and returns a value $penalty_{(c)}$ representing the associated semantic distance. Futhermore, if $\mathcal{T} \not\models A \sqsubseteq B$ then Concept Abduction computes a concept H (for *Hypothesis*) such that $\mathcal{T} \models A \sqcap H \sqsubseteq B$. That is, H represents what should be hypothesized (i.e., is underspecified) in A in order to completely satisfy B w.r.t. the information modeled in $\mathcal{T}$. Concept Abduction provides a related distance metric named $penalty_{(a)}$. Given these premises, the contextual score is calculated as:

$$f_{cs}(x_c, y_c) = \frac{\omega \cdot penalty_{(c)} + (1-\omega) \cdot penalty_{(a)}}{max\ penalty_{(a)}} \quad (3)$$

using as normalizing factor the maximum possible semantic distance, which is the one between x_c and the most generic $\top$ concept. The scoring mechanism is tuned by ω, which depends on the geometric score and is computed as $\omega = \delta \cdot f_{gs}(x_g, y_g)$ with the proportional factor $\delta \in [0.8, 1]$ and the weight ω, which emphasizes explicit incompatibility measured by Contraction as geometric distance increases.
3. Semantic-based matchmaking: leverages inference services in [3] to compare the semantic characterization of the context with descriptions of instances in the object Knowledge Base (KB), so giving a semantic interpretation to the raw data. The *overall distance* F is computed as:

$$F(x,y) = (f_{gs}(x_g, y_g) + \epsilon)^{\alpha} \cdot (f_{cs}(x_c, y_c) + \gamma)^{1-\alpha} \quad (4)$$

It is a monotonic function in $[0,1]$ and ranks input training examples in a consistent way. It basically adopts a user-friendly scale distance, where lower outcomes represent better results. In a great detail, $\alpha \in [0,1]$ factor determines the relative weight of contextual and geometric scores. In case of contextual or geometric full matches, score is tuned by means of $\epsilon \in [0,1]$ and $\gamma \in [0,1]$, respectively. Each new data point or series acquired in the same observation window undergoes this process which terminates when the latest data points are integrated in the training set, while data older than a purging threshold are removed.

B. Knowledge Discovery

Throughout the objects lifetime, the semantic endowment is progressively enriched and completed so that it could be exposed to the outside world as in a blog. To achieve this, the proposed system exploits a pub/sub MOM. In this paradigm, topics of exchanged messages specify the type, structure and purpose of the message payload. Each node can act as a *publisher* to emit messages with a specific topic and/or as a *subscriber* to receive all messages related to a subscribed topic. In conventional pub/sub MOM architectures, resource discovery occurs through syntactic match of topics. Conversely, the proposed framework allows the support for a dynamic semantic-based resource retrieval. This is realized through the integration of additional functional layers to the standard MOM paradigm. As shown in Fig. 2, the proposed approach includes three layers: (i) Bee-DDS, an off-the-shelf pub/sub MOM; (ii) a ubiquitous Knowledge Base, a distributed model for information partitioning and on-the-fly materialization; (iii) Resource/Service Discovery, a decentralized collaborative resource/service discovery protocol exploiting non-standard inference services to enable a fine-grained categorization and ranking of resources matching a request.
1. Bee Data Distribution Service: it provides services for real-time data distribution by adopting the publish/subscribe model in order to guarantee the basic inter-node communication. Its software infrastructure comprises Data Local Reconstruction Layer (DLRL) and Data Centric Publish/Subscribe (DCPS).
2. Ubiquitous Knowledge Base Model: transparent access to information embedded in semantic-enabled devices of the network is granted by the *ubiquitous KB* (u-KB) layer. KB is partitioned in a decentralized way and scattered across multiple nodes. Specifically, the Terminological Box $\mathcal{T}$ (i.e., the ontology) is fragmented in one or more *chunks* managed by multiple distributed nodes. Individuals in the Assertion Box $\mathcal{A}$ are not centrally stored, but disseminated in the environment as they make part of the endowment of each node. Due to the generality of the proposed approach, all nodes within the same network can manage any domain ontology, even using multiple

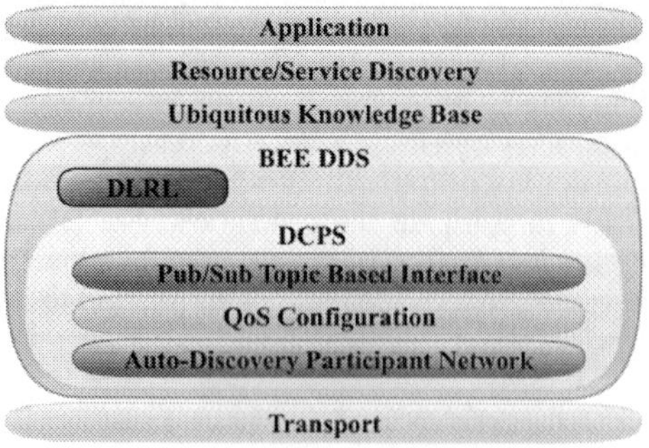

Figure 2. Bee DDS Layered Architecture

vocabularies in order to cover different application domains. Furthermore, the use of unique ontology Uniform Resource Identifiers (URI) ensures that all objects working with the same reference ontology can share parts of the u-KB dynamically without requiring preliminary agreement among them. In order to enable dissemination and on-the-fly ontology reconstruction, the ontology partitioning is based on associating each class with a unique ID, computed from its position in the taxonomy. The most generic class, named *Thing* in OWL 2 (*a.k.a. Top* or $\top$ in DL notation), takes ID 1. Each nesting level adds a further numerical suffix, separated by a . (dot). The ontology partitioning starts from an Upper Ontology (UO) chunk, comprising the topmost levels in the class hierarchy. The UO depth level can be set based on size and complexity of the ontology itself. Every node cache contains the UO as well as the chunk(s) required by detained semantic resource annotations. Before the discovery phase, a requester node must rebuild a subset of the ontology containing the classes used in the logical expressions of the involved annotations.To do so, it publishes a message with the *BuildTBox* middleware topic, which all semantic-enabled nodes must be subscribed to. The message contains: (i) the unique ontology URI, (ii) the list of requested class IDs, and (iii) the topic name (e.g., *MergeOnto_NodeID*) to be used in reply messages. If a node has one or more requested class IDs in its cache, it will publish on the above topic the compressed ontology chunk containing those classes. Requester node is subscribed to topic MergeOnto_NodeID to receive the ontology chunks and merge them.

3. Semantic Resource Discovery: discovery is based on a semantic resource request which consists of a logic-based annotation expressed w.r.t. a reference ontology. The requester starts inquiry by sending a *Discovery* message containing: (i) the reference ontology URI which implicitly defines the request domain, (ii) the topic *SemAnn_NodeID* to be used in reply messages. Through the *Discovery* topic, other nodes receive the request and check whether they own resources related to the same domain. Only in this case, nodes become publishers on the reply topic and send back the related compressed annotations; each annotation is associated with a resource-specific topic. The requester collects all descriptions and compares them with its request through the semantic matchmaking process described in [3] and recalled hereafter. The outcome of the match determines a ranked list of resources which best satisfy the request. Finally, the requester uses the topic(s) associated to the selected resource(s) in order to start fruition. In case of data gathering resources, such as from sensors, the requester will act as a subscriber to receive information; on the other hand, controllable resources require the service user to be a publisher on the topic to send commands and data. As for the above mining approach, this layer exploits non-standard inferences for semantic matchmaking implemented in the *Mini-ME* reasoning engine [5], which is suitable for computationally constrained nodes.

IV. Case Study: Save the Grapes

The proposed approach has a strong potential impact in supporting a wide range of applications including urban search and rescue, personal assistance, industrial maintenance, home automation, smart agriculture and many more. The case study proposed here is related to the smart agriculture field, where objects can share information in order to monitor crops by means of appropriate sensors or fulfill a product tracking system able to follow them from the farm to seller shelves. In order to evaluate the usefulness of the framework, a prototypical testbed is under development, exploiting a semantic distributed sensor network and a *3D Robotics Iris* drone [21] equipped with additional sensors and peripherals. The cooperation of these entities allows to detect the specific agricultural context state, formulate plans to reach the mission goals and act accordingly. In what follows, an illustrative example is presented to clarify functional and non-functional aspects of the proposal.

Downy mildew is a serious fungal disease of grapevine which can result in severe crop loss. It is caused by the fungus Plasmopara viticola. *The pathogen attacks all green parts of the vine, especially the leaves. In order to eliminate the fungus, a smart vine monitoring is realized by analyzing environmental parameters collected by a sensor network. According with this monitoring, a smart farming drone is able to automatically infer when, where and how spraying fungicides on susceptible cultivars.*

Environmental factors that influence development of

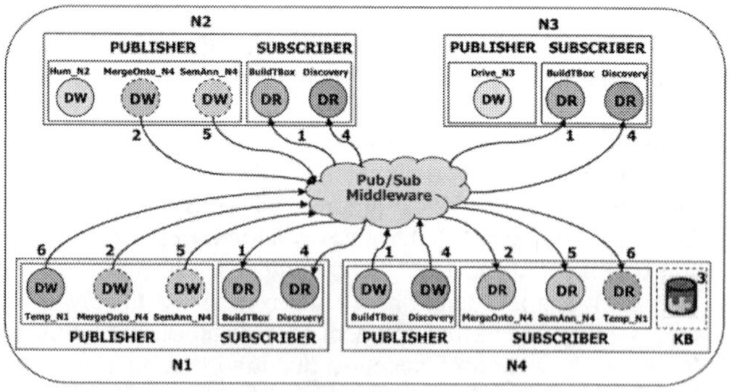

Figure 3. Temperature service discovery

Plasmopara viticola include relative humidity, atmospheric pressure, soil moisture, leaf wetness, rugged soil temperature, sun calibration quantum, meteorological data. Raw data are processed on the fly by the smart farmer drone leveraging the proposed semantic-based approach. As shown in Fig. 3, each node includes a Publisher for data dissemination, through one or more Data Writer (DW) objects and a Subscriber for data gathering through one or more Data Reader (DR) objects, each associated to one Topic subscription. N4 represents the drone that acts as a requester of knowledge about the environment in order to act on it. N1 is a temperature sensor, N2 is a humidity sensor and N3 is a cutter drive. They are distributed in the monitored area and play the role of resource providers. In the initial system state, they all subscribe to general topics *BuildTBox* and *Discovery*; furthermore, each provided service has a specific topic associated via the respective Publisher (*Temp_N1, Hum_N2, Drive_N3*). The knowledge discovery process is composed by the following interaction steps, also marked in Fig. 3.

1. N4 requires a soil temperature service, with high accuracy and precision, low measurement range and frequency, and high response time.

$\mathit{SoilTempSensor} \sqcap \forall \mathit{observes.SoilTemp} \sqcap \forall \mathit{hasMeasuremProp.}(\mathit{HighAccuracy} \sqcap \mathit{HighPrecision} \sqcap \mathit{LowFrequency} \sqcap \mathit{LowMeasuremRange} \sqcap \mathit{HighResponseTime})$

Before starting service discovery, N4 sends its request on the BuildTBox topic.

2. Through the DR on the BuildTBox topic, N1, N2 and N3 receive the metadata and check whether the URI in the request refers to some chunks of an ontology they own. If it does, they determine whether at least one item is in the list defined in their ontology chunk(s). In that case, a DW on MergeOnto_N4 is created on-the-fly (dynamically created DWs and DRs are shown with a dashed outline in Fig. 3) for sending selected chunk(s). In the example, N1 and N2 reply, whereas N3 does not manage the requested ontology.

3. Through the DR on MergeOnto_N4, N4 receives the needed ontology chunks and merges them to rebuild a minimal self-contained terminology subset for matchmaking.

4. N4 forwards its service request on the Discovery topic.

5. N1, N2 and N3 receive the metadata and check whether the URI specified in the request is the same of their service description(s). N3 has no service described by the specified vocabulary, while the check succeeds for N1 and N2 and they become publishers on the SemAnn_N4 topic.

N1: $\mathit{SoilTempSensor} \sqcap \forall \mathit{observes.SoilTemp} \sqcap \forall \mathit{hasMeasuremProp.}(\mathit{HighAccuracy} \sqcap \mathit{LowFrequency} \sqcap \mathit{MediumMeasuremRange} \sqcap \mathit{HighPrecision} \sqcap \mathit{MediumResponseTime} \sqcap \mathit{MediumResolution} \sqcap \mathit{LowLatency})$

N2: $\mathit{HumSensor} \sqcap \forall \mathit{observes.Humidity} \sqcap \forall \mathit{hasMeasuremProp.}(\mathit{LowAccuracy} \sqcap \mathit{LowFrequency} \sqcap \mathit{LowMeasuremRange} \sqcap \mathit{MediumPrecision} \sqcap \mathit{MediumResponseTime} \sqcap \mathit{LowResolution} \sqcap \mathit{LowLatency})$

6. N4 gets the messages of N1 and N2 and executes the matchmaking process between the annotated request and the semantic descriptions of discovered services. The best match (i.e., lowest semantic distance) is achieved by N1, while N2 is less relevant as a sensor, because its observed quantity is incompatible. So, N4 becomes subscriber on Temp_N1 topic for receiving temperature data from the sensor exposed by N1.

N4 executes these steps for all environmental data needed to detect the monitored area state. Furthermore, the drone exploits the proposed mining approach to analyze data collected by each sensor and to determine high-level feature values of the monitored factors for the whole observation window.

Soil temperature semantic-based classification value is calculated considering not only quantitative statistical parameters (mean, variance, kurtosis, skewness), but also relevant context features (*Altitude*, *Latitude*, *Season*; *PartOfDay*). Clusters are $\mathit{VeryLowSoilTemp}$, $\mathit{LowSoilTemp}$, $\mathit{MediumSoilTemp}$, $\mathit{HighSoilTemp}$ and $\mathit{VeryHighSoilTemp}$. By replicating this process for each sensed parameter, the smart object (e.g., the drone) creates a high-level representation of the considered grapevine status. A semantic description detected by the system follows as an example.

$\mathit{Grapevine} \sqcap \forall \mathit{hasSoilTemp.LowSoilTemp} \sqcap \forall \mathit{hasAtmosphPressure.}(\mathit{VeryLowAtmosphPressure} \sqcap \neg \mathit{HighAtmosphPressure}) \sqcap \forall \mathit{hasHumidity.HighHumidity} \sqcap \forall \mathit{hasSoilMoisture.HighSoilMoisture} \sqcap \forall \mathit{hasLeafWetness.}(\mathit{VeryHighLeafWetness} \sqcap \neg \mathit{LowLeafWetness}) \sqcap \forall \mathit{hasSunCalibQuantum.HighSunCalibnQuantum} \sqcap \forall \mathit{hasRuggedSoilTemp.}\ \mathit{MediumRuggedSoilTemp}$

The coordinator (drone) knows the influential environmental factors that directly interacting in the onset and evolution of vite disease states, hence it performs a second-level matchmaking process to detect whether the grapes is likely attacked by the pathogen. According to this detection, the smart farmer acts on the surrounding monitored environment spraying fungicides (if necessary).

V. Experiments

The proposed framework was implemented in a Java-based software prototype to early evaluate its feasibility. The semantic layer defined in this paper for the knowledge discovery phase was implemented by extending BEE DDS middleware [7]. The resulting architecture for each smart object consists of three basic modules:

– *Clustering*: performed with the *k-Means* algorithm provided by *Weka 3.7* library [22].

– *Advanced k-NN*: inference services for semantic-enhanced classification are provided by the embedded *Mini-ME 2.0.0* matchmaking and reasoning engine [23].

– *Semantic-based matchmaking*: also this module exploits Mini-ME to infer the environmental state from the semantic-based context description.

Object network performance tests were performed on 50 nodes that provide services and one requester node. They were connected through BEE DDS middleware enriched with the proposed semantic layer. The tests were conducted considering different system configuration variables: (i)annotation compression type: COX [24] or EXI [25]; (ii) upper ontology nesting level: 2, 3 or 4. Compressed size of messages exchanged between nodes, turnaround time and RAM usage were considered as performance metrics for both the ontology distribuition phase and the resource allotment step. Time was measured through timestamping instructions embedded in the source code. The system took less than 3 seconds for the first phase and less than 2 seconds for the second ones with EXI compression and considering the maximum nesting level of the upper ontology. With COX compression, the system performs both phases in a little more than 2.5 seconds. For memory usage analysis, an embedded thread was used to profile memory usage at runtime for both phases. RAM occupancy is always under 90 MB. It is important to note that the system appears to be stable and predictable. Intra-node performance evaluation was carried out on a Raspberry Pi [26] mobile host to simulate a real smart object with limited resources. Tests were conducted on a dataset of 400 real

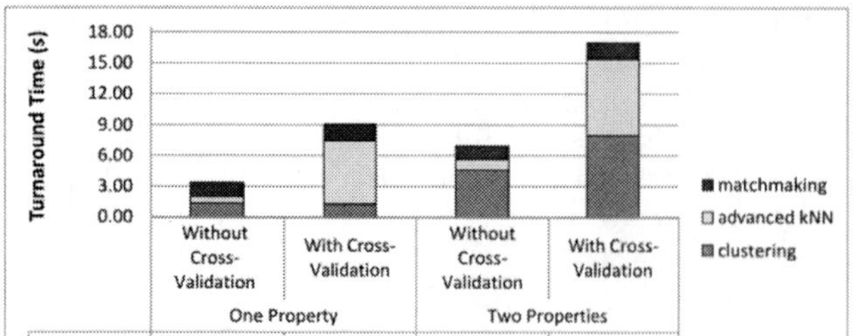

	One Property: Without Cross-Validation	One Property: With Cross-Validation	Two Properties: Without Cross-Validation	Two Properties: With Cross-Validation
matchmaking	1.388	1.618	1.377	1.617
advanced kNN	0.613	6.173	1.010	7.388
clustering	1.366	1.288	4.594	8.001

Figure 4. Turnaround time results

instances of weather sensor data (temperature and humidity, collected from Weather Underground Web Service [27]) to simulate sensor data gathering by a smart object. The tests were performed in two different conditions: with static value of k for the *advanced k-NN* phase and with cross validation (useful to set k dynamically). Turnaround time of data point processing and RAM usage were considered for each module of the mining proposed framework. Fig. 4 reports turnaround time results for the analysis of only one and both properties, with and without cross validation. As expected, turnaround time increased significantly when the system performed cross validation to set the best k value for k-NN. The most significant differences between results for one and two properties are in the clustering and matchmaking phases, but the time increase is less than linear. For memory usage analysis, RAM occupancy is always below 17 MB. Memory peaks correspond to the most data intensive tasks, i.e., cross validation and matchmaking. These preliminary results evidence the feasibility of the proposed framework, even though optimizations will be required.

VI. Conclusion and Future Work

The paper proposed a novel knowledge-based framework enabling a smart object to collect and annotate sensor data in a fully automated fashion. k-NN machine learning algorithm was modified including non-standard semantic-based reasoning services in order to achieve this goal. The proposal also allows the knowledge sharing in distributed systems, particularly targeted toward scenarios including large numbers of resource-constrained nodes. The framework was devised as a semantic-enhancement layer to be added on top of an off-the-shelf publish/subscribe middleware. The approach was implemented in a working prototype, embedding a mobile semantic matchmaker. Correctness and feasibility of the proposal were evaluated in a reference case study. Future work concerns further performance evaluation comparison with state-of-the-art approaches and improvement, as well as enrichment of semantic-based capabilities for the data mining approach.

References

[1] L. Da Xu, W. He, and S. Li, "Internet of things in industries: a survey," *Industrial Informatics, IEEE Transactions on*, vol. 10, no. 4, pp. 2233–2243, 2014.

[2] L. Atzori, A. Iera, and G. Morabito, "From "smart objects" to "social objects": The next evolutionary step of the internet of things," *Communications Magazine, IEEE*, vol. 52, no. 1, pp. 97–105, 2014.

[3] M. Ruta, E. Di Sciascio, and F. Scioscia, "Concept abduction and contraction in semantic-based P2P environments," *Web Intelligence and Agent Systems*, vol. 9, no. 3, pp. 179–207, 2011.

[4] W3C OWL Working Group. OWL 2 Web Ontology Language Document Overview (Second Edition). W3C Recommendation 11 December 2012. [Online]. Available: http://www.w3.org/TR/owl2-overview/ 2016.09.27

[5] F. Scioscia *et al.*, "A mobile matchmaker for the ubiquitous semantic web," *International Journal on Semantic Web and Information Systems (IJSWIS)*, vol. 10, no. 4, pp. 77–100, 2014.

[6] M. Ruta, F. Scioscia, and E. Di Sciascio, "Enabling the semantic web of things: framework and architecture," pp. 345–347, 2012, doi: 10.1109/ICSC.2012.42.

[7] BEE Data Distribuition System. [Online]. Available: http://sine.ni.com/nips/cds/view/p/lang/it/nid/211025 2016.09.22

[8] M. Martin *et al.*, "Learning to detect user activity and availability from a variety of sensor data," *2013 IEEE International Conference on Pervasive Computing and Communications (PerCom)*, pp. 13–13, 2004.

[9] K. Kapitanova, S. H. Son, and K.-D. Kang, "Using fuzzy logic for robust event detection in wireless sensor networks," *Ad Hoc Networks*, vol. 10, no. 4, pp. 709–722, 2012.

[10] L. Chen, C. D. Nugent, and H. Wang, "A knowledge-driven approach to activity recognition in smart homes," *Knowledge and Data Engineering, IEEE Transactions on*, vol. 24, no. 6, pp. 961–974, 2012.

[11] T. A. Nguyen, A. Raspitzu, and M. Aiello, "Ontology-based office activity recognition with applications for energy savings," *Journal of Ambient Intelligence and Humanized Computing*, vol. 5, no. 5, pp. 667–681, 2014.

[12] S. Kotsiantis, "Supervised machine learning: A review of classification techniques," *Informatica*, vol. 31, pp. 249–268, 2007.

[13] D. J. Russomanno, C. R. Kothari, and O. A. Thomas, "Building a Sensor Ontology: A Practical Approach Leveraging ISO and OGC Models," pp. 637–643, 2005.

[14] M. Compton *et al.*, "The SSN Ontology of the W3C Semantic Sensor Network Incubator Group," *Web Semantics: Science, Services and Agents on the World Wide Web*, vol. 17, 2012.

[15] T. Rybicki, "Ontology recomposition," *Knowledge Engineering, Machine Learning and Lattice Computing with Applications*, pp. 119–132, 2012.

[16] S. B. Mokhtar, D. Preuveneers, N. Georgantas, V. Issarny, and Y. Berbers, "EASY: Efficient semAntic Service discoverY in pervasive computing environments with QoS and context support," *Journal of Systems and Software*, vol. 81, no. 5, pp. 785–808, 2008.

[17] H. Li and G. Jiang, "Semantic message oriented middleware for publish/subscribe networks," *Defense and Security*, pp. 124–133, 2004.

[18] F. Baader, D. Calvanese, D. Mc Guinness, D. Nardi, and P. Patel-Schneider, *The Description Logic Handbook*. Cambridge University Press, 2002.

[19] R. Xu, D. Wunsch *et al.*, "Survey of clustering algorithms," *Neural Networks, IEEE Transactions on*, vol. 16, no. 3, pp. 645–678, 2005.

[20] K. Rasch, F. Li, S. Sehic, R. Ayani, and S. Dustdar, "Context-driven personalized service discovery in pervasive environments," *World Wide Web*, vol. 14, no. 4, pp. 295–319, 2011.

[21] 3D Robotics Iris. [Online]. Available: https://store.3dr.com/products/iris 2016.02.16

[22] Weka 3: Data Mining Software in Java. [Online]. Available: http://www.cs.waikato.ac.nz/ml/weka/ 2016.05.27

[23] Mini-ME 2.0.0. [Online]. Available: http://sisinflab.poliba.it/swottools/minime/ 2016.07.14

[24] F. Scioscia and M. Ruta, "Building a semantic web of things: issues and perspectives in information compression," pp. 589–594, 2009.

[25] Efficient XML Interchange-EXI. [Online]. Available: https://www.w3.org/TR/exi/ 2016.06.30

[26] Raspberry Pi. [Online]. Available: https://www.raspberrypi.org/about/ 2016.02.16

[27] Weather Underground Web Service. [Online]. Available: http://www.wunderground.com/ 2015.09.14

Knowledge-Enabled Complex Event Processing-based platform for health monitoring

Francesco Nocera, Tommaso Di Noia, Marina Mongiello, Eugenio Di Sciascio
Dipartimento di Ingegneria Elettrica e dell'Informazione (DEI), Politecnico di Bari, Via Orabona, 4 - 70125 Bari- Italy
email: {firstname.lastname}@poliba.it

Abstract—**An increasing number of applications that require real-time or near-real time processing of high-volume of data streams are changing the way that traditional data processing systems infrastructures operate. Timeliness and flow processing are crucial for justifying the need for developing a new class of systems that are capable of processing not only generic data, but also event notifications coming from different source to identify interesting situations, with respect to traditional Database Management System (DBMS). Accordingly, different systems emerged and are competing in the last years, namely Information Flow Processing (IFP) systems. In this paper we discuss how semantic technologies can contribute to the field of complex event and study their support in health monitoring domain. Complex Event Processing (CEP) systems associate a precise semantics to the information items being processing. We propose an approach that combines Semantic Web methodologies and CEP model in a health monitoring platform.**

Keywords–Complex Event Processing; Semantic Web; knowledge Representation; Health monitoring.

I. INTRODUCTION

Technological innovation is driving profound changes in all productive fields. Consequently it is contributing to a new definition of the organizations and processes, which increasingly require new skills and responsibilities profiles. This path has also involved the health field where technologies have taken a leading role, it is becoming an integral part of the health service and they are establishing more and more inseparable interconnections between health and technology. The progress in medical technology is driving a continuous improvement of health and predictive diagnostic and therapeutic outcomes. Throughout the industry that deals with health, but especially in hospitals, the significant presence of technology, must ensure safe and appropriate use in various phase of prevention, diagnosis and treatment. It is expected that the Healthcare Industrial IoT *(HealthIIoT)* will be one of the main players in the Industrial Internet of Things (IIoT)-driven healthcare industry. IIoT has had a remarkable influence across many large and small healthcare industries. As a result, an increasing number of wearable IoT devices, tools, and apps are being used for different monitoring applications (e.g., glucose monitors, ECG monitors, and blood pressure monitors) [1]. The concept of "Competence"covers a key role in each phase. Competence is the ability to orient themselves in certain situations. It does not reside in the resources to be mobilized but in the same mobilization of knowledge that are known to select, integrate and combine in a context and for a specific purpose. The emergency health situations represent a sudden event, often unpredictable, which endangers life if the person concerned is not made, within a few minutes, a rescue action in a timely and professional manner. There are many medical professions that are emerging, due to the complexity of the events, each with their own skills. We can say that Competence consists of three components: *Knowledge*, generally the scope of conceptual knowledge, *The ability (or skill)*: the operational aspect of competence, the implementation of principles that belong to the knowledge and the *The behavior (or way of acting)*: the performing tasks that affect relationships with others and the effectiveness of the mobilization of the entire competence itself. These three components are closely linked to each other and make up the complex areas of knowing how to act. The aim of this paper is to present an intelligent system architecture for the management of health data, in particular a support system in the prevention, diagnosis and treatment phases. According to G. Cugola and A. Margara [2] the concepts of timeliness and flow processing are crucial for justifying the need for a new class of systems. Indeed, traditional Database Management Systems (DBMSs): *(i)* require data to be (persistently) stored and indexed before it could be processed and *(ii)* process data only when explicitly asked by the users, that is, asynchronously with respect to its arrival. These limitations have led to the design of a number of systems specifically designed to process information as a set of flows according to a set of processing rules. Complex event Processing (CEP) is one of these emerging models to monitor and react to continuously arriving events in real-time or near-real. Critical factors for event-based systems are event detection and the enormous amount of information available on the events. The continuous streams of high-level events require real-time intelligent processors. Human knowledge domain will greatly affect the decision making support system. Knowledge Representation is the method used to encode knowledge in an intelligent systems knowledge base. Events-based semantic models can improve the quality of event processing by using metadata in combination with knowledge bases consisting of ontologies and rules. The proposed solution is based on the combination of this two discipline: CEP domain and Knowledge Representation. The remainder of this paper is structured as follows: Section 2 provides a background on CEP and ontology Knowledge Representation. Section 3 presents the application domain and Section 4 discusses the proposed approach and platform. Finally, Section 5 concludes and discusses future research work.

II. BACKGROUND

Currently, an increasing number of distributed applications requires continuous analysis of flows of data and real-time response to complex queries. Furthermore, it is very important decide the way data should be stored because this choice will determine later also the way in which data will be extracted.

Today ontologies are widely used to model and encode domain's knowledge and allow us to reason about this knowledge. The fusion of background knowledge with data from an event stream can help the event processing engine to know more about incoming events and their relationships to other related concepts. In this section, we provide a background on CEP and Knowledge Representation.

A. Complex Event Processing

The concept of CEP was introduced by David Luckham in his seminal work [3] as a "*defined set of tools and techniques for analyzing and controlling the complex series of interrelated events that drive modern distributed Information Systems (IS)*". This emerging technology helps IS and Information Technology (IT) professionals understand what is happening within the system, quickly identify and solve problems, and more effectively utilize events for enhanced operation, performance, and security."CEP systems can be classified as Advanced Decision Support Systems (ADSS) [4]. It is part of Event-Driven Architectures (EDA), which are architectures generally dealing with the production, detection, consumption of, and reaction to events [5]. The key characteristic of a CEP system is its capability to handle complex event situations, detecting patterns, creating correlations, aggregating events and making use of time windows. The capability of defining and managing the relationships between events is an important and integral part of event processing solutions. The relationship between events is called correlation and uses a collection of semantic rules to describe how specific events are related to each other [6]. When a problem or opportunity arises, it should be noticed in real time, to make sure the right action can be taken at the right moment. Otherwise there will only be historical data that reveals possible problems, which already have become a real problem or opportunities which already have vanished. With CEP it is possible to act in real time and make better use of the already available events. Specification languages for event patterns are frequently inspired by regular languages and therefore have automata based semantics [7]. CEP systems can be classified on the basis of the architecture of the CEP engine in *centralized, hierarchical, acyclic and peer-to-peer* [8], the forwarding schemes adopted by brokers [9], and the way processing of event patterns is distributed among brokers [10]. Several CEP systems have been developed in the last few years, each one proposing a different processing model. Currently, the most popular are: *Esper* [11], *Apache YARN* [12], *StreamDrill* [13].

B. Ontology for Knowledge Representation

The field of knowledge Representation tries to deal with the problems surrounding the incorporation of some body of knowledge in a computer system, for the purpose of automated, intelligent reasoning. In this sense, knowledge representation is the basic research topic in Artificial Intelligence (AI). Knowledge Management (KM) consists of techniques that use Information Technology tools for the information management, and its goal is to improve the efficiency of work teams; it studies methods for making knowledge explicit, and sharing professional expertise and informative resources. In the scientific literature, different approaches have emerged to classification of KM issues. Alavi and Leidner [14] group the problems of Knowledge Management, namely storage, creation, transfer and retrieval issues into four classes. Verwijs et al. in [15] analyzed different knowledge approaches in business processes, and categorized them as follows: *Knowledge storage approach, Knowledge processes approach, Learning processes approach, Intellectual capital approach.* A generic Knowledge Management System (KMS), supporting the creation and storage of knowledge, gives the opportunity to make data, information and knowledge from different sources readily available. It contains data and documents, and can also store tacit knowledge, which is more difficult to express, and includes peoples experiences, know-how and expertise. The issue of how to better capitalize and disseminate knowledge is one of the actual priorities in KM. To realize such goals, a KMS can make use of different technologies such as: *Document based technologies* for the creation, administration and sharing of different documents (e.g., doc, pdf, html); *Ontology/Taxonomy based technologies* which use ontologies and classification for knowledge representation; *Artificial Intelligence based technologies* which use particular inference engines to solve peculiar domain problems. The main components of a Knowledge-Based System [16] are the following: *(i)* the *Knowledge Base* is the passive component of a Knowledge-Based System. It plays a role similar to a database in a traditional informative system; *(ii)* the *Inference Engine* is the core of the system. It uses the Knowledge Base content to derive new knowledge using reasoning techniques; *(iii)*the *Knowledge Base Manager* manages coherence and consistency of the information stored in the Knowledge Base. KMS can represent knowledge in both human and machine-readable forms. Human-readable knowledge is typically accessed using browsers or intelligent search engine. Human-readable knowledge is represented using a wide range of approaches in Knowledge Management Systems. But in some case, as the development of an expert system for decision support, knowledge needs to be accessible in machine-readable forms. Therefore, one of the major questions of knowledge management is to obtain a method to represent knowledge in both human and machine-readable forms. To solve this problem, Ontologies [17] are generally used as knowledge containers for KMSs.

III. Application domain

The aim of this paper will be the design of an integrated platform consisting of integrated components designed to remotely manage the paths of prevention, diagnosis and treatment. With respect to the prevention processes, there are three levels of prevention: *Primary* that aims to intervene on external pathogens and/or the individual's defenses, prevent a disease from developing; *Secondary* that aims to early detect the disease process already begun before symptoms appears; *Tertiary* that seeks to remove or repair the results of a disease that has already manifested through symptoms. In order to comply these three levels of prevention, the platform should provide a monitoring system integrated with a module of management of clinic compliance (care process), the real time management of the events by a CEP system and a connection system to the own caregiver or physician for the management of teleconsultation (diagnosis process). The diagnostic process should provide the possibility of a consultation and remote activation of health facilities in the event of hospitalization or specialized investigation. We identified the following functionalities:

- the use of digital medical record;
- the connection to the Electronic Health Record;
- the ability to analyze the patient's medical history and retrieve digitally reports;
- the ability to link the medical plan allows one to manage the entire cycle in dematerialized form and to reduce the clinical risk related to patient care with unsuitable or contradict each other.

The process of care management involves the management of compliance and must include the link to the medical plan. Also, it must provide the delivery of care using any devices in the patient's home. In particular, all scenarios to the three health-related processes should include a system of systematic data collection and their organization in a knowledge base used by decision makers at all levels and the definition of dashboards for the governance of health care. A personal health monitor is one example application [18]. A health monitor is a personalized system that allows a person and their caregivers to monitor the persons health status. Health monitors may be particularly useful for chronically ill people as well as for elderly citizens [19]. The data may be captured from sensors and devices at the person as well as from stationary sensors in their home or in a specific clinical area for the atmosphere data collection. Alarms are set up to alert the person and, if necessary, doctors or a remote caregiver. Sensors automatically capture personalized health data such as heart rate, blood pressure, respiration rate, ECG, oxygen saturation in blood, the location of the person in reference to a room,. In addition, specific regular measurements for particular health conditions are performed by the person and the results are filtered for emergency situations, as well as kept for long term observation. Health monitors offer many challenges derived from the high volume of low level events and the need to derive higher level events that must be propagated. This application is particularly sensitive to false negatives and false positives.

IV. Proposed Platform

Healthcare has many applications for event-based systems. EDA integrates relational, non-relational and stream data structures to create a unified analytics environment. EDA enables discovery, or exploratory, analytics, which rely on low-latency continuous processing techniques and high frequency querying on real-time data. This type of architecture requires a different class of tools and system interfaces to promote a looser coupling of applications to streamline data access, integration, exploration, and analysis. Real-time data allows information to be disseminated in a timely manner, when and where it is needed. Real-time capability and related process automation assist in accessing data to build event-driven applications enriched with other relevant information and bringing them together in a scalable platform. This section of the paper describes the proposed architecture platform depicted in Fig. 1. The modeled real-time platform is based on CEP and semantic web technologies and approaches. Together, these components create an agile, high performance, scalable platform that can deliver fast insights through real-time queries, pattern matching and anomaly detection, continuous analytics and triggers notifications and alerts based on a CEP engine. Detection and Aggregation- oriented Complex Event Processing focuses on *(i)* detecting combinations or patterns of events; *(ii)* executing

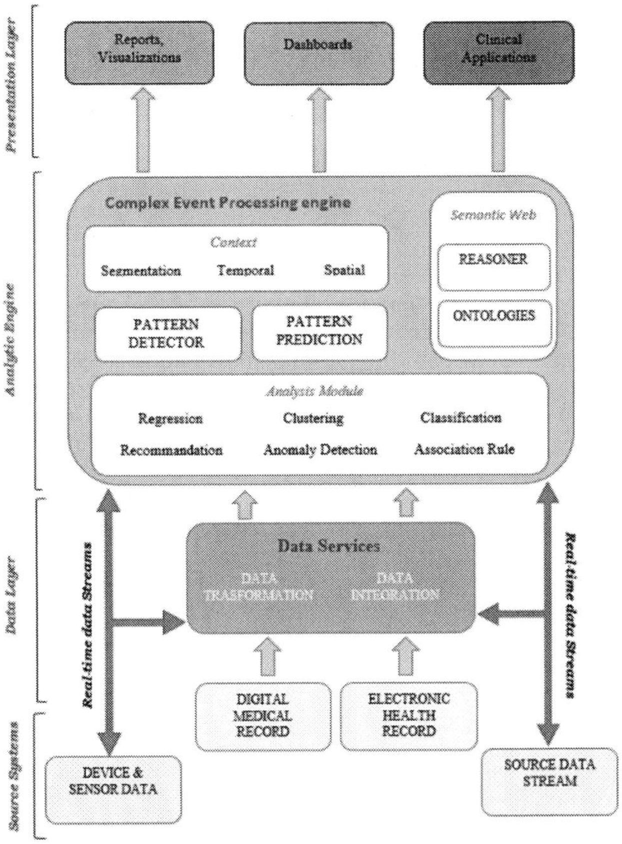

Figure 1. Proposed functional Architecture.

algorithms as a response to system input. Sources includes real-time data by sensors, medical devices, data stream generate real-time data that are captured by other systems for continuous monitoring, together with patient's historical data (Digital medical record, Electronic health record). Depending on the scenario, anomalies may be resolved by automated responses or alerts for human or machine intervention. CEP extends this capability by correlating multiple events through a common interface that invokes an embedded rules engine. Event filtering evaluates a specified logical condition based on event attributes, and, if the condition is true, publishes the event to the destination stream as a notification or alert. The main challenge is the huge amount of data collection and their organization in a knowledge base. Ontologies play an important key role in the knowledge-based CEP. They cover the conceptualization of the application domain to allow reasoning on events and other non-event concepts. We propose that event processing domain should be described by a modular and layered ontology model, which can be reused in different scenario application. Important general concepts, such as event, action, situation, space/place, time, agent and process should be defined based on meta-models and pluggable ontologies which are in a modularized ontological top-level structure. These general concepts defined in the top-level ontologies can be further specialized with existing domain ontologies and ontologies for generic tasks and activities.

V. CONCLUSION

For the healthcare industry, a real-time capability is required to exceed future standards of care, provider competence and patient engagement expectations and to accommodate the currently transformation in the healthcare industry focused on opening up health data to facilitate exchange between actors. All the challenges introduced in Section 2 necessitate next-generation technologies designed to extract value from very large volumes of disparate, multi-structured data by enabling high-velocity capture, discovery, and analysis. CEP systems offer the ability to detect, manage and predict events, situations, opportunities, rules, conditions and threats in very complex networks. The presented platform based on CEP and Semantic Web technologies, providers will be able to process high volumes of underlying technical events to derive clinical decision support. The modeled real-time platform is based on requirements for providing minimally acceptable timeliness of information based on feasibility and clinical necessity. In collecting, processing and analyzing real-time data, there is inherent latency depending on data rates, volume, aggregation method, processing power, embedded analytics and throughput. The presented platform is work in progress. We are currently preparing different case studies for the management of all different health data.

ACKNOWLEDGMENT

The author Francesco Nocera acknowledges support of Exprivia S.p.A Ph.D grant 2016.

REFERENCES

[1] M. S. Hossain and G. Muhammad, "Cloud-assisted industrial internet of things (iiot) enabled framework for health monitoring," Computer Networks, vol. 101, 2016, pp. 192 – 202, industrial Technologies and Applications for the Internet of Things. [Online]. Available: http://www.sciencedirect.com/science/article/pii/S1389128616300019

[2] G. Cugola and A. Margara, "Processing flows of information: From data stream to complex event processing," ACM Computing Surveys (CSUR), vol. 44, no. 3, 2012, p. 15.

[3] D. Luckham, The power of events. Addison-Wesley Reading, 2002, vol. 204.

[4] R. Rupnik, "Decision support system to support the solving of classification problems in telecommunications," Informacije Midem - Journal of microelectronic electronic component and materials, vol. 39, no. 3, 2009, pp. 168–177.

[5] D. Robins, "Complex event processing," in Second International Workshop on Education Technology and Computer Science. Wuhan, 2010.

[6] T. Moser, H. Roth, S. Rozsnyai, R. Mordinyi, and S. Biffl, "Semantic event correlation using ontologies," in On the Move to Meaningful Internet Systems: OTM 2009. Springer, 2009, pp. 1087–1094.

[7] J. E. Hopcroft, R. Motwani, and J. D. Ullman, "Introduction to automata theory, languages, and computation," ACM SIGACT News, vol. 32, no. 1, 2001, pp. 60–65.

[8] P. T. Eugster, P. A. Felber, R. Guerraoui, and A.-M. Kermarrec, "The many faces of publish/subscribe," ACM Computing Surveys (CSUR), vol. 35, no. 2, 2003, pp. 114–131.

[9] A. Carzaniga and A. L. Wolf, "Content-based networking: A new communication infrastructure," in Workshop on Infrastruture for Mobile and Wireless Systems. Springer, 2001, pp. 59–68.

[10] L. Amini, N. Jain, A. Sehgal, J. Silber, and O. Verscheure, "Adaptive control of extreme-scale stream processing systems," in 26th IEEE International Conference on Distributed Computing Systems (ICDCS'06). IEEE, 2006, pp. 71–71.

[11] "Esper," 2016, URL: http://www.espertech.com/esper/ [accessed: 2016-10-03].

[12] "Apache Hadoop," 2016, URL: http://hadoop.apache.org/ [accessed: 2016-10-03].

[13] "Streamdill," 2016, URL: https://streamdrill.com/ [accessed: 2016-10-03].

[14] M. Alavi and D. E. Leidner, "Knowledge management and knowledge management systems - conceptual foundations and research issues," MIS Quarterly, vol. 25, no. 1, 2001.

[15] M. Alvarez, J. Arana, I. Pradales, and J. Santos, "Review: Knowledge management in the extended enterprise." Fuzzy Sets, 2003.

[16] K. M. Hangos, R. Lakner, and M. Gerzson, Intelligent Control Systems: An Introduction with Examples. Springer Science & Business Media, 2001.

[17] N. Guarino and P. Giaretta, "Ontologies and knowledge bases: Towards a terminological clarification," in Towards very Large Knowledge bases: Knowledge Building and Knowledge sharing. IOS Press, 1995, pp. 25–32.

[18] W. B. Heinzelman, A. L. Murphy, H. S. Carvalho, and M. A. Perillo, "Middleware to support sensor network applications," Network, IEEE, vol. 18, no. 1, 2004, pp. 6–14.

[19] D. Jung and A. Hinze, "A mobile alerting system for the support of patients with chronic conditions," in First European Conference on Mobile Government (EURO mGOV), Brighton, UK, 2005, pp. 264–274.

AUTHOR INDEX